THE INDIAN POLICY OF PORTUGAL
IN THE AMAZON REGION, 1614-1693

THE CATHOLIC UNIVERSITY OF AMERICA

The Indian Policy of Portugal in the Amazon Region, 1614-1693

A DISSERTATION

SUBMITTED TO THE FACULTY OF THE GRADUATE SCHOOL OF ARTS AND
SCIENCES OF THE CATHOLIC UNIVERSITY OF AMERICA IN PARTIAL
FULFILLMENT OF THE REQUIREMENTS FOR THE DEGREE
OF DOCTOR OF PHILOSOPHY

BY

MATHIAS C. KIEMEN, O.F.M., M.A.

THE CATHOLIC UNIVERSITY OF AMERICA PRESS
WASHINGTON, D. C.
1954

PRINTED IN THE UNITED STATES OF AMERICA

BY THE SEEMAN PRINTERY, INC., DURHAM, NORTH CAROLINA

16757

This dissertation was approved by Manoel Cardozo, Associate Professor of Ibero-American History, as director, and by Antonine Tibesar, O.F.M., and John T. Farrell as readers.

CONTENTS

PREFACE

The purpose of this study is to analyze Portugal's Indian policy in the Amazon region of South America during the years 1614-1693 in terms of the missions, legislation affecting the Indians, and the laws regulating the relations between Indians and Portuguese as they worked out in practice. The Amazon region, as understood in this dissertation, included that part of modern Brazil known during most of the period covered by this study as the state of Maranhão and Grão Pará. This colonial state, which was politically not a part of Brazil proper, but was rather a separate and distinct administrative unit of Portuguese America, included, at least ideally, the area covered by the present Brazilian states of Ceará, Piauí, Maranhão, Pará and Amazonas.

In the course of this study, missions and missionary work will be discussed in some detail, but it is not my purpose to write mission history as such. I will dwell upon mission history only in so far as it is connected with the formation of Indian policy. Moreover, no attempt will be made to analyze the theological question concerning the genuineness of the conversion of the Indians to the Catholic Faith. Lastly, I shall make no attempt to present a complete political history of the region, but rather only those aspects of it that had a causative effect on the formation of Indian policy. My story, in other words, will be essentially about the development of Indian policy from the beginning of colonization in 1614 until 1693, when a more or less definitive policy was finally achieved.

The Amazon region as the locale of this study was chosen deliberately. It was precisely here (as well as in São Paulo) that the Indian worker was of paramount importance for the success of European civilization, and it was here that an honorable Indian policy was especially difficult to establish. The Portuguese will not always appear, therefore, in the best light, largely because of the ever-present economic burdens of the colonists, which often caused the home government to close its eyes to obvious abuses. In the rest of Portuguese America, on the other hand, São Paulo excepted, the Indian was spared quite early from the worst features of exploitation. This was due to the early introduction of African slaves in great numbers, a commodity which the settlers of the infinitely poorer state of Maranhão could not afford. In any case, I shall not as a rule pass judgment on the Christian or humanitarian character of the Indian policy as developed in the north, preferring to let the facts speak for themselves.

The main source of information has been the papers of the Portuguese Overseas Council (Conselho Ultramarino), the principal agency for colonial affairs, now in the Arquivo Histórico Ultramarino of Lisbon. I also consulted manuscripts and other documents in the Biblioteca Nacional of Lisbon, especially the papers of the *Collecção Pombalina*. Other pertinent materials were found in the Arquivo Nacional da Torre do Tombo of Lisbon, the Biblioteca da Ajuda, also of Lisbon, the Arquivo Distrital of Évora, the Biblioteca Municipal of Pôrto, and the Biblioteca Geral of the University of Coimbra. Some material was found in two Spanish archives, the Archivo Nacional de Simancas and the Archivo General de las Indias in Seville. In Rome I consulted the Archivio Segreto Vaticano and the Archivio della Propaganda Fide.

From the information supplied by these European archives and libraries, it was possible for me to make the first thorough study of Portugal's Indian policy as it was developed in the seventeenth century. I sincerely hope that this dissertation, however many its imperfections may be, will make clearer many aspects of the relations between Portuguese and Indians during a particularly critical period of colonization. This study will also be of possible value in any comparison of Portugal's policy with Spain's.

In the course of the preparation of this thesis, I have been placed under obligation to very many people, to all of whom I render my sincerest appreciation. In this connection it is fitting that I express my gratitude to the Directors of the various archives and libraries visited, especially to Dr. Alberto Iria of the Arquivo Histórico Ultramarino, who, during a period of almost a year, extended me every facility. A financial grant from the Instituto para a Alta Cultura of Lisbon helped, in part, to make my sojourn in Portugal possible. To the helpful officials of the Instituto, especially to its able secretary, Dr. A. de Medeiros-Gouvêa, I express my sincerest appreciation. My heartfelt thanks also to Dr.

Manoel Cardozo, my major professor, and to the readers of the dissertation, Dr. Antonine Tibesar and Dr. John Farrell. The Very Reverend Fathers Provincial of the Franciscan Province of the Sacred Heart have been most kind in allowing me the opportunity to pursue higher studies, and to undertake the traveling necessary for the preparation of this thesis.

ABBREVIATIONS

ABAPP— *Annaes da Biblioteca e Archivo Publico do Pará*, Belem, Pará

ABNR — *Anais da Biblioteca Nacional*, Rio de Janeiro

ADE — Arquivo Distrital de Évora

AGI — Archivo General de las Indias, Seville

AHU — Arquivo Histórico Ultramarino, Lisbon

ANTT — Arquivo Nacional da Torre do Tombo, Lisbon

BA — Biblioteca da Ajuda, Lisbon

BGUC — Biblioteca Geral da Universidade de Coimbra

BMP — Biblioteca Municipal do Pôrto

BNL — Biblioteca Nacional, Lisbon

RIHGB — *Revista do Instituto Histórico e Geográfico Brasileiro*, Rio de Janeiro

CHAPTER I

INTRODUCTION

The Portuguese of the seventeenth century did not share the naïveté of Pero Vaz de Caminha, who in 1500 had seen only primitive innocence in the Brazilian natives—people, in his opinion, of "good and of pure simplicity."[1] By the time of the conquest of Maranhão and Pará, the Portuguese colonists and soldiers knew the Indian for what he was: a turbulent man when aroused or attacked; a man proud of his freedom, well built physically, but incapable of heavy labor from which he soon sickened and died. The Indian, in other words, had the virtues and vices of other primitive men; he was not the childlike person the early chroniclers supposed him to be.

Modern anthropologists have divided the Indians of Brazil into two large groups: the Indians of *silval* culture and the Indians of *marginal* culture. To the first group belonged the larger number of Indians in the Amazon region; they occupied mainly the tropical rain-forest areas. The marginal, more primitive peoples lived for the most part in the unforested highlands of Brazil, and hence come very little into our story. There were, however, in the area of our study, isolated groups of these marginal Indians surrounded by their more advanced neighbors. The difference in culture between the two groups was, to be sure, not noteworthy or readily discernible to the naked eye; the more primitive did not practice horticulture, in the anthropological sense, but relied instead on hunting and gathering for subsistence.[2]

---

[1] "Letter of Pero Vaz de Caminha to King Manoel. Written from Porto Seguro of Vera Cruz, the first of May, 1500," William Brooks Greenlee (trans. and ed.), *The voyage of Pedro Álvares Cabral to Brazil and India from contemporary documents and narratives* (London, 1938), pp. 10 ff.

[2] This and the following information on Indian culture is taken largely from John M. Cooper, "Areal and temporal aspects of aboriginal South American culture," *Primitive Man*, XV (1942), 1-38. This article, on p. 9, has a map showing the location of the Indians of Brazil. See also Alfred Métraux, *La civilisation matérielle des tribus Tupí-Guaraní* (Paris, 1928); and Julian H. Steward (ed.), *Handbook of South American Indians* (6 vols.; Washington, D. C., 1946-1950), Vol. I: *The Marginal Tribes*, and Vol. III: *The Tropical Forest Tribes*.

1

In Brazil, including the Amazon region, the majority of silval peoples belonged to the Tupí-Guaraní family. It was the language of this family, the so-called *língua geral*, which was used extensively by the missionaries in instructing the Indians in the *aldeias*, or villages of Indians set up by Europeans. The Tupí Indians were horticulturists and depended upon manioc as their main food staple, although a good deal of maize, beans and sweet potatoes were also grown to supplement their diet. Clothing was virtually non-existent, but they ornamented the body in various ways. Their multi-family homes were made of a timber framework. Hammocks were used instead of beds. Handicrafts, such as weaving, carpentry and pottery-making, flourished, especially on the island of Marajó in Pará. The Indians were mainly concerned with the problem of finding enough to eat. They had not reached the stage of cultivating the fine arts. They had no writing. Yet in their use of medicinal herbs and roots they showed considerable knowledge and ingenuity. For music they made use or rattles, drums and simple wind instruments. They fashioned weapons out of stone or wood. They commonly used poison in fishing. They employed the blowgun and curare-poisoned darts in hunting and the bow and arrow in war. They smoked tobacco in the form of cigars. They drank alcoholic beverages.

Social organization among them was weak, family allegiance forming perhaps the strongest element of it. Their religion was largely shamanistic and animistic. The shaman, or medicine man, acted as sacrificial agent and physician. Clearly discernible, however, in the Tupí's maze of animal spirits and gods was a strong vein of theism. A most important trait of the Tupí Indians was their fondness of ritualistic cannibalism. Their almost incessant warlike campaigns led to the capture of hundreds of *índios presos a corda*, i.e., Indians captured in war and immolated subsequently in cannibalistic feasts. A wealth of ceremony surrounded the eating of captives. As Alfred Métraux writes:

Religious and social values of high importance clustered around war and the closely connected practice of cannibalism. Prestige and political power were derived mainly from the ritual slaughtering of prisoners. . . . The *Tupinamba's* excessive interest in ritual cannibalism contributed toward keeping the different tribes and even local communities in a constant state of warfare and was one of the chief causes of their ready subjection by Europeans. Their mutual hatred of one another, born of a desire to avenge the insult of cannibalism, was so great that the *Tupinamba* groups always willingly marched with the White invaders against their local rivals. Their bellicose disposition and craving for human flesh loom large in many aspects of their culture, such as education, oratory, poetry and religion. The rites and festivities that marked the execution of a prisoner and the consumption of his body were joyful events, which provided these Indians with the opportunity for merrymaking, esthetic displays and other emotional outlets.[3]

The marginal peoples in the states of Maranhão and Pará were in a definite minority. In many ways they had adopted the customs of their stronger neighbors; some of them even practiced cannibalism. The crafts were not so well developed among them, and their houses were not so elaborate. They were less stable in residence. They were accustomed to even less central authority than were the Tupí. Both the marginals and the silvals, however, were alike in their fondness for war. Before the advent of the Europeans they constantly fought among themselves. They continued to fight after the arrival of the invaders, but often on their side.

Maranhão and Pará were settled at the beginning of the seventeenth century, and as early as 1621 were to be made into a separate administrative unit, independent of the state of Brazil, with headquarters at Bahia. Yet from 1615 to 1624, the earlier legislation on Indian matters, drawn up for the state of Brazil, was applied in the north as well.

The first reference to Indian policy in Brazil is found in the *regimento*, or set of regulations, of the ship *Bretôa*, which went to Brazil in 1511 to pick up a cargo of brazilwood. Here it was declared that nobody was to harm or molest the Indians, under pain of punishment. The tone of the *regimento* in this connection is very harsh, as are the penalties to be levied upon the guilty.[4] The second reference is in the elaborate *regimento* of 1548, issued

---

[3] Alfred Métraux, "The Tupinamba," *Handbook of South American Indians,* III, 119.

[4] It is interesting to note that violators were to be punished as though they had harmed Europeans. For the text, see Carlos Malheiro Dias (ed)., *História da colonização portuguesa do Brasil. Edição monumental comemorativa do primeiro centenário da independência do Brasil* (3 vols.; Pôrto, 1924-1926), II, 344. Hereafter cited as *Colonização.*

in favor of Tomé de Sousa, the first governor-general of Brazil. Various of its sections concern the Indians. For instance, the governor was ordered to punish Indians who had fought against the Portuguese, but he was to be careful not to punish innocent Indians along with the guilty. He was ordered to rule them through their own chiefs. His principal object in dealing with the Indians was to keep them at peace, and thus more inclined to accept Christianity. If the natives should commit some crime for which they were later sorry, the governor was to treat them with kindness and to forgive them. Finally, Indians who became Christians were to be brought to live near the European settlements, so that they could be taught the truths of the Christian faith more readily.[5]

The first specific piece of legislation on Indian slavery, dated March 20, 1570, was the work of King Sebastian. After consulting the Mesa da Consciência e Ordens[6] and upon its recommendation, he prohibited the enslavement of natives in Brazil, with the exception of those taken in a just war. Such a war might be waged only with the permission of the king or of the governor.

---

[5] *Ibid.*, III, 345-350.

[6] The Mesa da Consciência e Ordens, a council for ecclesiastical affairs, was created by John III in December, 1532, to help the king in matters of conscience. During its early years, it seems to have had considerable influence in colonial matters. The Conselho da Índia (founded in 1604 and abolished in 1614) cut deeply into the Mesa's powers over colonial affairs, so that the Mesa thenceforth was restricted to matters regarding "defuntos e ausentes, redempção dos captivos e jurisdição contenciosa entre as partes." Cf. Francisco Adolfo de Varnhagen, *História geral do Brasil antes da sua separação e independência de Portugal* (3rd. ed.; 5 vols.; Rio de Janeiro and São Paulo, 1926-1936), II, 76 f. The Mesa retained its ancient power over the military orders. As time went on, especially after King Sebastian received papal approval for laymen to sit as judges in the Mesa, it became an instrument of regalism against the Church. It was finally abolished by King Peter IV on August 16, 1833. It had already been abolished in Brazil on September 22, 1828. See Oscar de Oliveira, *Os dízimos eclesiásticos do Brasil nos períodos da colônia e do império* (Juiz de Fora, Brazil, 1940), p. 75 f. See also António Caetano de Sousa, *Historia genealógica da casa real Portugueza, desde a sua origem até o presente, com as familias illustres, que procedem dos reys e dos serenissimos duques de Bragança* (Lisboa, 1737), III, 484 f. For documentation concerning this tribunal, see BNL, Collecção Pombalina, Cód. 645, fls. 1-33, and Fundo Geral, Cód. 251; also ANTT, Ministério do Reino, Consultas da Mesa da Consciência e Ordens, maço 406, docs. Dec. 19, 1747, July, 1749, and Aug. 13, 1753. In this last document, the councillors outline the functions of the Mesa at that time.

No permission was needed to wage war against Indians accustomed to assaulting the whites or who fought other natives to get captives for their cannibalistic feasts. The names of the natives taken captive by the Portuguese were to be recorded in the official treasury books of the district so that everybody might know that they were taken legally. Natives taken in any other way were to be declared free.[7] In 1595 Philip I further clarified the meaning of "just war" by defining it as a war expressly authorized by a particular command of the king.[8]

At the beginning of the seventeenth century, two strong laws in favor of the freedom of the Indians were promulgated. The first, on June 5, 1605, declared that

> . . . in no case could the natives of Brazil be taken captive, since, although there might be some legal reasons which permitted the said capturing in some cases, those to the contrary were of so much greater consideration, especially those pertaining to the conversion of the natives to our Holy Catholic Faith, that these latter must be placed before all the others.[9]

The second law, of July 30, 1609, went beyond anything that had thus far been done in protecting the Indians. Because of the excesses which followed when slave raids were allowed, the king, upon the advice of his council, declared that both Christian and pagan natives of Brazil were free, in conformity with law and nature. He also declared that they were not to be forced to work,

---

[7] For the complete text see Francisco Correa (ed.), *Leys e provisões que el Rey dom Sebastião, nosso Senhor, fez depois que começou à governar* (Lisboa, 1570), pp. 154 ff. There is a modern transcript of this law in the Oliveira Lima Library of The Catholic University of America, Washington, D. C., Historical Archive, Section I, Item 52, fl. 1.

[8] João Francisco Lisboa, *Jornal de Timon: Apontamentos, noticias e observações para servirem á historia do Maranhão* (São Luiz, 1865), II, 279 f. Hereafter cited as *Jornal de Timon*. See also Fortunato de Almeida, *Historia da igreja em Portugal* (Coimbra, 1912), III, Parte I, 670.

[9] ". . . em nenhum caso se pudessem captivar os gentios do Brazil; porque, conquanto houvesse algumas razões de direito para se poder em alguns casos introduzir o dito captiveiro, eram de tanto maior consideração as que havia em contrario, especialmente pelo que tocava á conversão dos gentios á nossa santa fé cathólica, que estas últimas se deviam antepôr a todas as mais." José Justino de Andrade e Silva (ed.), *Collecção chronológica da legislação portuguesa compilada e annotada, (1603-1612)*, (Lisboa, 1854), 129. This set of ten volumes gives synopses and texts of laws passed between the years 1603-1700. It will hereafter be cited as *Collecção chronológica*.

and that when they did work, they were to be paid for it. The Jesuits were given almost complete control over the Indians, since the law declared that they, and only they, were to go into the backlands to "domesticate" the pagans, assure them of their liberty, show them the way of salvation, and finally help them establish trade with the whites. The Indians were owners of their cultivated land, and of their forests, and these could not be taken from them. The governor, with the advice of the Jesuits, was to assign land to the Indians brought from the backlands; this land, once given, was not to change hands unless the Indians so willed it. A special judge was to be appointed to decide cases of lesser value involving Indians and merchants. There was also to be a special "curator," or advocate, who, under the direction of the Jesuits, would look after the Indians' interests in lawsuits. The Jesuit missionaries, although they were in charge of the domesticated Indians in their villages, had to pay the same wages as the colonists for the service of the Indians, their charges. The captains and donataries were to have no more jurisdiction over the natives than they had over the other free people in the colony. The captains could not impose tribute on the Indians; if they had done so, the governor was to force them to pay it back. Finally, the law freed all Indians who had been unjustly captured, contrary to the royal laws; those guilty of such unjust actions in the future would be punished for the crime of enslaving free persons.[10]

The law of 1609 put the Indian on an equal legal basis with the Portuguese. It forbade forced labor. Slavery, as a principle, was not condemned, but only the illegal capture of Indians. Unfortunately for the Indians, the law so aroused the opposition of the colonists that the king was forced to issue a new provision on September 10, 1611, which re-established in effect the conditions that had existed before 1609. The essential freedom of the natives was reiterated, but with outstanding exceptions. In case of war, rebellion or uprising on the part of the Indians, the governor, together with the ecclesiastical and civil officials, should hold a junta, or meeting, for the purpose of deciding whether to wage war or not, and whether or not it would be just to do so. If the junta approved the justness of the war, the colonists would be

---

[10] For the text of this law see *Collecção chronológica* (*1603-1612*), pp. 271-273; or *Boletim do Conselho Ultramarino: legislação antiga*, I (Lisboa, 1867), 204 f.

legally allowed to capture any natives involved in the same, The law obliged the junta to make known their decision to the king, who would then say whether or not the decision was fair. Only after the receipt of the king's permission could war be waged against the Indians, except in emergencies. In any case, no captured Indian could be sold until the king's assent to the decision of the junta had been received.

The law also allowed *resgates dos índios de corda*, i.e., expeditions sent to ransom Indians condemned to be killed by other Indians. In return for his ransom an Indian would be obliged to serve his benefactor for ten years, if the colonist paid no more than the sum stipulated by the governor. If he paid more, he could keep the servant proportionately longer. At the end of the period of servitude the Indian would regain his freedom.

The same law of 1611 provided for a married lay captain in each Indian *aldeia* to administer its affairs, thus displacing the Jesuits who had served in this capacity until then. It was to be the business of the lay captains to go into the interior in the company of a Jesuit or some other religious with a knowledge of the native language to persuade the Indians through peaceful means to settle in *aldeias* near white settlements. The governor was ordered to group about 300 of these Indian families in each village. The Indians could build their houses according to their own fashion. Sufficient land for cultivation would be given them by the governor. Each village was to have a church in charge of a Portuguese secular priest, or in his absence, a Jesuit, and in the absence of a Jesuit, a religious of another Order. The priest and the lay captain were to live in or near the village. The lay captain was required to govern the village, order the cultivation of the land, and assign the Indians as workers to the colonists for set wages. He had to be present when the Indians were paid; he was to see that they were not badly treated by their employers. He was to act as judge in his own village in all cases involving his charges. His authority in civil suits was limited to cases involving no more than ten *cruzados*; in criminal proceedings he could impose sentences of no more than thirty days in jail. In all other instances, he had to appeal to the *ouvidor*, or judge, of the district or to the higher courts of the land. The governor, with the advice of his councillors, was to draw up the *regimento* specifying the temporal powers of the captains and the resident priests, and the salary each was to receive. Such salaries were to be paid by the Indians.[11]

This was, in short, the legislation on Indians in effect in Portuguese America when the state of Maranhão and Pará was created. Brazil was discovered by the Portuguese in 1500, during the course of a voyage by Cabral to India. In the first years of the sixteenth century, the Portuguese Crown leased mercantile rights in Brazil to favored merchants, who were authorized to set up trading posts or factories along the coast, largely for the purpose of collecting dyewood.[12] When this system was unable to secure effectively the coastline for Portugal, King John III divided Brazil into captaincies and bestowed them on donataries or entrepreneurs.[13] Of the fifteen separate grants made to the twelve original donataries, three, corresponding roughly to the present-day states of Ceará, Maranhão and Pará, were given to António Cardoso de Barros, Fernão Álvares de Andrade, and João de Barros and Aires da Cunha respectively. Only Cardoso de Barros made no effort to colonize his grant. The other three donataries, Álvares de Andrade, João de Barros and Aires da Cunha, organized a joint expedition, to be led personally by Aires da Cunha. Setting out in 1535, Aires da Cunha and his men were shipwrecked off the coast of Maranhão, and all presumably lost their lives. No further efforts to colonize were made by the donataries in the Amazon region.[14] Spanish voyages down the Amazon during the sixteenth century had no other result than to focus attention on this area of South America.[15]

It was, therefore, not until the beginning of the seventeenth century that the history of colonization of Maranhão and Pará began, with the disastrous expedition of Pero Coelho de Sousa, who set out in 1603 from Olinda in Pernambuco to explore the coast of present-day Ceará and to capture Indians. In the region

---

[11] *Collecção chronológica* (1603-1612), pp. 309 ff.; *Boletim do Conselho Ultramarino*: *legislação antiga*, I, 206 ff.

[12] See Luiz Norton, "A colonização portuguesa do Brasil, 1500-1550," *Revista de Historia de América*, XI (1941), 14 ff.

[13] *Colonização*, III, 167 ff. See also Norton, *loc. cit.*, p. 37.

[14] For a detailed study of these early efforts, see *Colonização*, III, 167 ff., and especially pp. 207-211.

[15] On the Spanish voyages down the Amazon in the sixteenth century, see Raúl Reyes y Reyes (ed.), *Biblioteca Amazonas* (Quito, 1942), I-VII, where the original accounts are published.

of Ibiapaba in Ceará, his expedition was set upon by the Indians and he was forced to abandon his proposed base of operations along the Ceará coast. He returned to Pernambuco with a few Indian slaves, but these he was not allowed to keep. The king subsequently ordered Governor Diogo Botelho of Brazil to set free all these Indians on the grounds

> that the said capture was not lawful, nor in accordance with the laws passed concerning this matter, nor was it convenient for the good success of that conquest to scandalize the Indians of those parts with enslavement, which they fear and hate so much.[16]

Zeal for souls was to initiate the next step leading to the colonization of Maranhão. The Jesuits in Pernambuco, especially Fr. Francisco Pinto, had long had their eyes on this vast northern terra incognita, with its reputed millions of Indians. On January 20, 1607, Fr. Francisco Pinto and Fr. Luiz Figueira started out with sixty Christianized Indians, but with no guard of soldiers, to try to reach the wild Tapuia Indians of the coast of Ceará. After a hazardous journey, partly by boat and partly on foot, they arrived at Ibiapaba, which Pero Coelho de Sousa had earlier visited. Sousa's cruelty evidently was still remembered by the Indians, for they attacked the Jesuits' party and succeeded in killing many of them, including Fr. Pinto. Luiz Figueira, busy in a nearby

---

[16] "Ora, mandando eu ver os autos que se fizeram sobre o dito cativeiro e outras informações que tive da mesma materia e razões mui urgentes do serviço de Deos e meu, se achou que o dito captiveiro não era legitimo nem conforme ás leis que sobre isso são passadas, nem era conveniente para o bom proseguimento daquella conquista escandalisar os indios dessas partes com captiveiros, que elles tanto temem e aborrecem. . . e houve por bem de os haver a todos por livres e mandar que sejam tornados a suas terras. . . ." "Carta Regia a Diogo Botelho sobre os Indios do Ceará captivados por Pero Coelho de Sousa, 22 de setembro de 1605," Guilherme [Barão de] Studart, *Documentos para a história do Brasil e especialmente a do Ceará* (4 vols.; Fortaleza, 1904-1921), IV, 7 f. Hereafter cited as Studart, *Documentos Brasil*. These volumes of documents are of particular importance for the early years in the Amazon region, although their value is somewhat lessened, when, as often happens, the editor gives no source for the document. For the *Regimento do Capitão Mor Pero Coelho de Souza na jornada e empreza que por serviço de sua majestade vae fazer, 21 de janeiro de 1603,"* see *ibid.,* pp. 5-7. Cruz Filho, *História do Ceará* (São Paulo, 1931), pp. 44-54, has a good general account of the undertaking. For the part played by Pernambuco in these early expeditions, see J. F. Almeida Prado, *Pernambuco e as capitanias do norte do Brasil, 1530-1630. Historia da formação da sociedade brasileira* (3 vols.; São Paulo, 1939-1941).

clearing teaching Indian boys, heard the shouts, and returned to a spot near enough to the shouting to ascertain the hopelessness of the situation. He remained hidden, and, after the fierce band of Tapuias left, made his way laboriously back to Pernambuco, staying at Ibiapaba only long enough to give Christian burial to Fr. Pinto and the other dead. Figueira, in his reports on this journey, conceded that no missionary efforts could hope to succeed until the Tapuias along the coast were won over to the Portuguese, a task not made any easier by the growing interest of the French in this region.[17]

As early as 1604, the French had been directly interested in the Amazon country. In that year, Daniel de la Touche, Sieur de la Ravardière, together with Jean Moquet, explored the coasts of Guiana. Upon their return to France they obtained a royal grant to colonize Cayenne. Some beginnings were subsequently made, but on October 1, 1610, La Ravardière abandoned the venture. The French king now authorized him to found a colony south of the equator in Maranhão and granted him fifty leagues of land on either side of a fort to be constructed by La Ravardière. The site of the fort would later be known as São Luiz. For two years he struggled to organize a company and to get the necessary finan-

---

[17] For a complete account of this expedition, see *Relação do Maranhão, pelo P. Luiz Figueira, dirigida ao Preposito Geral da Ordem de Jesus, Claudio Aquaviva, 26 de março de 1609*, Studart, *Documentos Brasil*, I, 1-42. The "Carta Annua da Provincia do Brasil de 1607," dated Bahia, August 2, 1608, ANTT, Cartório dos Jesuítas, maço 83, has a brief account. See also Serafim Leite, *História da Companhia de Jesús no Brasil* (10 vols.; Rio de Janeiro, 1938-1950), III, 3 ff. Cited hereafter as Leite, *História da Companhia*. Figueira wrote another letter to the Jesuit General on August 26, 1609, in which he mentions the necessity of driving out the French. Studart, *Documentos Brasil*, I, 42-44. See also *ibid.*, pp. 46-49 for the "Noticia summaria da vida do bemdito martyr o Padre Francisco Pinto," copied from the second chapter of Cod. 15-2-11 of ADE. See also chapter 13 of the "Chronica da Missão da Companhia de Jesus em o estado do Maranhão," in *RIHGB*, LXXII, Parte I (1909), 39-43. Rubem Almeida, in his "A contribuição dos Antoninos para a historia do Maranhão," *Revista de Geografia e Historia do Maranhão*, II (1947), 115, says that Pinto was killed by the French, and not by the Indians, as was claimed later to dramatize the death. Leite, *História da Companhia*, III, 8, is probably more correct when he says: ". . . aos Franceses do Maranhão se deve atribuir a sua instigação." Leite repeats these words and most of the account of the mission to Ibiapaba in his *Luiz Figueira, a sua vida heróica e a sua obra literária* (Lisboa, 1940), p. 31.

cial backing. Finally, in March, 1612, he left France for Maranhão.[18]

Meanwhile the Portuguese government had begun to realize that it would be necessary to occupy the north country to keep it secure from other European nations. Some of the men needed for the undertaking were already at hand. Among those who had taken part in Pero Coelho de Sousa's ill-starred expedition was Martim Soares Moreno, nephew of Diogo de Campos Moreno, *sargento-mor* of Brazil. When Sousa returned to Pernambuco, Martim Soares remained behind. Martim, who was very young at the time, succeeded in making friends with the Indians, among whom he had lived for many years. He learned their languages and gained great influence over them. At this juncture, in 1611, the king asked Governor Diogo de Meneses of Brazil to obtain all possible information concerning Maranhão. The governor now ordered Diogo de Campos Moreno, commander of the fort at Rio Grande do Norte, to gather the information needed. Campos Moreno naturally turned to his nephew for help. Martim was accordingly sent farther along the coast where he built a small fort in Ceará and a church dedicated to Nossa Senhora do Amparo. For protection he depended almost entirely on a tribe of friendly Indians that accompanied him. Only a few soldiers were in his party. For a short time, this method of leading a life similar to that of the Indians in order to hold their confidence worked adequately, but when the influence of the French began to be felt again, Martim was forced to ask for immediate aid from Recife.[19]

---

[18] Varnhagen, *História geral*, II, 168 f. On the early French interest in Brazil, see Charles André Julien, *Voyages de découverte et les premiers établissements, XVe-XVIe siècles* (Paris, 1948), pp. 166-221. The book is particularly valuable for its extensive bibliography (pp. 446-497). See also the somewhat shallow book by Mario de Lima-Barbosa, *Les Français dans l'histoire du Brésil. Traduction et adaptation de l'original brésilien par Clément Gazet* (Paris, 1923), pp. 93-99. The standard works are those by Yves d'Evreux, *Suite de l'histoire des choses plus memorables advenues en Maragnan en 1613 et 1614* (Paris, 1615), and Claude d'Abbeville, *L'arrivée des peres capucins en l'isle de Maragnon et la conversion des sauvages à nostre saincte foy* (Paris, 1623).

[19] Details concerning these activities of Martim Soares Moreno are contained in an account of events in Maranhão written by his uncle, Diogo de Campos Moreno, "Jornada do Maranhão por Diogo de Campos Moreno," in Cândido Mendes de Almeida, *Memorias para a história do Maranhão cujo territorio comprehende hoje as provincias do Maranhão, Piauhy, Grão Pará e Amazonas* (2 vols.; Rio de Janeiro,

As a result of Soares Moreno's request, Governor Diogo de Meneses, on March 1, 1612, wrote to the king about the developments north of Pernambuco and the imperative need of taking quick action to aid Soares Moreno and settle Maranhão.[20] The governor included the suggestions of the *Sargento-mor* Diogo de Campos Moreno to found successively three settlements: at Ceará (Jaguaribe); the port of Camucim, between Ceará and Maranhão; and in Maranhão. An indication of the importance attached in Portugal to the matter was the rapidity with which the king answered by royal orders of October 9 and November 8, 1612, which authorized the settling of Camucim and eventually of Maranhão.[21] At the same time, to facilitate the northern venture, the new governor-general of Brazil, Gaspar de Sousa, was ordered to establish his residence in Pernambuco for the time being, instead of proceeding to Bahia. He appropriated for the royal undertaking the sum of five to six thousand *cruzados* belonging to a contested estate. As the leader of the colonizing expedition he chose Jerónimo de Albuquerque, who was well acquainted with the country and the Indians and knew many of the Indian languages.[22]

Albuquerque sailed to the settlement of Martim Soares Moreno

1860-1874), II, 160-265. For a letter of Governor Diogo de Meneses of March 1, 1612, describing Moreno's activities, see Guilherme Studart, *Documentos para a história do Martim Soares Moreno* (Fortaleza, 1905), p. 1 f. These two sources state that Moreno went with only two soldiers and one unnamed secular priest to Ceará, in order not to cause alarm to the Indians. Another source says that sixteen soldiers went with him. See "Carta de Gaspar de Sousa a El Rey em que falla nas differentes materias do governo e da fazenda, e trata da conquista do Maranhão e do modo com que se deve proceder nella, visto estar da sorte que se acha, feita em Olinda a 31 de janeiro de 1615," in "Documentos para a história da conquista e colonização da costa de leste-oeste do Brasil," *ABNR*, XXVI (1904), 311-320. This large and extremely informative collection of documents will hereafter be cited as *Documentos Leste-Oeste*, and the pagination of the *Anais* of 1904 will be followed. The same collection was also published separately, but with different pagination.

[20] "Carta do Governador do Brazil a El Rey sobre a utilidade desta terra e sitios por onde se podião dividir suas capitanias, modo de captar as amisades dos Indios, etc.," ANTT, Corpo Chronologico, parte I, maço 115, doc. 129. The letter has been published in *Documentos Leste-Oeste*, 307-310, and in Studart, *Dccumentos Brasil*, II, 65-68.

[21] Varnhagen, *História geral*, II, 140 f.

[22] To encourage Pernambucans to join the expedition, the king, on October 8, 1612, offered rewards to all who would accompany the expedition. See Studart, *Documentos Brasil*, I, 53.

on the borders of Ceará and conferred with him. It was determined that Soares Moreno would reconnoiter along the coast as far as Maranhão, while Jerónimo would found a settlement at Camucim and await Moreno's return. Moreno carried out his part of the arrangement on the outward voyage, and made contact with the French on August 12, 1612, a week after the large French expedition under La Ravardière had founded the town of São Luiz in Maranhão.[23]

La Ravardière had chosen the site for his fort with a good deal of care and soon attracted the good will of the nearby Indians with gifts and promises. When the fort was established he had set off with most of his men to explore Maranhão and Pará. Only a small part of his forces had remained behind at the fort. Martim Soares arrived on August 12, and seeing the weakness of the French, he landed some men, attacked the fort and burned some of the buildings. Hearing, however, of the approach of reinforcements, he fled, pursued for a time by a French ship. Contrary winds finally took him to Santo Domingo in the Spanish West Indies, from where he embarked for the Iberian Peninsula. Meanwhile Jerónimo de Albuquerque, after waiting in vain for Moreno's return, left a garrison of forty soldiers at Camucim and returned to Pernam-

---

[23] Varnhagen, *História geral*, II, 171 f. La Ravardière sailed from France on March 19, 1612, with a fleet of three vessels, carrying four Capuchin missionaries, many nobles and about 500 soldiers and colonists. Landing on the island of Maranhão, he founded the town of São Luiz on August 6, 1612. See *ibid.*, pp. 203 ff. For the work of the Capuchins see Yves d'Evreux, *op. cit.*, pp. 33-35, and Claude d'Abbeville, *op. cit.*, *passim*. For modern studies see Fidélis M. de Primério, *Capuchinhos em terras de Santa Cruz nos séculos XVII, XVIII e XXIX* (São Paulo, 1942), and Jacinto de Palazzolo, "Primeiros Capuchinhos no Maranhão," *Vozes de Petrópolis*, III (1945), 501-506. The magnitude of the French effort can be gauged by the fact that twenty Capuchins were in the settlement when the French were defeated in 1615. Rodolfo Garcia, in his annotations to Varnhagen's *História geral*, II, 203-205, gives us more details concerning the French expedition. The leaders were François de Rasilly, La Ravardière and Nicolas de Harlay de Sancy, the celebrated financier, who were named lieutenant generals of the king. The spiritual side was taken care of by Capuchin volunteers. Marie de Medici had written to Fr. Léonard, provincial of the Paris Capuchins, asking him to send four fathers. At the chapter of the Order, practically all the fathers offered to go. Four were picked: Yves d'Evreux as superior, Claude d'Abbeville, Arsène de Paris and Ambroise d'Amiens. Their letter of obedience is dated October 27, 1611. On May 23, the expedition arrived off Fernão de Noronha Island, where a Portuguese and about eighteen Indians had been exiled from Pernambuco. These people were taken to Maranhão. The three ships arrived at Maranhão Island on July 26.

buco.   For the time being this ended Portuguese efforts against
the French.   The only concrete advantage gained was the founding of a settlement in Ceará nearer to Maranhão.[24]

Diogo de Campos Moreno was already in Spain to acquaint the
Court with the seriousness of the situation when Martim Soares
Moreno arrived.   Diogo now received orders to return to Brazil
to lead the definitive expedition which was expected to overwhelm
the French.   When he reached Recife on May 26, 1614,[25] the
governor had already confided the leadership of a new Maranhão
expedition to Jerónimo de Albuquerque.   Diogo was thereupon
named Albuquerque's *adjunto*, with an equal vote in council.   Albuquerque with 200 to 300 Indians went by land, and Diogo de
Campos with 260 Portuguese soldiers and forty Indians, by sea.
Near Ceará the two groups united and moved forward together.[26]
The whole expedition, made up of about 500 men, including the
inconstant Indians, arrived across the bay from the French settlement on October 26, 1614.   The situation of the Portuguese was
far from enviable.   Of the two contenders, the French were the
stronger, protected by their fortifications and controlling the sea,
but they made the mistake of leaving their fort and of coming
across the bay to engage the jungle-trained Portuguese and Indians in battle.   The skirmish of Guaxenduba ended with a clear,

---

[24] *Ibid.*, II, 169; 170 f.; 203-205.   Almeida, *Memorias do Maranhão*, II, "Jornada
do Maranhão," pp. 165-167.   Martim Soares Moreno had an unlucky time of it.
When he finally arrived in Santo Domingo with twenty-seven soldiers and seventy
Indians, he and his men were starving.   In Santo Domingo he asked the governor,
Don Diego Gómez de Sandoval, for assistance, and after much bureaucratic delay,
received 230 ducats.   From the West Indies Moreno took ship for Seville.   See
"Carta del presidente de la Española con testimonio de una información del Capi-
tan Martin Suarez Moreno, que fué á examinar el Rio Marañon, por orden del
Governador del Brasil.   Santo Domingo, 15 diciembre, 1613," and other docu-
ments on the same subject in *Documentos Leste-Oeste*, pp. 151-191, or in Studart,
Documentos para a história do Martim Soares Moreno, pp. 3 ff., together with a
letter of Moreno to Governor Sousa written on Apr. 27, 1614, pp. 53-55.   For the
French account, see Yves d'Evreux, *op. cit.*, pp. 33-35.

[25] Almeida, *Memorias do Maranhão*, II, "Jornada do Maranhão," p. 168.

[26] See *Regimento dado a Jeronymo d'Albuquerque pelo Governador Gaspar de Sousa.
Olinda, 22 de Junho de 1614*, in Studart, *Documentos Brasil*, I, 83-92.   The governor
did not give complete power to Jerónimo.   He was to consult at every step with
Diogo Moreno and Manuel de Sousa d'Eça, another captain.   In case of accident
to Albuquerque, Diogo was to assume command.   The sea expedition left Recife
on August 23, 1614.   See Varnhagen, *História geral*, II, 173.

though not an overwhelming, victory for Albuquerque's men, but the French kept their control of the sea.   After a brisk interchange of letters, a one-year truce was agreed upon on November 27, 1614, to allow time for the two European monarchs to make up their minds about the disposal of this section of America.[27]

The situation in Maranhão after the truce of November 27, 1614, must have reflected the two commanding officers' uncertainty about their relative military strength.   Only in this light can we explain the unique and intensely formal actions which took place during those days.   Official charters were reciprocally examined, gun salutes were exchanged, joint religious services were held. On November 29, part of the Portuguese forces peacefully occupied a French fort on São Luiz Island.   The emissaries—one French and the other Portuguese—were sent to both European governments on December 16, 1614, and January 4, 1615.   Both sides then settled down uneasily to wait for a decision or for reinforcements.[28]

---

[27] The Portuguese were aware that they were in a position of inferiority in men and munitions.   In an "auto que mandou fazer o governador e capitão geral do Brasil sobre a jornada do Maranhão, Olinda, 26 de julho, 1614," the main point discussed was their weakness and the need for more aid from the king.   On this point all the captains agreed.   See Studart, *Documentos Brasil*, I, 92-96.   See also *ibid.*, pp. 102-114, for a letter of Gaspar de Sousa to the king, August 20, 1614, telling of his many problems in this expedition, and the difficulties in which the king placed him by delaying answers to important letters.   The best single source for this first campaign is the "Jornada do Maranhão," *loc. cit.*, pp. 167 ff., by the old soldier Diogo de Campos Moreno.   Its author was present for most of the activity.   This account is more than a diary, for it includes, e.g., official letters like that of Jerónimo de Albuquerque to the Spanish ambassador in France (pp. 253-255); copies of letters written by La Ravardière and Albuquerque before the truce on November 27 (pp. 219-228); lists of men killed on both sides (pp. 215-217); the ten points of the truce agreed upon (pp. 228-234), all this spiced with a typical European-trained soldier's remarks concerning every move.   The *Documentos Leste-Oeste*, pp. 263-276, contain the interrogations of the French captives by Diogo de Campos Moreno on November 20, and another eyewitness account in "Breve relación de la jornada dela conquista del Marañon," a translation of the original Portuguese account by Manuel de Sousa Dessa (d'Eça), a captain of the army, pp. 281-287.   See also Vicente de Salvador, *História do Brasil* (3rd ed.; revista por Capistrano de Abreu & Rodolfo Garcia; São Paulo, 1931), pp. 464-488.   These three sources should be used together to get a balanced picture.   For an account of the Pernambucan Albuquerque family, see Helio Vianna, *Estudos de história colonial* (São Paulo, 1948), pp. 196-245.

[28] See Almeida, *Memorias do Maranhão*, II, "Jornada do Maranhão," 235 ff., especially pp. 253 f. and 258.   For a reliable short account see Theodoro Braga,

The home government in Lisbon and Madrid, aghast at the turn of events in Maranhão, made immediate plans to send a large and strong expedition to break the stalemate. On October 5, 1615, Alexandre de Moura sailed from Recife for Maranhão with 600 men in nine ships. This force was enough to compel the French to surrender without a battle on November 4, 1615, putting an end to France's ambitions and efforts in the Amazon region proper.[29]

Even in these early troubled days the religious assistance of friars and Jesuits was not lacking, but little could be accomplished with the natives until the times became more peaceful. Two Franciscans had accompanied the first expedition of Jerónimo de Albuquerque in 1614, more or less in the position of chaplains to the fleet, and these two stayed in São Luiz until the beginning of 1616, when they returned to Pernambuco. While they were there, they took over the Capuchin convent for themselves and played an important part in keeping the Indians of the Portuguese from

---

História do Pará (São Paulo, n.d.), pp. 46-49. Varnhagen, *História geral*, II, 177 f., when used in conjunction with the notes by Abreu and Garcia, gives a well-documented account.

[29] What I have given above is only the general outline of this phase of the campaign. It may be of interest, however, to indicate some of the important source material. The minutes of the Conselho de Portugal and the Conselho de Estado for their meetings in April, May and June, 1615, in which strong and immediate attacks were ordered to expel the French, have been printed in *Documentos Leste-Oeste*, pp. 289-304. The "Carta do Governador Gaspar de Sousa a El Rey em que falla nas differentes materias do governo e da fazenda, e trata da conquista do Maranhão e do modo com que se deve proceder nella, visto estar da sorte que se acha, feita em Olinda a 31 de janeiro de 1615," *ibid.*, pp. 311-320, is important. Manoel de Sousa d'Eça's "Breve relación de la jornada de la conquista del Marañon, 1615," AGI, *Patronato Real*, leg. 272, ramo 4, which was printed only in Spanish in the *Documentos Leste-Oeste*, pp. 281-287, and in Studart, *Documentos Brasil*, I, 184-191, was consulted by the author in both the original Portuguese and the Spanish translation in the AGI in Seville. The "Roteiro do Rio das Almazonas," by the same author was also consulted in the original in the AGI, *loc. cit.*, ramo 5. This work also, was printed only in Spanish in *Documentos Leste-Oeste*, pp. 277-279, the original translator in 1615 giving "Derrota" for "Roteiro" in the title. Some idea of the internal strife going on among the various Portuguese leaders before the arrival of Alexandre de Moura is given in Studart, *Documentos Brasil*, II, 161-164, and *Documentos Leste-Oeste*, pp. 206-209. For the relief expedition of Alexandre de Moura see his own "Relatorio de Alexandre de Moura sobre a expedição á Ilha do Maranhão e expulsão dos Francezes. Lisboa, 24 de outubro de 1616," *ibid.*, pp. 193-242; Varnhagen, *História geral*, II, 168-202; 210 f.; and in Studart, *Documentos Brasil*, II, 175-177; 166-173.

deserting. They also were able to do some missionary work among the Indians, but on a very limited scale.[30]

Two Jesuits arrived a year after the Franciscans, with Alexandre de Moura's fleet. They also came as chaplains. Because of their influence they were able to add 300 Indian warriors to Moura's forces. They, too, had orders to return to Pernambuco in 1616, but an epidemic of smallpox broke out among the Indians, and the demands of charity, they said, kept them in Maranhão until March, 1618.[31]

The two Carmelite friars who accompanied Moura as chaplains remained in the colony. They founded convents in Maranhão and later in Pará. Their ministrations, however, were exclusively for the Portuguese in these early days.[32]

Maranhão was now relatively safe from the French, but Moura still had work to do. His *regimento* obliged him to found a settlement on the Amazon and also to expel all foreigners who might be there. For these tasks he chose Francisco Caldeira de Castelo Branco. The expedition set out on December 25, 1615, with 200 men, 150 of them trained soldiers. Sailing only by day, it took eighteen days of cautious navigating for them to reach the Amazon estuary. On January 12 Caldeira founded the city of Nossa Sen-

---

[30] See Apolinário da Conceição, *Primazia serafica na regiam da America, novo descobrimento de santos e veneraveis religiosos da ordem serafica, que ennobrecem o Novo Mundo com suas virtudes e acçoens* (Lisboa, 1733), pp. 121-123; Antônio de Santa Maria Jaboatão, *Novo orbe serafico brasilico, ou Chronica dos Frades Menores da Provincia do Brazil* (2nd ed.; 2 vols.; Rio de Janeiro, 1858-1861), I, 186 ff. See the "Jornada do Maranhão," *loc. cit.*, p. 172, for a tribute to the Franciscans and their work by Diogo Moreno. See also Bernardo Pereira de Berredo, *Annaes historicos do estado do Maranhão* (3rd ed.; 2 vols.; Florença, 1905), I, No. 157 f., 204 ("No." refers to paragraphs.); and Vicente do Salvador, *História do Brasil*, p. 440.

[31] See Serafim Leite, *História da Companhia*, III, 99 ff., and João Felippe Betendorf, "Chronica da missão dos Padres da Companhia de Jesus no estado do Maranhão," *RIGHB*, LXXII, Parte I (1909); Leite, *Luiz Figueira*, pp. 45 f.; *Documentos Leste-Oeste*, pp. 329-334, or Studart, *Documentos Brasil*, I, 273-288.

[32] See Manoel de Sá, *Memorias historicas dos illustrissimos arcebispos, bispos, e escritores portuguezes da ordem de Nossa Senhora do Carmo, reduzidas a catalogo alfabetico que entregou na Academia Real da Historia Portugueza e a seu protector augustissimo el rey D. João V nosso Senhor offerece e dedica o Academico Supranumerario Fr. Manoel de Sá, religioso da mesma ordem da provincia de Portugal* (Lisboa, 1724), pp. 324-327; hereafter cited as *Memorias Historicas O. Carm.*; Manuel de Mello Cardoso Barata, "Apontamentos para as ephemérides Paraenses," *RIHGB*, CXLIV (1925), 31 f.; Berredo, *Annaes historicos*, I, 163.

hora de Belém.   He called the region "Feliz Lusitânia," but the Indian name of Pará was destined to prevail.[33]

Ecclesiastical organization followed closely upon the founding of the city of Belém.   On July 28, 1617, four Franciscans arrived to take charge of the Indians, and at the same time, to care for the spiritual needs of the Portuguese settlers.   The four friars were Frei António da Merciana, Custos, or Superior, Frei Cristóvão de São José, Frei Sebastião do Rosário and Frei Filipe de São Boaventura, all priests.   These Franciscans were the first missionaries in the captaincy of Pará.[34]   The following year, 1618, Fr. Manoel Figueroa, or Filgueira, arrived in Belém, to be the first secular priest in the area.[35]

Ceará, Maranhão and Pará were now established definitively. Many were the trials to which they would be subjected, especially during the first fifty years of their existence.   But somehow they persevered, and it was to be from São Luiz and Belém that Portuguese influence spread north to French Guiana and west to the borders of Peru and Ecuador.

---

[33] "Regimento que Alexandre de Moura deixou a Francisco Caldeira de Castello Branco, 22 de dezembro de 1615," *Documentos Leste-Oeste*, pp. 239-242.   For an account of the expedition written by Captain António Pereira, who accompanied Caldeira, see "Relaçam do que ha no grande rio das Amazonas novamente descuberto," *Ibid.*, pp. 255-259.   For official letters concerning Belém, etc. see Studart, *Documentos Brasil*, I, 4-11.   There are good general accounts in Varnhagen, *História geral*, II, 168 ff., and Braga, *História do Pará*, pp. 51-54.

[34] See Conceição, *Primazia serafica*, pp. 122 f.; Vicente do Salvador, *História do Brasil*, Prolegomenos of Capistrano de Abreu, p. 440; Arthur Cézar Ferreira Reis, "A formação espiritual da Amazônia," *Cultura*, I (1948), 98 f.; Domingos Antônio Raiol (Barão de Guajará), "Catechese de Indios no Pará," *Annaes da Bibliotheca e Archivo Publico do Pará*, II (1903), 124 f. and Arthur Vianna, "Os exploradores da Amazônia," *Revista do Instituto Historico, Geographico e Ethnographico do Pará*, I (1900), 294 f.   In the AHU in Lisbon there is an undated document (Pará, Papeis Avulsos, [1615]) written by Francisco Caldeira do Castelo Branco, entitled: "Rol do q. deve ir para a conquista do Maranhão digo Pará," which begins: "Primeiramente religiozos para a conversão das almas de que ha centenas de milhares mostranse affeiçoados a capuchos [i.e., Franciscans] pello que delles lhes dizem os Indios do Maranhão."

[35] See "Carta do Padre Manoel Filgueira de Mendonça a el Rei expondo as cousas do Maranhão. Belém, 30 de novembro de 1618," AHU, Pará, Papeis Avulsos, doc. 30 de novembro de 1618.

CHAPTER II

THE FRANCISCANS AND THE INDIANS, 1617-1636

When the first four Franciscan missionaries arrived in Pará in 1617, the colony was little more than a year old, and in a very rudimentary state of development.[1] The home government had not yet found the time to carry out any of the many suggestions made by leaders who had looked over the possibilities of the region. But the suggestions were not wanting. Even as early as June 17, 1614, before the founding of Belém or São Luiz, Alexandre de Moura had urged the king to approve the concession of land grants in the area as a means to attract and hold permanent Portuguese settlers.[2] He had other suggestions to make along this line in 1616. The king, he felt, should send five of six hundred people from Brazil, especially from Pernambuco, where the population was large, as pioneer settlers, together with their domestic animals. Brazilians, he said, were to be preferred above other people because it would be easier for them to make their adjustment in the new environment. Supplies, however, should come from Portugal, because they were cheaper there than in Brazil, and also because it was easier to sail from Maranhão to Portugal than to Brazil. He focused attention upon the necessity of being on good terms with the Indians and thought that some religious ought to be sent, since they were respected by the Indians. Coopers, carpenters, calkers and weavers were also needed, as were such supplies as iron and copper tools, cloth, wine, olive oil and saltpeter. It was not easy for the Crown to put all these admirable suggestions into

---

[1] On the coming of the friars in 1617, see AHU, Pará, Papeis Avulsos, doc. 16 de dezembro, 1616, which is one of the oldest documents in that archive. In it the archbishop of Lisbon, who was viceroy of Portugal, says: "Os frades são quatro da ordem de São Francisco e eu ordenarey para cidade para se lhes dar o necessario. Arcebispo de Lisboa." See also ANTT, Santo António dos Capuchos, maço 1, no. 4, doc. 19, for the official grant of *ordinária*, or annual salary, for the four friars.

[2] "Carta de Alexandre de Moura a S. Magestade sobre repartições de terra. Pernambuco, 17 de junho de 1614," Studart, *Documentos Brasil*, I, 65-67.

practice at once, as would have been desirable, but some beginnings were made almost immediately.[3]

The suggestion of Moura concerning missionaries was carried out, as we have seen, in 1617, by the arrival of the four Franciscan priests. In 1618 the Franciscans were given official charge of the Indian missions in Pará.[4]

The amount of missionary work which four priests could do in such an immense territory was, of course, very limited. They were forced to confine their work pretty much to the territory near-by Belém, except when they accompanied soldiers on expeditions into the interior. More than that they could not do until the arrival of reinforcements in 1624.[5]

---

[3] "Relatorio de Alexandre de Moura sobre a expedição á Ilha do Maranhão e expulsão dos Francezes. Lisboa, 24 de setembro de 1616," AHU, Maranhão, Papeis Avulsos, doc. of September 24, 1616. This has been printed in *Documentos Leste-Oeste*, pp. 193-242, but under date of October 24.

[4] See ANTT, Santo António dos Capuchos, maço 1, no. 4, doc. 19, dated June 6, 1618. In a royal letter of June 20, 1618, the king speaks of his intention to separate Maranhão from Brazil and give it an independent governor. He continues: "E considerando quam importante he ao serviço de Deos e meu enviaremsse desse Reino relligiosos aquellas partes para tratarem de augmento de nossa santa fee e da conservação do gentio e celebrarem os officios divinos me pareceo que estes relligiosos devem ser de Sam Francisco da Provincia de Santo Antonio a que compete aquella commissão: os quais hirão com o novo governador no numero que parecer necessario." Studart, *Documentos Brasil*, I, 141-142, or II, 190 f. See also Vicente do Salvador, *Historia do Brasil*, Prolegomenos of Capistrano de Abreu, p. 440.

[5] The documents do not speak of anything specific concerning the missions of the Franciscans until 1624. For general remarks concerning missionary work during those first years, see J. Lúcio d'Azevedo, *Os Jesuítas no Grão Pará, suas missões e a colonização* (2nd ed. rev.; Coimbra, 1930), p. 257. Ferreira Reis, in his "A formação espiritual da Amazônia," *Cultura*, I, 98 f. has this to say: "A ação missionária, lembrada, pleiteada mesmo incessantemente pelos capitães-mores e outros funcionários que vieram servir nos cargos civis e militares do Pará, confiada, de início, aos Franciscanos de Santo Antônio, produziu resultados animadores. Cabildas Tupinambás e de outros grupos do Amazonas, do Marajó e do Tocantins, cedendo em suas dúvidas para com os lusitanos, à voz dos Frades aliaram-se àqueles nas justas contra os 'herejes' de Holanda e Britânia. E se deixaram nuclear nas cercanias de Belem, fruto promissor para o futuro da Capitania nascente." Governor Gaspar de Sousa, before passing the governorship of Brazil to his successor in 1617, suggested to the king the creation of a separate custody, or minor province, of Franciscans in Maranhão and Pará, so that the friars could increase the number of *indios aldeados*: "Tambem ha muito mister aquela conquista mais religiosos para o acrecentamento dos Indios aldeados e que estes sejão da provincia de Santo Antonio que forão os que a principiarão e não hão mister fazenda para. . . muito

It was unfortunate for the work of the Franciscans that the early times were so turbulent and uncertain in Pará. The first *capitão-mor*, Francisco Caldeira de Castelo Branco, was forcibly deposed on September 14, 1618. From that date until May, 1620, there were six changes in government, all by popular vote. It was not until June 18, 1621, that Bento Maciel Parente took office as a duly appointed *capitão-mor*, and he ruled only until October, 1626.[6]

The explanation for this instability may be found partly in the character of the settlers, partly in their attitude toward the Indians and partly in the danger of foreign intrusion. Castelo Branco, the first *capitão-mor*, was overthrown because he had allowed to go free a relative of his who had killed another man in cold blood. Two citizens protested at this flouting of the law, and to escape retaliation they found asylum in the Franciscan church. When Caldeira ordered them forcibly removed from the church, the people revolted and imprisoned him.[7]

---

facil la de prover fazendose a custodia do Brasil provincia pois tem casas bastantes para o ser e podem então a deste reino fazer nova custodia no Maranhão e provella de mais frades dos que la tem, que só são quatro." Studart, *Documentos Brasil*, I, 129. See also Conceição, *Primazia serafica*, pp. 121-123; Vicente do Salvador, *História do Brasil*, Prolegomenos of Capistrano de Abreu, p. 440, and Jaboatão, *Novo Orbe Serafico*, I, 208-218, who gives the longest account of Franciscan activities during this period, although accurate details are lacking.

[6] For a list of the captains and governors of the state, see Braga, *História do Pará*, pp. 137-158. It covers the period of 1616 to 1931. See also "Memoria dos capitães e governadores do Maranhão e Pará," BA, 51-VI-46, Num. 17, which contains a short account of each captain or governor of the state from 1614 to 1783. Hereafter it will be cited as "Memoria dos governadores."

[7] The following primary sources may be cited: AHU, Maranhão, Papeis Avulsos, doc. 1618, for a request from the Court for secret information on the revolt; and Manuel Soares de Almeida's answer to this request, AHU, Pará, Papeis Avulsos, doc. 8 de novembro de 1618. See also *ibid.*, doc. 27 de novembro de 1618, for an account of the uprising by Fr. António da Merciana, the Franciscan custos, who was intimately connected with the revolt. Another account of the same date is given by Baltasar Rodrigues de Mello. It is printed in Studart, *Documentos Brasil*, I, 153 f. under date of November 28, 1618. A report favorable to the deposed governor is the letter of Fr. Manoel Filgueira de Mendonça, the first secular priest in Pará, who arrived in Pará during the revolt. He blames the two Franciscans (probably Fr. António da Merciana and Fr. Cristóvão de São José) for everything. AHU, Pará, Papeis Avulsos, doc. 30 de novembro de 1618. Also printed in Studart, *Documentos Brasil*, I, 254-256. One of the charges against the deposed governor was his needless cruelties to the Indians around Belém. Governor Gaspar de Sousa in his instructions to his successor suggested that Caldeira Branco be recalled

Coincidental with this revolt in Pará, the Indians attacked the white settlements in both Maranhão and Pará in 1618. The revolt began in the captaincy of Cumá in Maranhão and spread from there to Pará at the time of the civil war. The Indian uprising continued into 1619. Clearly the Indians were making a desperate effort to rid their coast of Europeans, especially of Portuguese, who had been treating them cruelly.[8]

To take care of both the revolt and the Indian uprising, Bento Maciel Parente and Jerónimo Fragoso de Albuquerque were sent in March, 1619, to restore order in Pará and chastise the Indians in both Maranhão and Pará. Parente received a special *regimento* as *Capitão da guerra aos indios rebeldes do Pará* from Governor Luis de Sousa of Brazil. By this time the Indians in Maranhão were pacified, and Parente was told to center his attentions on the Indians in Pará. His instructions were explicit: if the Indians gave in, there were to be no reprisals. The intent of the war was to achieve peace, not to precipitate new wars. Parente was forbidden to make war on any tribe that was not involved in the conspiracy. His soldiers were forbidden to destroy or take anything from friendly Indians on the line of march; if they needed anything, they were to buy it from the Indians.[9] These counsels of moderation were not followed. Starting out from Belém with a strong force of soldiers and friendly Indians, he laid waste all the Indian villages for miles around and killed many hundreds of Indians and captured others. It was such a terrible raid that the Tupí Indians were never able to attack Belém again.[10]

These early years in Pará were also troubled by the intrusion of other Europeans in the Amazon Valley, drawn there by the

from Pará because of his handling of the Indians. Studart, *Documentos Brasil*, I, 124-130.

[8] See "Carta de Francisco de Azevedo a El Rei sobre o estado e necessidades do Pará e Maranhão, dezembro de 1618," *Ibid.*, 191-194. See also "Carta do Vice-Rei de Portugal a S. Magestade opinando sobre as medidas que se devem tomar com relação ao Maranhão, Pará e Ceará a vista de cartas de Antonio de Albuquerque e dos religiosos Christóvão de S. José e Antonio da Merciana, 31 de janeiro de 1619," AHU, Pará, Papeis Avulsos, doc. 31 de janeiro de 1619, printed in Studart, *Documentos Brasil*, I, 194 f.

[9] For the text of the *regimento*, dated Recife, March 22, 1619, see *ibid.*, IV, 13-22.

[10] Fr. Manoel Gomes, a Jesuit who stayed in Maranhão until 1618, in a letter written on July 2, 1621, accused the authorities of Pará of killing more than 30,000 Indians. In Cumá, 80 leagues wide, there was not a single Indian left. See BNL, Fundo Geral, Caixa 222, printed in Studart, *Documentos Brasil*, I, 273-288.

prospects of trade.   The Hollanders and Englishmen were especially interested in this.   Their trading posts, in the spirit of the times, were also centers of military and political activity.   In ridding the region of foreigners, the Portuguese authorities had to depend greatly upon the Franciscans, who enlisted the help (or at least secured the neutrality) of the Indians, since the friars were the only Portuguese who had any influence over them.   Ferreira Reis says in this connection:

> . . . the intervention of the Franciscans of Santo Antônio was an immediate consequence of the grave problem of the collaboration of the natives.   At the coming of the Portuguese, great masses of the natives were friends of the strangers from Britain and the low countries.   The enticing away of these natives from friendship with the exponents of Protestantism was one of the gravest problems of policy in setting up a secure domination.   Only after this was accomplished could the natives be made collaborators in the work to be done.[11]

An example of this Franciscan collaboration was given in 1623 when Luis Aranha de Vasconcelos was sent to expel the foreigners from Pará.   In his company was Frei Cristóvão de São José, who was "so respected by the Indians that in the few days of navigation up the river [to Gurupá] he managed to get forty canoes with more than a thousand friendly Indian bowmen to join him."[12]

Foreign outposts in the Amazon Valley had been discovered the very first year of the Portuguese settlement—in 1616.   In a letter to the king in 1616, Captain Caldeira de Castello Branco mentioned that he had heard that a Dutch expedition of fifteen ships had gone up the Amazon the year before.   Also he had been informed that there was an English settlement 120 leagues up the

---

[11] "A intervenção dos Franciscanos de Santo Antônio era uma consequência imediata do grave problema da colaboração do gentio.   Porque, à chegada dos ibéricos, grossa massa indígena andava acamaradada com os estrangeiros da Britânia e dos Países Baixos.   Subtraí-los à influência dêsses concorrentes, que, em última análise, se alistavam na corrente herética européia, constituía um dos capítulos mais sérios da política que se quisesse seguir para dominar seguramente.   Depois, transformá-los em colaboradores . . . para tôdas as aventuras que se tivessem de experimentar." "A formação espiritual da Amazônia," *Cultura*, I, 98.

[12] ". . . o qual era tão respeitado dos indios que em poucos dias de navegação pelo rio acima lhe ajuntou quarenta canôas com mais de mil frecheiros amigos. . . ." Salvador, *História do Brasil*, p. 500.   See also "Memoria dos governadores" under date of 1623.

river.[13] Military operations were evidently called for, and they
began almost immediately. The friars helped control the Indians
for these expeditions, but the natives were primarily taken care
of by military leaders who knew the jungle. The most successful
military leader that Portugal had in these campaigns against the
foreigner was Pedro Teixeira. Even as early as 1616, as he was
returning by land from São Luiz, he attacked and sank a Dutch
ship anchored offshore. As a reward he was promoted to the captaincy on August 28, 1618, by royal patent. In 1623 he took part
in the successful assault on the Dutch forts of Orange and Nassau
on the Xingú River. On May 23, 1625, he and his men attacked
and destroyed the Dutch fort of Mandiutuba, near the Portuguese
settlement of Gurupá, in retaliation for the burning of Gurupá by
the Dutch at the beginning of 1625. On October 24, 1629, he
helped to take the English fort of Torrego, on the north side of
the Amazon.[14]

Amidst all the trouble and instability that plagued Maranhão
and Pará during their first years, it must have been a refreshing
contrast in 1619 to welcome Azorean settlers into São Luiz, for
these settlers were the stuff from which well-ordered government
would proceed, not from the petty criminals and rough professional
soldiers who had made up most of the population until then. The
problem of securing the right kind of settlers for Maranhão had
engaged the authorities from the very beginning of settlement.
They realized full well that the sending of *degredados* would not
solve the problem.[15] Therefore, when Jorge de Lemos de Betancor,
a rich citizen of the Azores, offered to transport 200 Azorean families to Maranhão in 1617, the king ordered that every assistance

[13] For the remarks of Captain Caldeira, see Studart, *Documentos Brasil*, IV, 8-10.
Men offered themselves for the arduous job of expelling foreigners and seeking
Indian slaves in the very first year of the colony. See, for instance, the *consulta*
of the Council of the Exchequer concerning the petition of Captain Antônio Bar-
roso to make a "conquest of the Amazon River." AHU, Pará, Papeis Avulsos,
doc. 30 de dezembro de 1616.

[14] Manuel Barata, *A jornada de Francisco Caldeira de Castello Branco. Fundação
da Cidade de Belem* (Belém, 1916), pp. 21-23, gives most of the facts known about
Pedro Teixeira. See also Pedro Calmon, *História do Brasil. A formação, 1600-1700*
(2 vols.; São Paulo, 1941), II, 105 f.

[15] On July 18, 1617, a royal letter to the governor of Brazil commanded that all
the *degredados* of Brazil, i.e., those guilty of crimes punishable with exile and loss
of property and title, should be sent to Maranhão and Pará. See *Collecção chronológica (1613-1620)*, p. 250.

be given him.[16]   Difficulties ensued,[17] but finally on April 11, 1619, 400 Azoreans arrived at São Luiz.   The plan was to send half of these to Pará, but most of the immigrants decided to stay in Maranhão because of the civil war going on in the neighboring captaincy.   The arrival of so many poeple severely strained the slender resources of the captaincy, but the good services of Diogo da Costa Machado, the *capitão-mor* of Maranhão at the time, and a fellow-Azorean, caused means to be found to take care of the immigrants until they became self-supporting.[18]

The presence of the Azoreans soon made itself felt in Maranhão: a town council was organized in São Luiz, with its members elected from among the Azoreans and the older settlers.   In a letter to the king of December 9, 1619, the councilmen expressed great hopes for the future of the colony.[19]

In the mind of the king, one of the things which would serve to stabilize this new conquest as soon as possible was to set up the Amazon region as an independent governmental unit, separate from Brazil.   From the very first years of the conquest it became evident that the captaincies of the Amazon region could not be effectively governed from Bahia and that, therefore, they ought to be made independent of the state of Brazil.   A very telling reason was the prevailing sea current along the northern coast of Brazil, which seriously hampered communication with Pernambuco and Bahia.   This difficulty had been mentioned as early as 1609 by Fr. Luiz Figueira, after his return from Ceará.[20] Governor Diogo de Menezes mentioned it in 1612,[21] and in 1616 Alexandre de Moura said it was easier to go from Maranhão to Portugal than to go from there to Brazil.[22]

---

[16] The king's order was dated April 12, 1617.   For the text, see Studart, *Documentos Brasil*, II, 181 f.

[17] Storms drove the fleet back in 1618.   See the *auto* of December 13, 1618, concerning their forced return in *ibid.*, I, 162-164.

[18] See letter of Betancor, May 6, 1619 in *ibid.*, I, 209-214.   See also letter of Machado, December 10, 1619, in *ibid.*, pp. 243-250.

[19] *Ibid.*, I, 235-243.

[20] *Ibid.*, doc. of August 26, 1609, pp. 42-44.

[21] Letter of March 1, 1612, in ANTT, Corpo Cronologico, parte I, maço 115, doc. 129, printed in Studart, *Documentos Brasil*, II, 65-68, and *Documentos Leste-Oeste*, pp. 307-310.

[22] "Relatorio de Alexandre de Moura . . . 24 de outubro de 1616," *ibid.*, pp. 193-242.

Insofar as we know, the king made up his mind to separate the government of Maranhão from that of Brazil as early as June 20, 1618, apparently at the suggestion of Gaspar de Sousa.[23] In the following year, as seems likely, Dom Diogo de Carcamo, or Carcome, was named governor-general of the new state of Maranhão and Grão Pará,[24] although the new state itself came into being only with the royal letter of June 13, 1621.[25] The governor, however, seemed to be in no hurry to take over his post. As late as January 11, 1623, he asked for an *ajuda de custo* of 800 milreis to prepare for his journey.[26] It was on the same day that the king set his salary at 800 milreis per year.[27] Actually, Carcamo never

[23] The exact suggestion of Sousa has not been found in the sources, but the king wrote in part to the viceroy of Portugal: "E hei por bem que o governo do Maranhão se separe do do Brazil. E porque convem que o governador que ally ade aver seja pessoa que tenha experiencia do gentio, e daquellas terras Vos encommendo que veijaes o parecer de Gaspar de Sousa cuja copia hyra com esta carta em que aponta as pessoas que para este governo podem ser a prepozito, e me consulteis logo o que vos parecer." Studart, *Documentos Brasil*, I, 141 f. or II, 190 f.

[24] The nomination probably took place in October, 1619, because there is in ANTT, *Collecção de Leis*, Livro 3, fl. 107v, a "Regimento do ouvidor geral do Maranhão" given to a Sebastião Barbosa on November 7, 1619, and this *regimento* directs him to refer the larger cases directly to the Casa da Suplicação of Lisbon, and not to the *Relação* of Bahia, as would have been the case if Maranhão were still subordinate to the government of Bahia. See also the *consulta* of the Council of the Exchequer, AHU, Códices de Consultas de Partes, Num. 32, p. 128, doc. 14 de outubro de 1620, concerning Carcamo's petition to the king for twenty leagues of land in Maranhão. His reason for asking was that the *regimento* given to him as the new governor gave him the power to distribute land to others. The viceroy of Portugal sent the petition to the council for their opinion. Their reply was that he could have a piece of land ten leagues long and four leagues wide, that was not claimed by someone else before him. The king's answer is as follows: "Vi duas consultas do Conselho de minha fazenda que me inviastes com carta vossa de dezanove de outubro passado hua sobre Dom Diogo de Carcamo que tenho nomeado por governador da conquista do Maranhão ao qual se dira que despois que estiver naquellas partes mande hua rellação do districto da costa da dita conquista e das terras que nellas estão dadas para com isso lhe mandar responder como foi servido."

[25] See Varnhagen, *História geral*, II, 185 f.; Braga, *História do Pará*, p. 62; Cruz Filho, *História do Ceará*, pp. 87 f.; *Revista do Instituto Historico e Geographico do Pará*, I, 30. I was not able to find the original *carta regia*.

[26] "Carta a D. Diogo de Carcome," ANTT, Chancelaria de Filipe III, Livro 18, fl. 73.

[27] "Alvará de ordenado do Governador Diogo de Carcome, 11 de janeiro de 1623," ANTT, Chancelaria de Filipe III, Livro 18, fls. 80 ff.

left Portugal. Finally, on September 23, 1623, Francisco Coelho de Carvalho was appointed in his place.[28]

The new state was called "the state of Maranhão and Grão Pará," and included the following component parts: the present-day states of Ceará, Piauí, Maranhão, Pará and Amazonas. Of these five, the last three were permanent parts of the state; the other two remained in it only part of the colonial period. During the period covered in this book, Piauí belonged to the captaincy of Bahia, becoming part of Maranhão only in 1715. This lasted until 1758, when Piauí became an independent captaincy.[29] Ceará, on the other hand, was part of the new state of Maranhão from the beginning in 1621, but remained so only until 1656, when it passed over for all practical purposes to the jurisdiction of Pernambuco. It became an independent captaincy only in 1799.[30]

The plans of the home government for the new state naturally included some sort of ecclesiastical organization for both Maranhão and Pará to take care of the spiritual needs of the settlers and the

---

[28] Berredo, *Annaes históricos*, I, No. 516; Braga, *História do Pará*, p. 63. For his *regimento*, which contains several general commands concerning the freedom of the Indians, see Studart, *Documentos Brasil*, II, 236-243.

[29] The *alvará* of January 11, 1715, transferred Piauí to the jurisdiction of Maranhão. The *alvará* of November 18, 1718, created Piauí as a separate captaincy, independent of Maranhão, but this latter letter was never put into execution, so that until 1758, Piauí remained under the administration of Maranhão. In the latter year, on July 29, Piauí was formed into a separate independent captaincy definitively. See Arthur César Ferreira Reis, *Estadistas portugueses na Amazônia. Estudos históricos e literários* (Rio de Janeiro, 1948), p. 134.

[30] From 1621 to 1656 Ceará formed part of Maranhão. On July 27, 1656, by royal order, it passed to the jurisdiction of Pernambuco, because of reasons of finance, although, legally, it remained a part of the state of Maranhão. It was most difficult for Maranhão to support Ceará at all times, and help from the home government was slow in coming. The system followed during the years 1621-1656 was for the governor of Maranhão to ask the king to command the authorities of Pernambuco to send supplies to Ceará—a most unsatisfactory arrangement. See Cruz Filho, *História do Ceará* (São Paulo, 1931), pp. 87 f. Studart, in *Documentos Brasil*, I-IV, *passim*, has collected practically all the available documentation on early Ceará. Practically speaking, Ceará had importance in the seventeenth century only as a way station between Pernambuco and Maranhão and Pará. The land was poor. Ceará was little more than a military fort all during the period covered by this book. It is clear that the captaincies of Maranhão and Pará were the important sections of the new state. Ceará became an independent captaincy in 1799, on January 17. See Cruz Filho, *op. cit.*, p. 88.

Indians. It is true that there were four Franciscans in Pará, a few Carmelites in Maranhão and perhaps three or four secular priests. But organization was lacking. The better men of the colony, such as Manoel de Sousa d'Eça, whom Capistrano de Abreu has called "the most sympathetic figure of the early days of Maranhão,"[31] had long been pleading for more missionaries, especially Franciscans and Jesuits. As early as 1618 Sousa d'Eça wrote:

> Senhor: In Grão Pará there is no secular priest, although many are necessary since there is a great quantity of pagans whose conversion must be accomplished. And the Franciscan fathers here are only four in number and cannot take care of the least part of what is necessary.[32]

Responding to these requests, the Crown at first thought to found a bishopric in São Luiz, but the idea was shelved in favor of sending Franciscans, with a major superior who would have quasi-episcopal powers.[33]

Acting upon this advice, the Franciscans of St. Anthony Province in their chapter of 1622 elected as custos, or major superior, Frei Cristóvão Severim, usually called Frei Cristóvão de Lisboa, brother of the historian and chanter of the Cathedral Church of Évora, Manoel Severim de Faria.[34]

---

[31] For Capistrano de Abreu's estimate and biographical details on Manoel de Sousa d'Eça, see Varnhagen, *História geral*, II, 208-210.

[32] "Sñor. No Gram Pará não ha nenhú sacerdote clerigo de missa sendo necessarios muitos por ser muita a quantidade do gentio, em cuja conversão se a de trabalhar. E os Padres capuchos que laa ha são quatro, e não podem acodir a menor parte do que he necessario," AHU, Pará, Papeis Avulsos, doc. 20 de fevereiro de 1618. On July 28, 1621, the Council of the Exchequer discussed another petition of Eça (which I could not find) in which he asks for Jesuits and Franciscans as missionaries. The council proposed to send to Pará two Jesuits and two Franciscans with Manoel de Sousa himself, who was soon to leave for the colony. The plan failed because the colonists in Pará did not care to have Jesuits. See AHU, Pará, Papeis Avulsos, doc. 28 de julho de 1621. See BA, 51-V-48, fl. 52v. for a *consulta* of the Mesa da Consciencia e Ordens concerning the same. The *consulta* is dated July 26, 1621.

[33] Varnhagen, *História geral*, II, 186.

[34] The biography of Frei Cristóvão has never been written. Dr. Luisa da Fonseca, formerly archivist at the Arquivo Histórico Ultramarino in Lisbon, has published some notes concerning his life and activity. See "Frei Cristóvão de Lisboa, O.F.M., Missionary and Natural Historian of Brazil," *The Americas*, VIII (1952), 289-303. Diogo Barbosa Machado, *Bibliotheca lusitana, historica, critica e crono-*

On April 30, 1622, the Franciscans, through their elected representative, Frei Cristóvão, asked the Crown for money (350$000)
to provision ten friars, six for Maranhão and four for Pará.[35] On
June 9, 1622, the king approved the selection of Fr. Cristóvão as
custos, as appears in a letter from the Court of that date.[36] During the next two years, while still in Portugal awaiting the departure of the new governor, Frei Cristóvão devoted himself to
the work of his future custody. Profiting from the experience of
the four Franciscans already in Pará, he formally asked the king
on October 17, 1623, to abolish the office of lay captains, which
the previous law of September 11, 1611, allowed,[37] and thus to
remove the Indians from laical control. In this connection he
wrote:

> The custos and the other religious which Your Majesty is
> sending for the conversion of the Indians of Maranhão and
> Pará declare that some Portuguese, Your Majesty not being
> well informed, obtained from Your Majesty the *capitanias*
> [direction] of the Indian villages of those regions. This re-
> sults in great harm to the service of God and of Your Majesty,
> because the aforesaid captains, as experience has shown both
> on the whole Brazilian coast as well as in the Spanish Indies,
> having their eyes cast exclusively on temporal profit, on ac-
> count of which they apply for the said captaincies without
> any remuneration, maltreat the Indians in various manners:

---

logica (4 vols.; Lisboa, 1741-1759), I, 581 f., has a few facts concerning his life and
the various works published by him. The family was of the lower nobility. The
most famous member of the family was Manoel Severim de Faria, the historian
chantre da Sé de Évora. Frei Cristóvão spent twelve years in Maranhão and Pará
(1624-1636), and upon his return to Portugal in 1636 took up again the life of a
simple friar. His advice was sought several times by the Overseas Council in the
first years of its existence. In 1644 he was named Bishop of Angola, but was
never consecrated. He died in 1652. I shall refer to various of his letters and
writings later on in this chapter.

[35] AHU, Códices de Consultas de Partes, Num. 34, p. 49v. The same petition,
apparently the original, is found in an incomplete form in AHU, Maranhão, Papeis
Avulsos, doc. 1622. It is signed by the future custos.

[36] ANTT, Santo António dos Capuchos, maço 6, doc. 9 de junho de 1622.

[37] See above, p. 7. Frei Cristóvão probably also had before him the memorial
written by the Franciscans in Pará, entitled "Memorial que aprezentão os religiosos
capuchos que ora estão no Pará os quais pedem a S. Magestade lhes mande dar
resolução de como se hão de haver no serviço de Deos e de S. Magestade sobre
algumas duvidas que se lhes offerecem, as quais são as seguintes," ANTT, MSS. da
Livraria, Livro 1116, fls. 593-598. The memorial bears no date, but from the
context it is clear that it was written between the years 1617 and 1622.

They hire them and overburden them with work, withholding the just wage for their labor; they even dare to take away from them their wives and daughters. They treat all Indians with asperity and immoderate rigor, neglecting to help them and to relieve their necessities. On the contrary, they do not even give them enough time to care for their own fields from which these Indians maintain themselves and also the Portuguese. Being interested only in having them working, they do not provide an opportunity for teaching them Christian doctrine, even though instruction in the faith is the major reason why Your Majesty, with such great expenses to your treasury, commands the settlement and conquest of these regions.

Since, as regards the aforesaid *capitanias*, the Indians need to be guided with meekness, they are scandalized to the point that they, as one solid group, flee into the interior, taking with them such reports about the Portuguese, to the others, that these then consider and treat us as mortal enemies. In consequence the country remains desolate without anyone to cultivate it and therefore there is so great a lack of food and game and fish, which they used to provide, that it is impossible to settle it and to have anyone to perform the services. Moreover, the conversion of those people and the propagation of the Catholic faith is entirely impeded and prevented, since those who accepted it abandon it by fleeing into the interior, and the rest of the Indians, who avoid contact with the Portuguese, cannot receive knowledge of it. Furthermore, the subjugated country is exposed to the risk of being badly defended, since we do not have any friendly Indians with whose aid we can defend ourselves from those who are not friendly, and without their help we can hardly manage it on account of the country being covered with dense vegetation, where only the Indians, natives and experts of the country know how to fight, being used to combat in such places with their weapons, bows and arrows, which we do not use, our weapons being of little effect in such places. Hence, one cannot help but conclude that Brazil and the Castilian Indies have been conquered with the aid of the very same Indians, our allies, whom our captains obtained as friends, understanding that without them they could not attack the others nor defend themselves. The undersigned ask that Your Majesty be pleased to command that the grant of the aforesaid captaincies be without effect, since, for these reasons, they are a detriment to the service of God and Your Majesty.[38]

---

[38] "Requerimento do Custodio e mais religiozos que V. Magestade manda para a conversão dos gentios do Maranhão e Pará, 17 de outubro de 1623," AHU, Maranhão, Papeis Avulsos, doc. 17 de outubro de 1623. There is another slightly

The petition was considered by the Council of the Exchequer, which decided to ask the opinion of ex-Governor Gaspar de Sousa. He agreed fully with Lisboa:

> All that is said by Father Frei Cristóvão de Lisboa, Custos, and the other fathers in this request is entirely the truth. . . . The conservation and the progress of this new *conquista* of Maranhão depends upon Your Majesty's commanding the execution of what the fathers ask in this request. . . . Your Majesty should decree that, if some appointments for the direction of villages have been made, these be void, and for the future no other appointments be made.[39]

The petition and Sousa's opinion were sent to the king, who, on March 7, 1624, approved the proposal and told the council to draw up the required enactment. On March 15, 1624, the law was finally passed which abolished the system of lay captain for the Indian villages.[40] The *ordinária*, or annual salary, of the friars was authorized by the Crown on March 19 and May 20, 1624. It consisted of cloth for their habits, wine for Holy Mass, olive oil and other necessary articles.[41] It was also during this time that Frei Cristóvão received ample ecclesiastical and temporal authority. He had already been appointed the superior of the friars. Now he was placed in charge of the administration of the Indians and given the quasi-episcopal powers of ecclesiastical visi-

---

longer petition by the friars in AHU, Maranhão, n.d. [1624]. Luisa Fonseca has published both of these petitions in *The Americas*, VIII (1952), 357-359. The translation used here, with some few changes, appeared in *The Americas, loc. cit.*

[39] AHU, Maranhão, Papeis Avulsos, n.d. [1623 or 1624]. This badly water-stained MS. was transcribed by Dr. Luisa Fonseca and published, in translation, in *The Americas*, VIII (1952), 294 f.

[40] The royal order to the council is found in AHU, Maranhão, Papeis Avulsos, doc. 7 de março de 1624. The text of the law, entitled "Alvará para se extinguirem as capitanias das aldeas do Maranhão, 15 de março de 1624," is found in ANTT, Chancelaria de Filipe III, Livro 39, fl. 77. This was the law brought over to the colony by Frei Cristóvão and published after his arrival.

[41] AHU, Códices de Consultas de Partes, Num. 34, fls. 78 f., doc. 19 de março de 1624; and *ibid.*, Pará, Papeis Avulsos, doc. 19 de maio de 1624. Earlier in the year, Frei Cristóvão had asked the Crown for additional money with which to outfit his friars. He pointed out that the objects purchased in 1622 had, due to the long delay, badly deteriorated; clearly some of them ought to be replaced. The request was favorably acted upon by the Council of the Exchequer on January 17, 1624, when each friar was granted an additional 20 milreis, a decision which the king later approved. AHU, Livros de registo de Consultas de Partes, Cód. 35-A, fl. 6, doc. 17 de janeiro de 1624.

tor. He was likewise given the powers of Commissary of the Holy Office, largely for the purpose of uprooting the heresies left by the Dutch and French traders.[42]

When the new governor, Francisco Coelho de Carvalho, finally left Lisbon on March 25, 1624, the friars left with him. The ship eventually arrived in Pernambuco, where the governor chose to remain for some time to help in the war effort against the Dutch at Bahia. Frei Cristóvão, however, was anxious to begin his work. He left Pernambuco a few days after his arrival in the company of his original band and five friars of the Brazilian custody who were persuaded to join him, partly, no doubt, because some of of them were skilled in the Indian languages. After a two-week stay in Ceará, Frei Cristóvão and eighteen of his brothers in religion continued to São Luiz, where they arrived on August 5 or 6, 1624.[43]

The friars were well received in São Luiz. The *capitão-mor* at the time was António Moniz Barreiros, a young man personally in favor of the missionaries and their work.[44] Berredo mentions

[42] Berredo, *Annaes históricos*, I, No. 522; Conceição, *Primazia serafica*, pp. 123 f.; Frei Agostinho de Santa Maria, *Santuario Mariano, e historia das imagēs milagrosas de nossa Senhora, e das milagrosamente apparecidas, em graça dos prégadores e dos devotos da mesma Senhora* (10 vols.; Lisboa, 1707-1723), IX, 363-365. Hereafter cited as *Santuario Mariano*. Manoel Severim de Faria, in his *Historia portugueza e de outras provincias do occidente desde o anno de 1610 até o de 1640* (new ed.; Fortaleza, 1903), pp. 19, 22, mentions two facts probably told him by his brother, Frei Cristóvão. The first one was that when the king asked the Province of Santo António to create a new custody in Maranhão, the province agreed, on condition that the province could have five new houses in Portugal, and stipends for twelve more collegians in Coimbra, so that thus it could get more new members who were lettered to continue the custody (p. 19). The second was that the king's intention was to send eventually eighty friars to this new custody from the Province of St. Anthony (p. 22).

[43] There is some confusion concerning the exact number of the friars from Lisbon and from Pernambuco, although it is generally believed that nineteen arrived in São Luiz. Expense money was allotted only for ten friars. The custos probably had his own grant of money from the king. It is conceivable that other friars were taken from Lisbon, without royal aid. The additional friars may have been lay brothers. Studart, in a footnote on p. 39 of Severim Faria, *op. cit.*, speaks of the five friars taken from Pernambuco: "Em Pernambuco chamou a si mais cinco religiosos da Custodia do Brasil, que foram Frei António do Calvario, excellente lingoa dos indios, Frei Manoel Baptista, Frei João da Cruz, e os leigos Junipero e Domingos. . . ." Conceição, *Primazia serafica*, p. 123, says that Frei Cristóvão left two friars at Ceará to take care of the Portuguese and Indians there.

[44] Barreiros held the post of captain-major from April 20, 1622, to September 24, 1626. See "Memoria dos Governadores."

how "the colonists [of Maranhão] venerated the new Franciscan custos immediately." Upon his arrival, Frei Cristóvão

> showed them the royal letter of March 15 of that same year, to which they gave entire compliance without the least doubt, although this was a great blow to their interests; of course, it is certain that the good offices of Captain António Moniz helped towards this joyful success.[45]

The friars began their missionary work immediately, probably in the Indian *aldeias* around the city. They also began to build a convent or monastery, which was completed before February 2 of the following year.[46]

Lisboa was anxious to promulgate the law of 1624 concerning lay captains also in the captaincy of Pará. For this purpose he journeyed to Belém, where he arrived on May 14, 1625. He was at first received with honors and expressions of joy. When, however, he presented to the city council the text of the law, the attitude towards him suddenly changed. The people of Pará, less docile than those of Maranhão, would have none of it. Because of the threat of a riot Frei Cristóvão was forced to postpone the promulgation of the law in Pará. To let tempers cool, he left the city, and in the company of three other missionaries, he made an evangelical tour as far as the Rio Tocantins, setting up missions and baptizing Indians.[47] He returned to Una, the Franciscan convent and Indian *aldeia* near Belém, on October 3, saddened by the miserable state of the Indians and the knowledge that they had learned to mistrust all Portuguese. His trip up the Amazon

---

[45] Berredo, *Annaes históricos*, I, No. 522.

[46] *Santuario Mariano*, IX, 364. In 1615 Jerónimo de Albuquerque had turned over to the two Franciscan chaplains, Frei Cosme de S. Damião and Fr. Manoel da Piedade, the little convent of the French Capuchins. During their stay there they had given hospitality to the two Jesuit chaplains. After the departure of the friars in 1616, the Jesuits continued to live in the Capuchin convent until they, in turn, left in 1618. In 1622, when Luiz Figueira, the Jesuit missionary, arrived in Maranhão with *Capitão* António Moniz Barreiros, he was granted title to the Capuchin convent and property by the said captain. In this location, well situated as it was, arose the Jesuit college and church. See Leite, *História da Companhia*, III, 117. Because of this, Frei Cristóvão and his friars had to find another location for their new convent in 1624.

[47] Berredo, *Annaes históricos*, I, No. 532-534; 543 f. The same author says that Fr. Cristóvão was accompanied on this trip by Fathers Sebastião de Coimbra, Domingos and Cristóvão de São José.

had, however, strengthened his resolve to be firm. On December 21, the day before he left for São Luiz, he promulgated the new law of 1624 by having it read in the Igreja Matriz of Belém, together with a letter threatening major excommunication to those who contumaciously continued to function as lay administrators. The populace was dumbfounded at the friar's action. There was a spontaneous meeting of the members of the city council and other influential citizens, who drew up a resolution against the new law. The law, they argued, did not cover Pará, but only Maranhão. Bento Maciel Parente, the ruling *capitão-mor* of Pará, had appointed the lay administrators legally, and the Crown, since then, had not condemned his action. The government of the two captaincies, they added, was distinct; therefore Frei Cristóvão had exceeded his authority. He had, moreover, made a great mistake, spiritually and temporally: spiritually, by imposing the penalty of excommunication on so many good men, and temporally by attempting to cause so many Indians to return to their natural domiciles, where they would continually be involved in bloody wars, and where they could not be used to protect Pará against foreign invasions. They asked Lisboa to allow things to remain as they were until the Crown settled the question definitively or until the new governor would arrive from Pernambuco. Lisboa saw the futility of his efforts, particularly in view of the fact that the *capitão-mor*, Bento Maciel Parente, did not support him, and he reluctantly allowed the existing state of affairs to continue. The next day, December 22, 1625, he returned to São Luiz.[48]

The prelate immediately began preparations for a trip to Ceará. A caravel had lately arrived from Pernambuco and Fr. Cristóvão hoped that he might sail on it as far as Ceará. But *Capitão-mor* António Moniz Barreiros refused to permit it. Whereupon the custos, saddened by this unexpected refusal from one he thought a friend, nevertheless set out by canoe, with one priest companion and a few soldiers and Indians. The little band was set upon by Tapuia Indians after landing near Perea. The ensuing battle was so fierce that Frei Cristóvão himself had to join in the fighting.

---

[48] *Ibid.*, No. 544-551. Certainly the fact that the new governor-general had not yet taken possession of his office lent strength to the arguments of the *Belenenses*. Francisco Coelho de Carvalho arrived in São Luiz only on September 3, 1626. Berredo, in No. 547, gives the entire document of protest presented to Frei Cristóvão by the people of Belém.

After winning this skirmish, the party finally arrived in Ceará on June 25, 1626, where it was warmly received by Martim Soares Moreno, the captain of the garrison.[49] Meanwhile the new governor-general had left Recife toward the end of July and arrived at Ceará within a few days. On August 15, Frei Cristóvão accompanied the governor to São Luiz, where the usual ceremonies of reception were held for the governor in the presence of the *câmara* on September 3, 1626.[50]

The new governor brought with him a royal order allowing the colonists to ransom "Indians of the cord" for a price fixed by the governor, and in return the Indians would have to serve the ransomer for a period of ten years.[51] On September 29, 1626, the governor called a meeting of all the civil and ecclesiastical officials in São Luiz in order to fix a just ransom price. It was decided that slaves which had cost the colonists more than five axes or their value, which was ten *patacas* (about 3$000), would remain captives for their whole life. All the officials present agreed to

---

[49] *Ibid.*, I, No. 552-554.

[50] See *ibid.*, No. 558-560 for details.

[51] The only source for this statement is Manuel Guedes Aranha, a procurator of the city of São Luiz at the Court of Lisbon, who made the assertion in his "Papel politico sobre o estado do Maranhão aprezentado em nome da Camara ao Senhor Rei D. Pedro Segundo por seu procurador Manuel Guedes Aranha, anno de 1685," *RIHGB*, XLVI, I Parte (1883), 18 f. I have found nothing about this law anywhere else. There is something concerning a similar law, apparently promulgated during the years 1617-1623, in the "Memorial que aprezentão os religiosos capuchos que ora estão no Pará os quais pedem a S. Magestade lhes mande dar resolução de como se hão de haver no serviço de Deos e de S. Magestade sobre algumas duvidas que se lhes offerecem, as quais são as seguintes," ANTT, MSS. da Livraria, Livro 1116, fls. 593-598. See above, p. 29. According to this information, this law was promulgated for the state of Brazil and extended by Governor Luis de Sousa to Maranhão. One of the questions asked by the friars in this memorial was concerning the opinion of the theologians on the new law promulgated in Pará by Governor Luis de Sousa, which permitted a white man to make use of the services, for ten years, of Indians who had been brought peacefully and willingly from the interior. The reply was that the law was unjust and the king should annul it because a white man under these conditions had no claim on the services of the Indians. But the same theologians, in answer to the question as to whether it was right for the Portuguese to keep ransomed *indios presos a corda* in perpetuity, answered that it was, since such Indians were rescued from death, and therefore were permanently bound to their ransomers whenever the ransom price was a fair one. But if the ransom price was less than the established one, Indians so acquired were obliged to serve only for a limited time.

this procedure, including the Franciscans and Jesuits present.[52] Meanwhile, Frei Cristóvão continued to organize mission work in Maranhão and Pará. By January 20, 1627, he was able to state that his friars took care of all the *aldeias* of Indians in Maranhão except one, which they only visited, while in Pará the friars resided in only one *aldeia*, but visited many others. The number of friars engaged in missionary work was twenty, in both captaincies.[53] In another place he mentioned that he had fifteen of his friars working in Maranhão, which left only five for Pará. This reflected the better atmosphere in Maranhão where the law prohibiting lay administrators was being observed, at least to some degree.[54] But both in Maranhão and Pará, Frei Cristóvão and his companions were finding out what a difficult assignment had been given to them. In both these captaincies throughout their history, in fact, it was to be an axiom that whoever controlled the Indians became the target of much opposition. Lisboa in 1626 and 1627 spoke especially of the opposition from the *capitão-mor* of Pará, Bento Maciel Parente, and from the Jesuit, Luiz Figueira.[55]

His complaints against Parente were especially vehement. He accused the captain of unparalleled cruelties against the Indians, whom he worked without cease until they died of weakness. As if that were not enough, he accused him also of great immoralities

---

[52] Aranha, *loc. cit.*, pp. 18 f. Leite, *Luiz Figueira*, p. 55, states that Luiz Figueira, who was the Jesuit representative at this meeting, after his initial agreement, began to have his doubts concerning the legality of this procedure, and, in 1631, submitted five questions concerning it to theologians in the mother country. Frei Cristóvão's doubts had apparently been taken away by the answers given to the friars' memorial before 1624. Another possibility, of course, since the memorial is undated, is that the memorial of the friars was actually written after 1626, after the meeting of the officials. This, however, seems unlikely, from internal evidence. For instance, the title of the memorial mentions the "Franciscans now in Pará," not "Maranhão and Pará," as would have been the case after 1624. Then, too, the friars request that the king send someone with ecclesiastical jurisdiction from Pernambuco to Maranhão. Would Franciscans have been likely to make such a request after the arrival of Frei Cristóvão, who already had the required ecclesiastical powers?

[53] "Cá ha este so mosteiro; no Pará uma aldeia com um recolhimento. Curão os religiosos esta e vizitão muitas outras, e de ordinario uma que está dahi a 4 leguas. Aqui curão todas aldeas tirando uma que a vizitamos; não assistimos nella por falta de frades, os quais nesta Custodia são 20." BNL, Fundo Geral, Caixa 29, Num. 28, printed in Studart, *Documentos Brasil*, II, 216. This paragraph is a postscript of a letter written by Lisboa to his brother on January 20, 1627.

[54] *Ibid.*, p. 204.

[55] *Ibid.*, pp. 200 f.

with the Indian women, young and old, married and unmarried.[56] The friar also said that the captain would not recognize his powers over the disposition of the Indians, saying that all Indian affairs were under the rule of the captain or governor, and not of the priest.[57]

Concerning the Jesuit priest, Figueira, Frei Cristóvão was also vehement. He accused the Jesuit of causing much of the opposition which the friars met in their administration of Indian affairs. He also accused him of slandering the work of the friars, and of fawning upon people whom Lisboa had to reprimand.[58] It must be remembered, in this connection, that Frei Cristóvão had also been given the offices of Ecclesiastical Visitor and Commissary of the Holy Office of the Inquisition, which would necessarily cause him to be stern also with Europeans who were not leading good lives. In the words of the *Santuario Mariano*, Frei Cristóvão

> . . . burned many books, which he found to belong to the heretical French, and many playing cards and superstitious prayers, which many people used. He separated those living in concubinage and did many other things in the service of our Lord and for the good of souls, in which he not only suffered much trouble, but many persecutions.[59]

The Franciscan also accused Fr. Figueira of impugning his authority in ecclesiastical matters, as, for instance, when he publicly disagreed with Lisboa concerning the prohibitions Lisboa had set up for all the people, viz., the prohibition against eating *jabotins*, a certain kind of turtle, on days of abstinence, and the prohibition against the capture and selling of Negroes as slaves.[60] To explain

---

[56] *Ibid.*, p. 201.

[57] *Loc. cit.*

[58] *Ibid.*, p. 202.

[59] "Queymou muytos livros, que achou dos Francezes herejes, e muytas cartas de tocar e orações supersticiosas, de que muytos usavão; apartou os amancebados das concubinas, e fez outras muytas cousas do serviço de nosso Senhor e bem das almas, em que não so padeceu muyto trabalho, mas muytas perseguiçoens. . . ." *Santuario Mariano*, IX, 363-365.

[60] Frei Cristóvão says, in part: ". . . e ao padre da Companhia andar dando liberdade de consciencia a todos para deste modo se fazer bemquisto, e odiarnos a nós com o povo porque fallando eu conforme a verdade e doutores disse que algumas couzas não erão licitas, como forão os Jabotins, cativeiro dos negros, compra delles . . . ." Studart, *Documentos Brasil*, II, 203. Concerning the *jabotins*: the friars and the Jesuits evidently differed on the question whether this type of turtle should be considered flesh meat, and hence prohibited on days of abstinence. Lisboa

the animosity of Frei Cristóvão toward Fr. Figueira, which Serafim Leite is at a loss to understand,[61] it is only necessary to remember the heavy burden of responsibilities the custos was bearing and the constant defiance which met his best efforts. This would have tended to magnify in his mind any lack of co-operation he received from another clergyman who he thought should have been aiding him, and not hindering him.

The biggest drawback, however, to the work of the Franciscans in Maranhão was their poverty. Franciscans, because of their special vow of poverty which forbade their use of money or their amassing of property, which would have paid their expenses, were particularly dependent on the royal help throughout the colonial period, and when that help was not forthcoming, or was delayed, as during these early years, they were literally reduced to penury. The complaints of Frei Cristóvão concerning poverty were particularly strong. There was not even any cloth in the country, he explained, from which to make habits for the friars, nor even linen for underclothing.[62] The king's promise to pay their salary in kind, i.e., in cloth and Mass wine and the other necessary things, was not being kept. He concluded that either the *ordinária* must be paid without fail, or else the friars could not continue to live in Maranhão.[63] The ultimate in poverty was reached by January 20, 1627, when, as Lisboa stated, the friars did not even have wine for Holy Mass.[64] Is it any wonder that the religious orders, later on in the century, began to take care of their own needs?

Under such circumstances of poverty, the friars could not continue to carry out their mandate from the king for any great length

---

thought the question was doubtful until resolved by higher authority. Figueira was so sure it was not flesh meat that he said he would have eaten it "in front of the pope" (*diante do Papa*) on a day of abstinence (p. 202). The question of *cativeiro dos negros* is of more interest to moderns. It is true that *negros* may possibly mean Indians and not black Negroes. But if *negros* be taken in its primary sense, then Figueira, and not Fr. António Vieira, must be charged with speaking in favor of Negro slavery for the first time in Maranhão.

[61] Leite, *Luiz Figueira*, p. 52, states that nowhere in the writings of Luiz Figueira do we find anything that would justify such animosity.

[62] Studart, *Documentos Brasil*, II, 204.

[63] *Ibid.*

[64] *Ibid.*, p. 213. ". . . fico agora no Maranhão bem avelhantado com os trabalhos corporaes, e principalmente com os da alma porque até o pasto do Sacramento nos falta, porque o vinho que el rei manda dar para as missas o não dão seus ministros nem a terra tem algum, tão miseravel está."

of time.   Leite claims that the friars had already abandoned their work in the *aldeias* in 1630, and returned to their convents in Belém and São Luiz.[65]   Although Leite gives no reference for this remark, it must be based on Luiz Figueira's statement in 1631:

> . . . the religious of St. Anthony here in Maranhão relinquished *this past year* the office they had of the administration of the *aldeias* of Indians, even though these religious were so zealous and even though they were put into the *aldeias* by a special provision of His Majesty.[66]

There can be no doubt that Figueira actually made this statement in 1631.[67]   Nor can it reasonably be doubted that the lack of resources caused the friars to slacken their efforts.[68]   But it does not seem probable that the friars abandoned mission work *completely* in 1630.[69]   We know, for instance, that Frei Cristóvão remained active in Maranhão and Pará until 1636.   He himself tells us concerning his labors:

> By order of His Majesty and in obedience to my prelates I

---

[65] Leite, *Luiz Figueira*, p. 55: "Em 1630 os religiosos de S. Francisco deixarem a cuidado dos Indios; pois a Luiz Figueira e aos Jesuítas se recorria para os casos emergentes."

[66] ". . . os religiosos de Santo António neste Maranhão . . . largaram êste ano passado o cargo que tinham da administração das aldeias do Gentio, sendo os ditos religiosos tão zelosos, e sendo providos nelas por provisão particular de Sua Magestade." *Ibid.*, p. 177, appendix.   The title of the work of Figueira is "Relação de vários sucessos acontecidos no Maranhão e Grão Pará, assim de paz como de guerra, contra o rebelde holandês, ingleses, e franceses e outras nações."

[67] The *Relação* of Figueira has been published several times.   Leite (*Luiz Figueira*, pp. 167-177); *ABAPP*, I, 15-25; and Studart (*Documentos Brasil*, II, 243-253) all used as master text the one found in BNL, *Collecção Pombalina*, Cód. 475, fls. 364-366.   This MS text, as I verified myself, is undated.   The *ABAPP* dates it 1631, but gives no reason for so doing.   Leite gives an emended and edited text based on BNL, and mentions that the *Relação* was published in Lisbon in 1631 by one Matias Rodrigues.   He admits, however, that he has not been able to find a copy of the published pamphlet, although he mentions that the *ABAPP* states it received a copy of the MS. from "um Sr. Espada."   The "Sr. Espada" referred to is Márcos Jimenez de la Espada, who found an original copy of the *Relação* in the library of the Academia Real de la Historia in Madrid, and published it in *Viaje del Capitán Pedro Texeira aguas arriba del rio de las Amazonas, 1638-1639* (Madrid, 1889), pp. 122-131.

[68] See above, p. 38.

[69] The collection in the ANTT entitled "Santo António dos Capuchos," consisting of twenty-five *maços*, or bundles of documents, would be the natural source of firsthand documentation on this matter.   Unfortunately, maço 18, entitled: "Di-

went to the regions of Maranhão and Pará to found a new custody of Franciscan religious of my Province of St. Anthony. I was obliged to travel to Brazil, to stay there for awhile, and thence I embarked for Maranhão where I remained for twelve years, traveling, visiting many times the regions of those conquests, dedicating myself to the conversion of the Indians and the instruction of the Christians, also trying to remedy and to settle many affairs with which I came in contact, by reason of the commissions given me by different tribunals; latterly, according to orders received from my superiors, I returned by way of the Castilian Indies, whence I embarked for Spain.[70]

His words do not give the impression that the latter half of the twelve years was spent only within the convents of the cities. It must be admitted, however, that the happenings in Maranhão and Pará during these early years must have been greatly discouraging to the Franciscan pioneers. For one thing, lack of recruits must have made an impression upon them. According to the available Franciscan documentation, levies of new missionaries were lacking during the years 1623 to 1652.[71] This meant that

---

versos documentos do conventos do Pará e Maranhão de S. Antonio, a saber: administração, missões, correspondencia, contas, noticias do hospicio de S. Boaventura do Pará, etc. 156 documentos," has been misplaced for some years, according to information afforded me at the ANTT, and up to November of 1951 it had not been found.

[70] "Por ordem de Sua Magestade e obediência de meus prelados passei às partes do Maranhão e Pará a fundar uma nova custodia dos religiosos capuchos da minha Provincia de Santo Antonio. Fui forçado tomar o Brasil, deter-me nele algum tempo e daí me tornei a embarcar para o Maranhão, onde assisti doze anos, correndo, visitando, por varias vezes as terras daquelas conquistas, ocupando-me na conversão dos gentios e doutrina dos cristãos, remediando e compondo tambem varias coisas que me vinham à mão por razão das comissões que tive de differentes tribunais, ultimamente segundo a ordem de meus superiores me recolhi por Indias de Castela, donde me embarquei para Espanha." Taken from the "Prologo" of Lisboa's *Santoral de vários sermões de Santos: oferecido a Manoel de Faria Severim, Chantre da Santa Sé de Evora* (Lisboa, 1638), quoted by Luiza da Fonseca, "Frei Cristóvão de Lisboa, O.F.M., missionary and natural historian of Brazil," *The Americas*, VIII (1952), 296. The same article describes an unpublished work by Fr. Cristóvão entitled "Historia dos animais e arvores do Maranhão. Pelo muito reverendo Padre Fr. Cristóvão de Lisboa, calificador do Santo Offício e fundador da custodia do Maranhão da recolecção de Santo Antonio de Lisboa. Anno . . . ." in 194 folios. The author mentions in a letter to his brother on January 20, 1627, Studart, *Documentos Brasil*, II, 214, that he is correcting and making improvements on it. The work at the present time is in the AHU in Lisbon. It contains many colored illustrations, hand-drawn, of plants, fishes and animals of the region.

[71] See the "Relação dos religiosos mais qualificados em ciencia e virtudes que

as the men died from sickness or other causes, there were no others to take their places. This factor alone could have forced the custos to diminish the number of *aldeias* under his care as time went on.

Another factor, not to be forgotten, was that of the failure, disastrous as it was, of the small salary paid the friars by the king. There is a *consulta* of the Overseas Council of March 20, 1629, giving a favorable reply to the petition of the custos for the sending of the Franciscans' *ordinária*, which had not been sent "for many years."[72]

There is no further mention of a request for their salary by the friars until after 1640. But perhaps the friars begged the necessary things from spiritual friends, in accordance with their Franciscan rule. An indication of this is given by Frei Cristóvão in a letter to his brother in 1627 when he says, "If by chance my successor as custos has not yet come, send me the order of iron tools that I asked you for. . . ."[73]

---

por ordem dos Senhores Reys Felipes 3 e 4 de Castella reynando em Portugal forão mandados a conquista do Maranhão e Grão Pará," ANTT, Santo António dos Capuchos, maço 6. According to this document, the main levies of Franciscan missionaries were sent in 1614, 1623, 1652 and 1653. See also the "Relação sumaria do que obrou a Provincia de Santo Antonio por seus filhos em serviço de ambas as magestades," Cód. 1086, Biblioteca e Arquivo Publico do Pará. Dr. Arthur Cézar Ferreira Reis transcribed this document in Belém and sent it to me before publication.

[72] AHU, Códices de Consultas de partes, Num. 38, p. 70. The *ordinária* consisted of: "Vinho para missas, farinha para hostias, cera, azeite e burel." The council agreed to send only enough for one year, saying nothing about the years before. Is it possible that the friars were not able to celebrate Holy Mass since 1627, when Frei Cristóvão mentioned the lack of wine?

[73] ". . . se acaso me não tem vindo successor mandaime a encommenda de ferramenta que vos mandei pedir." Studart, *Documentos Brasil*, II, 215. As far as can be ascertained, no successor came for Frei Cristóvão as custos after his three-year term, and he remained in the office for all the twelve years he stayed in Maranhão. It is true that Capistrano de Abreu, in his Prolegomenos to Salvador, *História do Brasil*, p. 462, mentions that, after 1627 "Frei Cristóvão de São José, Pregador regio," was "custodio dos capuchos." But from the context, it seems to me to be clear that this Frei Cristóvão was merely the Franciscan superior in *Pará*. On the other hand, a MS chronicle of the Province of St. Anthony, written in 1688, quoted by L. Wadding, *Annales Minorum seu trium ordinum a S. Francisco institutorum, continuati a P. Aniceto Chiappini*, XXX (Florentiae, 1951), XXX, 41 f., states plainly that the "secunda custodis electio facta est" in 1651. The first election of a custos took place in 1622. It is probable, therefore, that Frei Cristóvão de Lisboa remained as custos until 1636. This conclusion is much strengthened

In 1629 there had occurred an event which must have caused many Franciscans to lose heart: one of their number was killed by a Portuguese mob. It happened that in January, 1629, a group of Irishmen under the command of Bernard O'Brien sailed up the Amazon and built a fort at Torrego. Manoel de Sousa d'Eça, the *capitão-mor* of Pará, thereupon sent 200 soldiers and thousands of Indians to attack them, but without success. In September, 300 Portuguese and even more Indians made another unsuccessful attack. At this juncture men from an English ship landed near the fort and demanded that the Irish render obedience to the king of England under pain of treason. The angry Irish now entered into negotiations with Teixeira to surrender the fort. A solemn agreement was signed in the presence of Frei Luis de Assunção, a Franciscan who had accompanied the expedition, but it was scandalously broken. The Irish were imprisoned in Caité and their goods confiscated by the Portuguese officials, especially by the governor, Francisco Coelho de Carvalho.[74] This perfidy to fellow Catholics, together with the complaints against the rapacity of the Coelhos, the father as well as the son Feliciano, and the death of the well-liked Manoel de Sousa d'Eça, who was unjustly imprisoned by Governor Coelho, caused general dissatisfaction, and Frei Cristóvão de São José voiced it publicly in a sermon. This led to the stoning of the Franciscan convent in the middle of the night, and the killing of a friar while he was lighting a candle on the high altar of the church.[75]

by a remark made by the Franciscans in 1652, when they asked for "viaticum" for the proposed trip to Maranhão of a new custos and seven companions: The Franciscan superiors in 1623 "imviarão o P. Frei Christovão de Lisboa que assistio naquelle estado *mais de doze anos por Custodio.*" (Italics mine.) AHU, Maranhão, Papeis Avulsos, doc. 7 de março de 1652.

[74] These Irish traders were actually working for Dutch companies. An account of this expedition is contained in George Edmundson, "The Dutch on the Amazon and Negro in the Seventeenth Century, Part I: Dutch Trade on the Amazon," *English Historical Review,* XVIII (1903), 642-663. The numbers of Portuguese and Indians involved are given as somewhat less. These encounters were the last major encounters against the Dutch on the Amazon. Edmundson writes (*loc. cit.,* p. 662): "The Portuguese were from this time onwards (sc. 1630) masters of the Lower Amazon. After 1625 ingress to the main stream was barred at Gurupá and after 1629 such desultory trading on the part of the Dutch as still continued was confined to the immediate neighborhood of the Cabo do Norte, and owed its existence to the passing visits of vessels laden with stores for one or more of the colonies on the Guiana coast."

[75] Salvador, *História do Brasil,* p. 462. Frei Cristóvão said: ". . . não espanta

Under the circumstances, the question of their effectiveness might also have caused some of the friars to lose heart. It is true that the law of 1624, which abolished lay administrators, was enforced in Maranhão; but in Pará, where there were many more Indians, it was a dead letter. As we will remember, the colonists of the latter captaincy had appealed to Fr. Lisboa to wait until the arrival of the new governor before publishing the law there. When, however, Governor Coelho de Carvalho finally visited Pará in 1627, he allowed the existing situation to continue. This obviously displeased the Franciscans.[76]

In 1628 the Franciscan superior in Pará, Frei Cristóvão de São José, protested against a proposed *entrada* to the region of the Tapuia Indians, because he believed that such *entradas* would endanger the continued existence in organized villages of all the pacified Indians of Pará,[77] but no one listened to him, and the *entrada* was carried out under the authority of Feliciano Coelho, the son of the governor. The purpose of the *entrada* was ostensibly to ransom captives. When Governor Coelho, in São Luiz, heard of this expedition, he forbade all *resgates* for the future, even those permitted by law, and although he soon afterwards changed the ruling to pacify the people, he insisted that in the future only two official *resgate* expeditions be made each year, and that in each case Franciscans must be taken along.[78] When the *Câmara* of Belém received word of the new ruling at the end of the year 1628, they organized an expedition early in January and asked the Franciscan superior, Frei Cristóvão de São José, to accompany it. The friar, knowing that the expedition would inevitably perpetrate cruelties on the Indians, excused himself and his subjects from the undertaking on the ground that it was repugnant to the Order's rules.[79] The *câmara* now appealed to the governor, who gave permission for the expedition to be carried out without benefit of

que uma cobre mate um veado; em Pernambuco ouvi dizer que um coelho tragou um navio com toda a sua enxarcia."

[76] Berredo, *Annaes históricos*, I, No. 572. According to Berredo it is not clear whether the governor allowed new administrators to be appointed.

[77] *Ibid.*, No. 577. The protest was made on July 9, 1628.

[78] *Ibid.*, No. 578.

[79] *Ibid.*, No. 579 f. The formal reply of the friar was made on January 30, 1629. After 1688, the Jesuits used the same argument as the friars did in 1629, to avoid accompanying this type of expedition.

clergy.[80] Clearly, moral considerations did not carry much decisive weight with the state administration.

Another source of discouragement to the Franciscans was the rise in royal favor of Bento Maciel Parente, the most successful Indian slaver in the country. After his term as *capitão-mor* of Pará was over in 1626, Parente had traveled to Spain and Portugal and remained there for some time, making many suggestions to the king concerning Maranhão and Pará.[81] Finally in 1636 he was named governor of Maranhão and Pará, and in the following year he was granted the captaincy of Cabo do Norte.[82]

Still another blow was the riot against the friars in São Luiz in which a Franciscan was shot to death on May 10, 1637.[83] By this time the friars had, practically speaking, given up the fight. It remained only to try to explain the decline of the Indian *aldeias* and to rally to the defence of the friars after it was too late. This the Chancellor of the Exchequer, Jácome Raimundo de Noronha, did in several documents in 1637. He explained the situation as follows:

> The principal cause of the lack of these people [the Indians] proceeds from the fact that the said governor, Francisco Coelho de Carvalho, took the fathers of Saint Anthony from the *aldeias* which Your Majesty by your royal provision had given to them, which they administered with much charity and without self-interest, but when the great covetousness of the

[80] *Ibid.*, No. 580.

[81] Parente suggested the parcelling out of private captaincies within the limits of Maranhão and Pará to deserving men. This the kings carried out from 1633 onwards, giving out six captaincies of the eight Parente suggested, sc., Cumá, Caeté, Camutá, Marajó, Cabo do Norte and finally, years later, in 1685, Xingú. See Helio Vianna, *Estudos de História Colonial* (São Paulo, 1950), p. 276. See also *Revista do Instituto Historico e Geographico do Pará*, I, 30, and BNL, Fundo Geral, Cód. 7627, fl. 131, printed in Studart, *Documentos Brasil*, II, 270, for the delineation of the various captaincies, royal or private. Most of Parente's suggestions were concerned with the adoption in Portuguese America of the Spanish system of encomiendas. See AHU, Pará, Papeis Avulsos, doc. 10 de janeiro de 1635, where he ends his suggestions with a request for 3,000 families of Indians, 1,000 of them for six lives and 2,000 for one life. On September 3, 1636, he asked for 1,000 families, see AHU, Códices de Consultas de Partes, Num. 41, pp. 226-229. These particular suggestions were not followed in Portuguese America.

[82] For the royal grant of Cabo do Norte, see ANTT, Chancelaria de Filipe III, Livro 34, fl. 2, doc. 14 de junho de 1637.

[83] Studart, *Documentos Brasil*, III, 46. See also Leite, *História da Companhia*, IV, 44.

said governor entered into the scene the Fathers, not being able to support his insolences, gave them up and returned to their convent of St. Anthony in São Luiz, where the said governor persecuted them, and his son, Feliciano Coelho, also persecuted them, which resulted in the killing of a friar within the same convent at night with a musket, many people having entered it through its grounds and surrounded the convent and church to the great scandal of all these people, for they all cried out for justice to fall upon the criminal.[84]

The interior of the country, Noronha continued, was still not securely in the possession of Portugal. He thought that a company of soldiers should be sent to the back country to make friends with the natives by offering them gifts, but this could be achieved only by taking along a Franciscan:

. . . there must be in the same company a priest of the Order of *Capuchos* of St. Anthony, whose fame has penetrated to the most remote peoples of these conquests, and the Indians love them and respect them very much for the virtues and charities with which they treat them.[85]

The Franciscans were indispensable, to his mind, for the friendship of the Indians, and the friars must, he insisted, be sent back to the *aldeias*

because when Your Majesty sent them [to the *aldeias*], and they lived in the *aldeias*, they [the *aldeias*] progressed greatly, and after they gave them up for the above-mentioned causes,

[84] ". . . a cauza principal da falta desta gente prosedeo do dito governador tirar os padres de Santo Antônio das aldeas que V. Magestade por provizão sua lhe tinha dadas, as quaes elles admenistravão com muita caridade e sem interesse nenhum mas como entrou a grande cobissa do dito governador não podendo os padres suportar suas insolencias as largarão e se recolherão ao seo convento de Santo Antônio aonde o dito governador os perseguia, e seu filho Felisiano Coelho de que prosedeo matarem a hum frade dentro no mesmo convento de noite com hua espingarda indo muita gente entrandolhe por sua serca e sercandolhe o convento e igreja com grande escandalo de todo este povo que todos clamaváo justissa ao reo." The *Relação* is dated May 10, 1637. Studart, *Documentos Brasil*, III, 45-54.

[85] ". . . ade hir na mesma companhia hum religioso de missa da ordem dos Capuchos de Santo Antonio cuja fama tem chegado athe os mais remottos gentios destas conquistas, e os amão e respeitão muito por suas virtudes e caridades que com elles uzão." *Ibid.* Noronha in the same place recalls the time when the king wrote a letter to Luis do Rego Barros, *capitão-mor* of Pará, and told him to get the opinion of Noronha and of the father custos of St. Anthony. He now suggests that the custos should, in general, advise the rulers on Indian matters.

and their custos left for Portugal, the *aldeias* became very diminished. And the friars also left, some to Portugal and others to Pernambuco, so that today between Maranhão and Pará there are no more than three priests and two brothers and one cleric.[86]

Noronha sums up thus:

The thing most necessary in those parts to keep the Indians under control is for the Franciscans of St. Anthony to visit them and protect them, for the friars are held in great veneration and are loved as the only remedy for their necessities, because they know the charity with which they treat them, and the dangers which they undergo to defend them in peace as in war, which they have well experienced in all those [wars] that have been fought in that conquest. For the religious of this Order were always found there for their [the natives'] remedy, as Father Frei Cosme and Frei Manoel were in the beginnings and the taking of Maranhão from the French, [as] Father Frei António da Merciana and Father Custos Frei Cristóvão de Lisboa and Father Frei Cristóvão de São José were in the continuation of the wars of Pará; [they] and all the other religious have always offered themselves for the labors of that conquest; . . . wherefore it would be convenient for His Majesty, for the security of those great ports, and navigations to send the said religious from this kingdom [Portugal] in sufficient numbers to go to the aid of such a prolonged conquest, and to command that they be esteemed and venerated by the governors and captains, and that the crimes committed against them in that conquest be punished as crimes against the service of God and of His Majesty.[87]

---

[86] ". . . porque no tempo que V.M. os mandou, e elles asestirão nas aldeas forão ellas em muito aumento e despois que elles as largarão pellas cauzas sobreditas, e o seu Custodio se foi para o Reino ficarão muy desmenuhidas. E os frades se forão tambem huns para o Reino e outros para Pernãobuquo de modo que não ha hoje entre o Maranhão e Pará mais que tres padres saserdotes e dous leigos e hum corista." *Ibid.*

[87] "A couza mais necessaria que ha naquellas partes para ter o gentio dellas sogeito, é visitalos e emparalos dos religiosos Capuchos de Santo Antonio, aos quaes todo o gentio tem em muita veneração, e os amão como o unico remedio de suas necessidades, porque conheçem delles a charidade com que os tratão, e os perigos, em que se poem para os defenderem assi na paz como na guerra, o que tem experimentado bem em todas as que ouve naquella conquista, que sempre nella se acharão por seu remedio os religiosos desta religião como foi nos principios e tomada do Maranhão aos Francezes o P. frei Cosme, e frey Manoel, é na continuação das guerras do Pará o P. frey Antônio da Merçeana, e o p. Costodio frey Christóvão de Lxa. e o p. frey Christóvão de S. Joseph, e todos os mais religiosos se offerecerão sempre aos trabalhos daquella conquista . . . por onde convê a S. Magestade para

The initial attempt of a religious order to stand between the Indians and the Europeans and protect the weaker race had failed, but the failure had nonetheless taught valuable lessons. The Franciscans had tried, though unsuccessfully, to get along without money payments of any kind: as their salary they received only objects essential for their spiritual and conventual life, such as cloth for habits and articles for sacramental purposes. They had also put too much faith in a somewhat general royal grant, which gave them the administration of the *aldeias*, without any of the details as to how they were to be run, and without sufficient safeguards. There were too many loopholes in the early laws on the Indians. Perhaps none learned more from the Franciscan failure than the Jesuits. Fr. Luiz Figueira, in particular, had been in Maranhão onwards from 1622 and learned from the Franciscan effort what really had to be done. When he left for Madrid and Lisbon in 1637, he had definite ideas about what was necessary for success, and he proceeded very wisely to secure adequate financial help and wide ecclesiastical powers for his Order. When seen in this light, the failure of the mendicant friars was not quite as complete as it seemed.[88]

---

segurança daquelles grandes portos, e navegações, mandar os dittos religiosos deste reino em quantidade para acodirem a tam perlongada conquista, e mãdar que sejão estimados e venerados dos governadores e capitães, e que sejão castigados os delictos que contra elles se tem commetidos naquella conquista tanto contra o serviço de Deos e de S. Magestade." "Relação de Jácome Raimundo de Noronha, sobre as cousas pertençentes á conservação e augmentação do estado do Maranhão, 1637," *Ibid.*, IV, 46-52.

[88] José Francisco da Rocha Pombo, *História do Brazil* (10 vols.; Rio de Janeiro, n.d.), V, 47-51, tells how Figueira capitalized on the Franciscans' withdrawal for his Order's benefit: "Era o momento azado, e Luiz Figueira não o perdeu" (p. 48).

CHAPTER III

THE JESUITS AND THE INDIANS, 1636-1652

We have already mentioned the initial efforts of the two Jesuit fathers who came as chaplains of the fleet of Alexandre de Moura in 1615, and remained in São Luiz until 1618, when they left.[1] In 1622 the Jesuits returned to Maranhão—they were not allowed in Pará—and this time they stayed. Fr. Serafim Leite has told the story of his colleagues of the Maranhão mission in his books on the Society of Jesus in Brazil and his biography of Luiz Figueira, but parts of it, at any rate, must be repeated here.[2]

When Diogo de Mendonça Furtado, the governor of Brazil (1622-1624), who was a friend of the Jesuits, appointed António Moniz Barreiros as *capitão-mor* of Maranhão, he included in his *regimento* a clause naming Fr. Luiz Figueira Barreiro's counsellor. Figueira and a Jesuit companion, Benedito Amodei, a Sicilian, subsequently left for São Luiz in the company of the new captain. At first the *Câmara* of São Luiz did not want to permit the Jesuits to stay, but the new captain insisted. When Figueira signed a declaration that he would have nothing to do with matters involving Indian slavery, the *câmara* gave way and the Jesuits were allowed to remain.[3]

The exact province of Figueira's counselling powers after he signed the above declaration is not too clear. Leite maintains it was "in all matters touching on the Indians and their liberty, and in matters that might arise concerning war with the Indians, and in all others of greater moment and consideration."[4] He maintains also that Figueira kept his powers after signing the declara-

---

[1] See *supra*, p. 17. For the disastrous trip of Fr. Francisco Pinto and Fr. Luiz Figueira to Ceará in 1607, see *supra*, p. 9.

[2] Leite, *História da Companhia*, III, 99 ff., IV, 44 f.; *Luiz Figueira*, pp. 45-50.

[3] The *câmara* briefly replied to Barreiros' demands: "Fiquem os Padres Jesuitas visto ser mandado o Padre Luiz Figueira pelo regimento do Governador Diogo de Mendonça Furtado, para conselheiro dos negócios e govêrno desta conquista. S. Luiz em Camara, 2 de abril de 1622." Leite, *Luiz Figueira*, p. 50.

[4] ". . . nas matérias tocantes ao gentio e sua liberdade, e nas materias tocantes a guerra com o gentio que se oferecerem e em tôdas as mais de maior momento e consideração." *Ibid.*

48

16757

tion, because he added the condition to his pledge, "except if conscience or obligation oblige it."[5] But whatever we may think of the matter, it became a purely academic question, since the king had already determined to turn over the care of the Indians in Pará and Maranhão to the Franciscans of St. Anthony Province and to give ecclesiastical powers to a Franciscan custos.[6]

Figueira and his companion now began to build their college in São Luiz on the grounds of the old French Capuchin convent, which Moniz Barreiros turned over to them.[7] Figueira turned all his attention to the building up of the property of the Order and of its prestige with the colonists, since, after the arrival of Frei Cristóvão in 1624, he and his companions no longer had anything to do with Indian policy. Soon the Jesuits had the first stone building in the city, finished before 1628.[8] At the same time the Jesuits were active in their public relations and so successfully that even their worst enemies reputedly became their friends.[9] Part of their success may doubtless have been due to the school they opened for Portuguese children.[10]

After 1630 Figueira saw more and more the possibility of the Jesuits becoming the protectors of the Indians in place of the Franciscans, who were unable to cope with the situation created by the attitude of the captains and governors and their own poverty of resources. He asked theologians in Spain and Portugal to clarify certain points regarding Indian slavery.[11] He began to think of recruiting Jesuits for the work. He wrote to the Jesuit father general in Rome about these matters, and in 1635 the general ordered him to go to Portugal to acquaint the king with the sad situation of the Indians and the willingness of the Jesuits to take over their administration.

Figueira did not leave at once for Lisbon. He was anxious to see Pará first and explore its possibilities, so that he might include

---

[5] "Salvo se a consciência ou obrigação assim o requeresse." *Ibid.*
[6] See above, p. 28.
[7] Leite, *História da Companhia*, III, 117.
[8] Leite, *Luiz Figueira*, p. 53.
[9] ". . . contra êles [the Franciscans] as iras! . . . Daí a pouco, ainda os maiores inimigos dos Jesuítas se converteram em amigos dedicados." *Ibid.*, p. 52.
[10] *Ibid.*, p. 53.
[11] See BNL, Collecção Pombalina, Cód. 474, fls. 347-360. Leite, *Luiz Figueira*, p. 55, says in point: "O parecer de Madrid é minucioso, monumento de paciência, erudição,- é de fastio."

this area in his proposed negotiations. There was also another reason for the trip. Governor Francisco Coelho de Carvalho had bestowed on his own son the private captaincy of Camutá in 1635, and the son, Feliciano, had invited the Jesuits to establish themselves there as soon as possible. In January, 1636, Figueira left for Pará in the company of a lay brother, João de Avelar, whose own brother was captain of Gurupá.

In Belém, Figueira stayed with the Franciscans in their convent in the city and spent the Lenten season in preaching and teaching Christian doctrine to the Indian slaves of the region. Some of the people of Belém wanted the Jesuit to establish a house there immediately, but the enthusiasm quickly cooled and for the time being nothing was done. Immediately after Easter, Figueira left on a quick trip through the back country as far as Camutá and Gurupá. The Indians, who were already used to Catholic priests because of the activities of the Franciscans, received him gladly and begged him to remain with them. Those of the *aldeia* near Gurupá offered to turn some of their boys over to the priest in order that they might learn Portuguese more easily. Figueira actually selected two of them, and took them with him to Portugal. Upon his return to Belém, Figueira was stricken with intermittent fever, but it did not incapacitate him for long. On June 14, 1636, he was back in São Luiz whence he left for Portugal at the end of 1636 or beginning of 1637.[12]

Shortly after his arrival in Lisbon, Figueira published his *Memorial sôbre as terras e gente do Maranhão, Grão Pará e Rio das Amazonas*.[13] The country, he wrote, was fertile and the forests were rich in materials for shipbuilding. The soil was well adapted for the growing of sugar cane, and better crops could be harvested in Maranhão than in Brazil. Money, however, was needed for new sugar mills, of which there were only four in Maranhão with a few others in process of construction. The area had an enormous number of Indians, whose help in defending the country against the Dutch had been indispensable. Spiritually, the In-

---

[12] The above account is taken from Leite, *Luiz Figueira*, pp. 57-62. The custom of taking young boys from among the Indians was begun in 1625 by Frei Cristóvão in the Tocantins region. The good results achieved at that time no doubt influenced the Indians to make the same offer to Figueira ten years later. See Berredo, *Annaes históricos*, I, No. 544.

[13] Reprinted in full in Leite, *Luiz Figueira*, pp. 207-211.

dians were much abandoned. Not a single cleric or religious worked among them. The remedy, of course, was within the king's reach. All he had to do was to send some religious to minister to the Indians, for no more than the wages of an ordinary soldier and transportation. Temporally, the Indians were also badly treated. They were enslaved unjustly and subjected to extremely hard work. They were rigorously punished for the slightest faults. The result was that the Indians often escaped to the interior, abandoning their *aldeias*. Yet the religious who spoke against these cruelties were hated and persecuted. Such was the experience of the Franciscans of St. Anthony, who were forced to give up the administration of the Indians and return to their convents. Figueira believed that the mission field was so vast that it might more profitably be divided among the various religious orders. The existing clergy was woefully insufficient. There was a single secular priest in all of Pará and only four in Maranhão. Proper ecclesiastical control was also lacking. The bishop of Brazil was 500 leagues away, and the war with the Dutch made it impossible to reach him. Figueira thought that the king should send a bishop to Maranhão-Pará, or at least an ecclesiastical administrator, and also additional secular priests. Finally, the moral life of the settlers suffered because of the lack of Portuguese women. He advised that 100 women should be sent immediately to Pará, where they would all easily find husbands.

Figueira's *Memorial* was discussed in the Council of State in Madrid in August of 1637. The discussion brought out much information concerning the state of Maranhão-Pará. The Conde de Prado, who was Dom Luiz de Sousa, an ex-governor of Brazil, stated that there were about 230 citizens in São Luiz, four old secular priests, twelve Carmelites, four Franciscans of the Province of St. Anthony and four Jesuits. In Belém, which had at the time some 200 citizens, mostly soldiers, there was one secular priest, six Carmelites and two Franciscans. Between Maranhão and Pará lay the private captaincy of Caité of Alvaro de Sousa, which had no priest. About twenty-five leagues up the Rio do Pará from Belém was the private captaincy of Camutá, given by Governor Francisco Coelho de Carvalho to his son, Feliciano Coelho; this also had no resident priest. Seventy leagues beyond Camutá was the fort of Gurupá with forty soldiers, many Indians and no priest. The solution for the want of clergy, said the Conde de Prado, was to turn over the whole Indian administration to the Jesuit fathers, who had a particular aptitude for this sort of work.[14]

The Procurator of the Crown thought that there was no necessity of having the Jesuits in the colony, since the Franciscans, who had originally been assigned to the area, could, with twelve or thirteen men, take care of the needs, especially if they were helped by the Carmelites in the *aldeias* near to Belém and São Luiz. The Council of State, however, agreed with the Conde de Prado that the ecclesiastical administration and the missions should be entrusted to the Jesuits. The king approved the decision, but made it clear that the Jesuits would not be allowed to acquire property without the permission of the Crown.[15]

These deliberations were legalized by the *alvará* of July 25, 1638, which placed the Indian *aldeias* as well as the entire ecclesiastical government of the colony in the hands of the Society of Jesus. The law provided that the Jesuit superior of the house in São Luiz would be ecclesiastical administrator, with quasi-episcopal powers, with a salary of 200 milreis per year. Six vicars, each with a salary of 40 milreis per year, were to be assigned to as many Portuguese settlements. The Jesuits were to be the administrators of all the *aldeias* in the colony and each administrator was to receive the salary of a soldier to enable him to live decently.[16]

The ecclesiastical provisions of the law of 1638 aroused great opposition. The Mesa da Consciência e Ordens was strongly against allowing the Jesuits the ecclesiastical administration of Maranhão. So was the bishop of Brazil who on September 27, 1638, had formally asserted his powers over the Maranhão area and threatened to take up the matter in the law courts. Luiz Figueira asked the Mesa on September 17, 1638, and again on November 9, to advise the king to uphold the law as it had been promulgated, but the Mesa would not do so. On October 22, 1639, the Mesa agreed that Maranhão needed an ecclesiastical

---

[14] "... porque se bem naquella conquista ha tambem relegiosos do Carmo, nunca elles se applicarão as aldeas nem no Brasil aonde ha quatro ou sinco conventos tiverão administração de yndios, que depende de hua mecanica que so se acha nos padres da Companhia de Jesus." See AHU, Códices de Consultas de Partes, Num. 43, pp. 110-120, or Studart, *Documentos Brasil*, III, 26-40.

[15] AHU, Códices de Consultas de Partes, Num. 43. p. 118. The *parecer* of the Council of the Exchequer is given in Studart, *Documentos Brasil*, III, 41 f.

[16] *Ibid.*, pp. 59-61.

administrator independent of Brazil, but that the position should be given to a secular priest, not to a Jesuit. The members of the Mesa also opposed giving the vicarages exclusively to Jesuits, as they thought the law in a sense provided.[17]

These rebuffs left Figueira undaunted; he was determined to safeguard the position of his Order, to avoid a repetition of the failure of the earlier Franciscans. He continued to make requests and to write letters. Thus, in May and June, 1639, he asked that the salaries of his missionaries be paid from the proceeds of the tithes on the sugar mills, a secure source of income. This was granted by the Council of the Exchequer on June 22, 1639, and confirmed on June 27.[18] On June 3, 1639, Figueira was named the Jesuit Superior of Maranhão.[19] In July, 1639, Fr. Luiz declared in a letter that he then had twenty-two Jesuits ready to go, and asked for a *subsidio de mantimentos* such as the Franciscans had received in 1622. This was granted on July 23, 1639. On July 29 he asked for *viaticum* as the Franciscans had received. In August and September his documents referred strongly to the need for religious in Maranhão and Pará. On September 4 he swore that there were in Maranhão only three convents of religious: Carmel with ten or twelve members, Santo António with four or five, and the Jesuits with three religious. In Pará, he said, there was the convent of Carmel with five or six men. He did not mention the Franciscan house in Pará.[20] During the same month, he asked for *matalotajem*, i.e., provisions put on board ship, for himself and his twenty-two Jesuits.[21]

In 1640 Figueira finally achieved a partial success. On August 8 the king confirmed the *alvará* of July 25, 1638, insofar as care of the Indians was concerned. He did not confirm the ecclesiastical authority earlier granted to the Jesuits.[22]

---

[17] See ANTT, Livraria, Cód. 1116, pp. 241-249, for a more exact text of the *consulta* of October 22, 1639. The copy in the BGUC, Cód. 493, fls. 84 ff. or Cód. 488, fls. 281-286 is not complete. Leite, *Luis Figueira*, pp. 66 f., refers only to the copy in BGUC.

[18] Studart, *Documentos Brasil*, III, 59 ff.

[19] Leite, *Luiz Figueira*, p. 66.

[20] Studart, *Documentos Brasil*, III, 59 ff. The document of September 4, 1639, is also in AHU, Maranhão, Papeis Avulsos, doc. 4 de setembro de 1639.

[21] Studart, *Documentos Brasil*, III, 59 ff.

[22] Leite, *Luiz Figueira*, p. 66 f. The text is in *Collecção chronologica (1640)*, pp. 237 f.

Figueira's victory, however, was not yet complete, for the two Jesuit fathers who had journeyed down the Amazon with Pedro Teixeira in 1639-1640 and who now arrived in Spain, claimed the Amazon Basin for the Spanish Jesuits.[23] Fortunately for Figueira, the restoration of Portuguese independence of Spain occurred on December 1, 1640, and the Spanish Jesuits and Figueira now no longer argued before the same monarch. Figueira shifted his attention to Lisbon, but again there were delays, caused no doubt by

[23] In 1636 two Franciscans and six Spanish soldiers drifted down the Amazon River to Belém, arriving there in 1637. Jácome de Noronha was acting governor, and he dispatched Pedro Teixeira and a large flotilla to Quito. Frei Domingo Brieva, the Spanish Franciscan lay brother acted as guide for the seventy Portuguese, 1,200 Indians and four Spaniards. They left Belém in the beginning of August, 1637. See BA, 51-VI-46, "Relacion del descubrimiento del Rio de las Amazonas e San Francisco del Quito y declaracion del mapa donde está pintado," which bears no date but is certainly from before 1640. Printed in Jiménez de la Espada, op. cit., pp. 70-95. The flotilla left Gurupá, the farthest Portuguese outpost, on October 17, 1638, and struck out for the headwaters of the Amazon in present-day Ecuador. The chaplain of the expedition was the Portuguese Franciscan, Fr. Agostinho das Chagas, the superior of the Franciscan house in Belém. The expedition arrived in Quito in June of 1639. When Teixeira returned to Pará he had with him two Jesuit fathers: Cristóbal de Acuña and Andrés de Artieda, four Mercedarians, two Franciscans, Frei Domingo Brieva and Fr. Agostinho das Chagas. The expedition arrived in Belém early in 1640. The two Jesuits continued on to Spain, and asserted the Spanish Jesuit claim to the Amazon Valley. For the Jesuit account of the journey, see Cristóbal de Acuña, "Nuevo descubrimiento del gran Rio de las Amazonas," in Cândido Mendes de Almeida, Memorias do Maranhão, II, 57-151; also printed in Coleccion de libros que tratan de America, Vol. II (Madrid, 1891). For the Franciscan account, see Fr. Laureano de la Cruz, "Nuevo descubrimiento del Rio de Marañon llamado de las Amazonas hecho por la religion de S. Francisco, 1651, siendo misionero el Padre Fr. Laureano de la Cruz e el padre Fr. Juan de Quincoces," printed in Fr. Marcellino da Civezza, Saggio di bibliografia geografica storica etnografica Sanfrancescana (Prato, 1879), pp. 269-300. This account is primarily concerned with a voyage down the Amazon made by the above two friars, in 1651, but it includes accounts of earlier Franciscan trips, including the one of 1636-1637. Concerning the expedition of Pedro Teixeira, see also AHU, Pará, Papeis Avulsos, doc. 29 de maio de 1645, for a consulta of the Overseas Council on the matter. Concerning the Mercedarians, see Manuel de Mello Cardoso Barata, "Apontamentos para as Ephemérides Paraenses," in RIHGB, CXLIV (1925), 19-24. They founded a convent in Belém. After 1640 they had much difficulty in the colony because they were Spaniards. See AHU, Pará, Papeis Avulsos, doc. 23 de setembro de 1645, 3 de setembro de 1646. Finally the king, on September 9, 1665, ordered that the Mercedarians be not disturbed in their possessions or work. They could, however, accept only Portuguese into the Order. See ANTT, Livraria, Livros do Brasil, Cód. 33, p. 6.

the chaotic state of affairs and the occupation of Maranhão by the Dutch (1641-1644). Figueira succeeded, nevertheless, in getting from the new sovereign, John IV, most of the things he demanded, including the right to administer the Sacraments to the Indians without outside interference, the administration of all the Indian *aldeias*, annual salaries of twenty-eight milreis for each missionary and the permission to found three Jesuit houses, in São Luiz, Belém and Camutá. There were two notable restrictions. The governor, not the Jesuits, would see that the Indians were paid for their work by the colonists; and the Jesuits could not acquire property without the king's authorization.[24]

Figueira and his band of Jesuit missionaries finally left Portugal on April 30, 1643. Twenty-two Jesuits had earlier volunteered for the venture, but their number dwindled as the departure was successively delayed. As it was, only fifteen Jesuits, including the superior, left for America at this time—eight priests and seven lay-brothers. On June 12 they arrived off São Luiz, but they did not land because the town was then in the hands of the Dutch. Continuing their voyage to Belém, they were shipwrecked off the island of Marajó, and twelve of the fifteen Jesuits, including Figueira, were killed. Some were drowned; others were eaten by the Tapuia Indians of Marajó. So ended Figueira's attempt to place the Jesuits in control of the Indians of the state of Maranhão and Grão Pará.[25]

The tragedy of Marajó was a severe blow to the Jesuits, whose plans for the future of the Indian missions in Maranhão and Pará had to be abandoned for some time. They were not able to recover from this disaster until the time of António Vieira in 1652. In the interval, various attempts were made to protect the Indians

---

[24] Leite, *Luiz Figueira*, p. 67 f. For the grant of administration of the Indians see AHU, Maranhão, Papeis Avulsos, doc. 20 de setembro de 1652, under which is included a copy of the document of January 14, 1642, on which day the king granted Figueira's requests.

[25] The account of the voyage was written by Nicolau Teixeira, one of the lay brothers who was saved. He did not stay in the colony, but returned to Portugal, where he wrote "Successo da viagem do Maranhão," printed by Studart, in *Documentos Brasil*, III, 91-96. There were 173 on the ill-fated ship. Of these only forty-three were saved. Brother António Carvalho later died in the Carmelite monastery in Belém. Father Francisco Pires was the only one of the three religious who stayed in the colony. He was called to São Luiz to be superior of the Jesuit house there. See Leite, *Luiz Figueira*, pp. 69-73.

although long-range planning was out of the question, because of chaotic conditions and lack of missionaries in the state.

Conditions were extremely uncertain in the colony. The Dutch had spread their rule and influence as far north as Maranhão; São Luiz fell to them in 1641. Pará was never conquered by the Dutch, but it was cut off for a time from the rest of Portuguese America. The friendship of the Indians again was the crucial factor in the campaign that ensued to drive out the Dutch. Initially many of the Indians along the coast had turned against the Portuguese. But through the efforts of men like António Moniz Barreiros and António Teixeira de Melo, who kept up a continuous guerrilla warfare against the invader, and of the missionaries who exhorted the Indians to be faithful to Portugal, the Dutch were finally defeated on February 28, 1644.[26] At least one lesson was learned by the settlers from the Dutch occupation of Maranhão, and that was how much they were dependent on the good will of the Indians for their own security.

In Portugal, meanwhile, colonial administration was reorganized and centralized with the creation in 1642 of the Overseas Council (Conselho Ultramarino). Before 1642 colonial affairs were in the hands of many different royal officials. With the new council a greater unity was achieved; the council's business was exclusively the empire, and it was the king's principal advisory body in matters involving the overseas possessions. Maranhão and Pará fell of course within the province of the new council, and the records that have survived bear eloquent testimony of the council's interest in this unpromising region of Portuguese America.[27]

By the royal letter of March 27, 1642, João Pereira de Cárceres was named a "captain of the Amazon River" for six years, with the obligation of searching for mines and introducing white settlers.[28]

---

[26] For details, see Leite, *História da Companhia*, III, 99 ff. and Varnhagen, *História geral*, II, 409 ff. On the Dutch wars, see Varnhagen, *História das lutas com os Hollandeses no Brasil desde 1624 a 1654* (Lisboa, 1872) and Hermann Waetjen, *Das holländische Kolonialreich in Brasilien* (Haag, 1921).

[27] For a brief history of the Overseas Council, see Marcelo Caetano, *Do Conselho Ultramarino ao Conselho do Império* (Lisboa, 1943). Members of the councils, their presidents, etc., are listed in an appendix.

[28] ANTT, Chancelaria de João IV, Livro 11, fl. 365. This grant did not include territorial rights. It was rather like the grant given to Luis Aranha de Vasconcellos in 1623—a grant of exploration. See above, p. 23.

One of the first documents received by the Overséas Council from Maranhão was one written or dictated by one of the Indian chiefs in that territory, which related past cruelties to the Indians and suggested means to better their lot.   Frei Cristóvão de Lisboa and the other Franciscans were called upon by the chief to attest to the truth of what he wrote.[29]

With Maranhão in the hands of the Dutch since 1641, however, it was but natural that the newly founded council should devote much of its time to this emergency.   There is, for instance, the *consulta* of February 21, 1643, which speaks of sending help and supplies to the Portuguese fighting against the Dutch occupation troops.[30]

The Indian problem, however, was never quite forgotten, and it came to the fore after the expulsion of the Dutch.   In 1643, in the *auto* of João Velho de Vale, the captain of the fort of Cabo do Norte, north of the island of Marajó, the defendant was accused, among other things, of treating the surrounding Indians badly and of using the *resgate* illegally.[31]

In the same year the council took note of a letter on the local situation from an Indian chief of Maranhão.   The writer suggested that much more could be done by governors and captains who understood the Indian language.   It was especially important to treat the Indians with kindness, particularly at a time when the Dutch were a danger.   For his loyalty the council thought that the chief should be given 200 *cruzados* and a habit in the Order of St. James.[32]   The feeling of gratitude for the help of the Indians against the Dutch was also expressed in two documents of 1644.   One was a *consulta* on the report of *Capitão-mor* João Vasquo on the activities of the Indians of Maranhão against the Dutch in the last campaign of 1644.   Vasquo mentions by name six Indian chiefs in Maranhão and three in Ceará who helped the

---

[29] "Papel do Principal do Grão Pará," AHU, Pará, Papeis Avulsos, doc. 1642.

[30] AHU, Maranhão, Papeis Avulsos, doc. 21 de fevereiro de 1643.   For an eye-witness account of the successful campaign against the Dutch, see Studart, *Documentos Brasil*, III, 122-137.

[31] AHU, Pará, Papeis Avulsos, doc. 27 de novembro de 1643.   This is a document of almost 100 pages, badly waterstained and poorly written.   It is a good example of the *auto*, or *residência*.

[32] AHU, Consultas do serviço de partes de todas as conquistas, Cód. 278, fls. 1 f. Since this is a copy, the *parecer* of the king is not given.   I could not find the original *consulta*.

Portuguese, and he asked for a *mercê* for each.   The council agreed
in principle, but did not state the nature of the honorarium, nor
is the king's reply given in the document.[33]   The second document
concerned the request of Captain Paulo Soares de Avelar for money
for the widows of three Indians who were killed fighting the Dutch.
The council agreed to give each of them twenty milreis and so did
the king.[34]

The Overseas Council also concerned itself with the problems
of lack of manpower created by the epidemic of smallpox which
had depopulated the Indian *aldeias* of Maranhão at about the time
of the Dutch defeat.   The *capitão-mor* of Maranhão, António Teixeira de Melo, told in a letter of the defeat of the Dutch and the
entry of the Portuguese into São Luiz on March 2, 1644, and the
appalling lack of Indians in Maranhão.   The Indians of four *aldeias*, he thought, should be brought from Pará to Maranhão to re-
populate the villages wiped out by smallpox.   He also was in
favor of opening the back country to unrestricted *resgates* of pagan
Indians.[35]

In 1645 the petitions of Álvaro de Sousa and Bento Maciel
Parente the Younger, two land holders of Pará, for grants of *índios
encomendados*, after the Spanish American style, led to a lengthy
re-examination of Indian policy by the Conselho Ultramarino.[36]
The Overseas Council turned down the requests of these land
holders on October 24 of that year, because it feared that the
Indians would be mistreated.   Instead of *índios encomendados*,
the council was ready to solve the problem by once more turning
the administration of the Indians over to the Franciscans of St.
Anthony Province:

> . . . since Your Majesty has earnestly entrusted to this council
> the providing of everything that might be proper for the wel-
> fare of the overseas territories, and their growth and good
> government, and in particular the things of the religion of the

[33] AHU, Pará, Papeis Avulsos, doc. 9-XI-645.   Included in this document is an
appeal, written on August 13, 1644, immediately after the defeat of the Dutch,
in which the Town Council of São Luiz asks for freedom from paying *dizimos*, or
tithes, for ten years, so that the colony could build up to its former strength again.

[34] AHU, Maranhão, Papeis Avulsos, doc. 26 de novembro de 1644.   The king's
confirmation was given on December 9.

[35] "Consulta sobre duas cartas de António Teixeira de Melo. . . ."   Studart,
Documentos Brasil, III, 122-137.

[36] AHU, Maranhão, Papeis Avulsos, doc. 24 de outubro de 1645.

Holy Gospel, as a thing of the greatest obligation to Your
Majesty, and which you want and desire most, and since the
sacred Order of St. Anthony has for a long time with a great
increase of our Holy Faith. . . promulgated the Holy Gospel,
edifying both the Portuguese and the Indians with their re-
nouncing of private property, and of all kinds of business so
that it does not need the sweat of the wretched Indians, it is
the opinion of the council that Your Majesty should command
the provincial of this religion to send missionaries to Maranhão on the first boats sailing from here, with a custos of strict
life, morals and education, so that together with those of his
confreres who are now there, they may with the name of *pais
dos cristãos*[37] as is done in India, take care of the conversion,
the souls and the persons of the Indians and protect them from
the injustices (not to say tyrannies) of the powerful—teaching
and drilling them all in Christian doctrine, teaching their children to read and write our language, and that Your Majesty's
judges, captains and governors give them all favor and aid, so
that they may fulfill their obligation.   Finally [it is the opinion
of the council] that in the *residencias* of these officials, it shall
be inquired in a special way concerning their conduct in this
matter.[38]

[37] The office of *pai dos cristãos* was earlier created in Portuguese India to protect
the Indian converts.   The holder of the office could be a "sacerdote secular, ou
religioso de qualquer ordem, que outrora, no Oriente português, tinha a seu cargo
superintender nas conversões dos naturais, proteger os seus interesses morais e
mesmo materiais e administrar a instrução e a justiça aos neo-conversos."   The
title was first used in 1543 in Goa by Fr. Diogo Borba, who founded a confraternity
for the protection of the converts.   As time went on the office was limited to
Jesuits.   Through it they attained to great power and prestige.   Since the *pai
dos cristãos* had so much authority, especially in lawsuits, and in official documents
concerning native matters, his income was very great.   Rules were laid down for
the office by Jesuit Visitors in 1595.   No date is given for the extinction of the
office.   See *Grande enciclopédia Portuguesa e Brasileira*, XIX, art. "Pai dos
cristãos."

[38] "E por V. Magestade encarregar tanto a este Conselho, prover tudo o que
convier ao bem dos estados ultramarinos, e a seu acrescentamento, e bom governo,
e em particular as cousas da religião do Santo Evangelho, como couza da mayor
obrigação de V. mgde, e que mais quer e deseja, e a sagrada religião de Santo
António tenha de longo tempo com grande augmento de nossa Sancta Fee, culti-
vadas em boa parte aquellas terras barbaras, e plantado nellas a sua çemente, e
promulgado o Sancto Evangelho, edificando juntamente asi aos Portuguezes, como
aos gentios com a denegação de bens proprios, e de todo o genero de negoçiagião,
com o que não necessita do suor dos mizeraveis gentios.- Pareçe que V. Mgde
mande ao Provincial desta religião invie nas primeiras embarcações que daqui
partirem para o Maranhão missionarios, com custodio de reformada vida, costumes,
e letras, para que juntos com os outros seus religiosos que la andão, com nome de

The council's proposal was not accepted immediately by the king and it was only on November 10, 1647, that His Majesty wrote to the Franciscan provincial along the lines earlier suggested in the council. The king, however, took exception to the general use of *pais dos cristãos* and limited the office to the custos.[39] Affairs moved even more slowly in Franciscan circles. The new custos and his seven companions did not leave Portugal until 1652.[40]

The Jesuits also were interested in the Indians of Maranhão and Pará. In 1646 they asked to be given the administration of an Indian *aldeia* and confirmed in the administration of another *aldeia* which they had received from the local authorities. In support of their petition the Jesuit provincial referred to their work in the past with the Indians and pointed out that they could no longer operate without some *aldeias*, since it was only in the *aldeias* that they could find Indian linguists to accompany them on missionary trips to the interior. In view of the fact that the Franciscans had not yet been able to send more missionaries, as the king had ordered, the council looked with favor upon the Jesuits' petition. Actually the council now felt that the Jesuits, rather than the Franciscans, should administer the Indian *aldeias* of Maranhão and Pará, but the king, on March 28, 1647, decided against this opinion.[41]

The council also concerned itself with the problem of *índios de corda*, and asked the Franciscan guardian of St. Anthony in Belém for his opinion regarding their protection. The council had heard

---

pais dos Christãos (asi como na India se faz) tratem da converção, almas, e pessoas dos gentios, e os amparem e defendão das injustiças (por não dizer tiranias) dos poderozos, emçinando, e doutrinando a todos a doutrina christãa, e a os filhos a ler e escrever a nossa lingoa, e que as justiças de V. Mgde, Capitães e governadores lhes dem todo o favor e ajuda, para bem poderem cumprir sua obrigação e que nas residências destes ministros se pergunta (?) em particular pelos proscedimentos que tiverão nesta materia." AHU, Maranhão, Papeis Avulsos, doc. 24 de outubro de 1645. The same *consulta* is found in AHU, Livros de registo de Consultas Mixtas, Num. 1, pp. 258 f.

[39] AHU, Cód. 275: Registo de cartas officiais para todas as conquistas e mandadas do Ultramar, fl. 121-121v.

[40] See AHU, Maranhão, Papeis Avulsos, doc. 7 de março de 1652, where Fr. Francisco de Alcântara and his seven companions ask for *viatico* for the journey.

[41] AHU, Maranhão, Papeis Avulsos, doc. 19 de dezembro de 1646. The same *consulta* is found also in AHU, Livros de registo de consultas mixtas, Num. 13, p. 385. The king wanted more information before acting: "Peçasse informação a governador e com ella se me torna a consultar esta materia."

that the donatary of Caité, Álvaro de Sousa, had some ransomed Indians, and in such cases it was anxious to prevent free Indians from being included among the *indios de corda*. At the same time, the guardian was asked to advise the council of anything else which occurred to him concerning this matter.[42] On April 27, 1647, Father Luis da Assunção, Franciscan guardian of Belém, answered the request. He had spent twenty-four years in Maranhão, having come with Frei Cristóvão de Lisboa in 1624, and therefore was familiar with the problem. In his letter he suggested means of preventing the unlawful seizure of Indians who were not *de corda*. First, royal officials should not be allowed to buy any *indio de corda* acquired in *resgate* expeditions, if the Crown expected them to be just in judging violations. Secondly, the town councils should be allowed to send one or two *entradas* a year to areas outside of effective Portuguese control. This was obviously a concession to the realities of the situation, since the friar realized that Indians were necessary for the economic life of the colony. Thirdly, before the departure of a ransoming expedition a list should be drawn up of the colonists needing Indians most, so that their requirements might be filled first. Fourthly, these expeditions should pay for the manioc flour (*farinha*) they took from the Indians along the line of march, and for the services of the Indian rowers and other workers. These expenditures should be entered into a special book, signed by the town council members and the *procurador dos índios*, the latter an officer specially appointed to look after the welfare of the Indians. Fifthly, men—laymen as well as ecclesiastics—who habitually traveled through the back country to capture *negros*[43] should be punished. Sixthly, no violence or harm should be done to the Indians in any way. In this connection, the buying of captives from the Indians should be a free, not a forced transaction, so that God would not be offended and the Indians would forget past violences and live in peace with the Portuguese. Finally, the governors should hold

---

[42] *Carta Régia* of July 20, 1646, to the Guardian of St. Anthony in Belém, in Arthur César Ferreira Reis (ed.), "Livro Grosso do Maranhão," *Anais da Biblioteca Nacional do Rio de Janeiro*, Vol. 66, Ia. Parte (2 vols.), I, 23. Hereafter cited as *Livro Grosso*. An identical letter was sent to the governor on July 20, 1646. *Ibid.*

[43] The use of the term "negro" is unusual and is not explained. The whole context demands that the sense be "Indian" and not "Negro."

an annual *devassa* to round up the infractors of these regulations.[44]

The council sent Fr. Luis' suggestions to Frei Cristóvão de Lisboa, then bishop-elect of Angola,[45] who was living in Portugal at that time, and asked for an opinion, which was forthcoming on October 29, 1647. A letter of the Town Council of Belém, asking for more unrestricted *resgates*, was sent to the bishop-elect at the same time, and in his reply he took up both sets of suggestions.

Frei Cristóvão mentioned first the letter of the town council, which asked for a blanket permission to conquer the interior. Lisboa pointed out that this conquest presupposed war and violence "without which we cannot subject these Indians, who have done us no wrong, nor have they shown repugnance to the promulgation of the law of God, and they are in their own country where they were born."[46] There was no territory near São Luiz, he pointed out, where such conquests could be carried out; there was not a single Indian village in the 100 leagues between São Luiz and Belém, and only domesticated Indians within 100 leagues from Belém westward. But there were other difficulties which militated against granting this petition. "When the Portuguese go to these conquests, so many scandals result that they make odious the promulgation of the Faith, the Indians taking the Portuguese for unjust men."[47] The town council, Lisboa said, asked for *resgates* in the ancient style, as practiced in the beginning of the conquest. But this old form only led to the destruction of that land. Though the law forbade buying free Indians as captives, "any door left open for capturing would be entered by the governors and by all those they sent out. . . ."[48] The destruction had been widespread.

---

[44] AHU, Maranhão, Papeis Avulsos, doc. 27 de abril de 1647. For more details on the life of Frei Luis, see Wadding, *op. cit.*, XXX, 42.

[45] He was nominated Bishop of Angola on September 2, 1644, but never occupied his see. See Fonseca, "Frei Cristovão de Lisboa," *The Americas*, VIII, 298.

[46] ". . . porque o conquistar suppoem guerra, e força sem que não podem invadir, nem suggeitar aquelles Indios, que não nos fizerão aggravo nenhum, nem repugnancia a promulgação da Ley de Deus, e estão em suas proprias terras donde são naturaes." AHU, Maranhão, Papeis Avulsos, doc. 29 de outubro de 1647.

[47] ". . . e quando os Portuguezes vão a estas conquistas, resultão dellas tantos scandalos, que fazem odioza a promulgação da Fee, tendo aos Portuguezes por homẽs injustos. . ." *Doc. cit.*

[48] ". . . qualquer porta, que deixarem aberta para o cattiveiro os governadores e todos os que elles mandarẽ hão de faser entrar por ella. . . ." *Doc. cit.*

In the district of Ceará there were in less than sixty leagues sixty Indian villages; today there is no more than one, for all the others were destroyed through the *resgates*. In Maranhão were thirty-two Indian villages, and on the mainland of Cumá and Taputaperá, which is right in front of the island, to Pará, a great number of them, and all came to an end through the vexation of *resgates*. In Pará and on the great rivers of that district, there were so many Indians and the settlements were so continuous that everybody remarked about it, and today very few villages exist that have escaped, for all the rest perished in *resgates*, for the Indians, seeing that little by little they were all being captured against all justice and reason, in desperation would set fire to the villages and flee into the forest, and since they are weak and go without supplies and with great sorrow and disconsolately, and the forests are very sterile, in a few days nearly all of them die of hunger and despair.[49]

In this connection Lisboa compares the Portuguese unfavorably with the *gente do Norte*, i.e., the Dutch, the French and the English. They were in Pará, he said, long before the Portuguese and took out thousands of *cruzados'* worth of tobacco and other products, but they never captured Indians. The Indians voluntarily lived near the Europeans and served them, but they were paid for their work. In such a situation the natives were happy, and the foreigners were made rich.

Frei Cristóvão obviously could not be in favor of the town council's petition:

> . . . it is my opinion that His Majesty. . . should send an order to the governors of that land that they should with mildness and kindness bring Indians out of the more remote interior to live alongside the Portuguese, by which means the land

---

[49] "No distritto do Seará havia em menos de 60 legoas 60 aldeias, hoje não há mais que hũa, que todas as outras se consumirão por occasião dos resgattes. No Maranhão 32, e na terra firme do Cumá e Taputapera que fica logo defronte da Ilha até o Pará grande numero dellas, e todas se accabarão com a vexação dos resgattes. No Pará, e nos grandes Rios que naquelle destritto ha, habitavão tantos Indios, e Herão as povoações tam continuas, que todos se admiravão, e hoje são muy poucas as aldeas, que escaparão, que todas as mais perecerão pelas injustiças de que uzão os que vão fazer resgattes, porque vendo os Indios que pouco a pouco os vão cattivando a todos contra toda a justiça e rezão, desesperados poem o fogo as aldeas, e se mettem por o sertão dentro, e como são fracos e vão sem mantimento, e com grande tristeza, e desconsolação e os mattos sejão muito steriles, em poucas jornadas morrem quasi todos as mãos da fome e desesperação." *Doc. cit.*

would again be populated; there would be a place to teach them the law of God, and the Portuguese would have people to serve them and help them cultivate the land, and the custom of eating each other would cease out of fear of Our Nearness, which custom already in my time was not had for more than one hundred leagues around where we lived. For His Majesty to permit expeditions of *resgate* would be the occasion of depopulating the country of Indians, and of making odious the name of Christian, as has happened until now.[50]

The second item taken up by Frei Cristóvão concerned his opinion of the conditions for *resgates* set up by Frei Luiz. Frei Cristóvão thought the seven conditions were good, if *resgates* must be had, but he believed that no amount of regulation would control the evils that the system inevitably provoked:

... morally speaking I hold for certain that none of these safeguards will be observed, for those who go to make these ransoming expeditions, and those who authorize them in order to buy the Indians, and principally those who govern are interested in breaking all the said conditions, for the land of those conquests is very poor, does not have mines of gold or silver or pearls or precious stones, and all who entered the country commonly entered it as poor as the land is, and some want to leave it with many thousand *cruzados*. Others live as though they possess great income, and in the country there is nothing else for this purpose than to capture Indians, to sell and make them work, because of which in a short time they all perish. This is my opinion, according to God, and my conscience, and what experience has shown me in the twelve years that I lived in those parts, and traveled over them many times, seeking information with great diligence. . . .[51]

---

[50] "Pello que o meu parecer he que S. Magestade que Deus guarde mandasse ordem aos que governão aquella terra para que com brandura, e suavemente trouxessem os Indios dos sertões mais remotos a viverem juntos aos Portugueses, com que se tornaria a povoar a terra, haveria lugar de lhes ensinarem a ley de Deus, e terião os Portugueses quem os servisse, e ajudasse a cultivar a terra e cessaria o costume de se comerem hũs aos outros com medo de Nossa Vezinhança, o qual costume já em meu tempo o não havia mais de cem legoas ao redor donde nos assestimos. O permittir S. Magestade jornadas de resgattes ha de ser occasião de se despovoar aquella terra de indios, e de se odiar o nome Christão, como ategora tem sucçedido." *Doc. cit.*

[51] ". . . mas moralmente fallando tenho por certo, que nenhua destas cautelas se ha de observar, porque os que vão fazer estes Resgattes, e os que os dão para lhe comprarem Indios, e principalmente os que governão vão interessados em se quebrarem todas as dittas condições, porque a terra daquellas Conquistas hé muito pobre, não tem minas de ouro, nem pratta, nem perolas, nem pedras preciosas e

The council also asked the opinion of Governor Coelho de Carvalho, called "o Sardo," i.e., the Freckled One, to distinguish him from the earlier governor with the same name.[52] The governor thereupon called a meeting of the highest ecclesiastical and civil officials of São Luiz to seek their ideas on the practice of ransoming Indians. Their reports all agreed in allowing *resgates*, but with certain rules to govern them and prevent abuses.[53] The governor gave a separate reply in which he praised the Indians for the aid they give the state in peace and war, and said they did not deserve to be made slaves under any conditions.[54]

While the question of *resgates* was being discussed in this fashion, two royal decrees were issued on Indian matters. The royal letter of November 10, 1647, revived in part the law of March 15, 1624, which had abolished the office of lay administrators in the *aldeias*, and had substituted the Franciscans as administrators. The law, we will remember, had never been fully carried out, especially in Pará. The royal letter of 1647 did not, however, entrust the administration of the Indian villages to a religious order in Maranhão and Pará. Instead, it abolished all administrators and placed the Indians on a par with the whites. Henceforth they would be at liberty to work for whomsoever they chose, and for whatever

todos os que la passarão ainda entrarão commumente tam pobres, como a terra hé, e querem sahir hūs com muitos mil cruzados e outros viver como quem possue grandes rendas, e na terra para este fim não ha mais que cattivarem Indios para os venderem e fazer trabalhar, com o que em breve tempo pereçem todos. Isto hé o que me pareçe, segundo Deus, e minha consciencia, e o que a experiencia me tem mostrado em 12 annos, que assesti naquellas partes, e as corry muitas vezes informando me com grande diligencia. . . ." *Doc. cit.* This document has been published by Luiza da Fonseca, "In defense of the Maranhão Indians of Colonial Brazil. A report of Frei Christóvão de Lisboa, O.F.M., to the Conselho Ultramarino," *The Americas*, VII (1950), 218-220. I have a microfilm copy of the original from AHU. The translation is mine.

[52] Luiza Fonseca, *The Americas*, VIII, 290, errs when she says the opinion was asked of the elder Carvalho, who died in 1636. See "Memoria dos governadores."

[53] The official report of the junta, or meeting, is found in AHU, Maranhão, Papeis Avulsos, doc. 17 de junho de 1647. The reply for the Franciscans was given by Frei Francisco do Presepio, the president of the Franciscan convent in São Luiz. His ideas agree substantially with those of Frei Luis da Assunção. The vicar general of Maranhão, Fr. Mateus de Sousa, also wrote a separate report, dated June 30, 1647, See AHU, Maranhão, Papeis Avulsos, doc. of that date.

[54] "Informação de Governador Francisco Coelho de Carvalho o Sardo, AHU, Maranhão, Papeis Avulsos, doc. 20 de maio de 1647.

wage they could get. This was an obvious attempt to establish a free labor market for the Indians, but the attempt was quixotic in the extreme, since it presupposed that the Indians could deal on a footing of equality with the white colonists.[55] By the *alvará* of November 12, 1647, the Crown determined that the wage and performance scales for the Indians, men as well as women, were to be established by the town council of each city, with the assistance of the vicar general, the *ouvidor* and the *pai dos cristãos*, i.e., the Franciscan superior. The assumption was that an Indian would work for a given master so long as the conditions of employment were carried out. If the master did not live up to his obligations in this regard, the law gave the Indian the right to sell his services to one who would. At the request of the *pai dos cristãos* or of the Indians themselves, the officers of justice were required to see that the stipulated salary was paid. The Crown felt that with these guarantees Indians would remain contented and serve the Portuguese with good will.[56]

In the course of this section, it has been necessary to rely almost exclusively on reports sent to the Overseas Council. This was truly an interim period, and nowhere does it become clearer than in a consideration of the question of administration of the Indian *aldeias*. Various opinions were expressed; various plans were tried. But our actual information on *aldeias* themselves is very scanty.

[55] ". . . hei por bem mandar declarar por lei (como por esta faço), e como o declararão já os senhores reis deste reino, e os summos pontifices, que os Gentios são livres, e que não haja administradores, nem administração, havendo por nullas e de nenhum effeito todas as que estiverem dadas de modo que não haja memoria dellas, e que os Indios possão livremente servir e trabalhar com que bem lhes estiver, e melhor lhes pagar seu trabalho." *Livro Grosso*, I, 17 f. The text is also given in Alexandre José Melo Morais, *Corographia historica, chronographica, genealogica, nobiliaria e politica do Imperio do Brasil* (5 vols. in 4; Rio de Janeiro, 1858-1863), IV, 496 f. Hereafter cited as Melo Morais, *Corographia*. The papal pronouncement referred to is the Breve "Commissum Nobis." of Pope Urban VIII of April 22, 1639, which is published in full in Leite, *História da Companhia*, VI, 569-571.

[56] ". . . hei por bem que se faça hua taxa com acordo da Camara de cada Cidade, Villa ou Capitania com asistencia do Vigario Geral, Ouvidor e Pae dos Christãos em que se declare conforme a qualidade do lugar quanto hão de ganhar por dia cada um destes gentios asim homens como mulheres e o trabalho que podem e devem fazer, e que não se lhes pagando ao tempo devido o seu jornal possão elles livremente servirem a quem quizerem, e as justiças da terra, á requerimento do pae dos Christãos, ou dos mesmos gentios lhe farão pagar vervalmente o seu jornal, com que ficarão contentes e servirão de boa vontade. . . ." *Livro Grosso*, I, 18.

We know, however, that at least some of them were in the hands of the clergy during this period. This we know from the report of the *capitão-mor* of Pará, Sebastião de Lucena de Azevedo, who complained that the governor ordered him to give two *aldeias* to the Franciscans of St. Anthony, another to the vicar general and still another to the Mercedarians, all of whom would thenceforth be freely in charge of their administration. Azevedo was not pleased at this transfer of authority; he felt that clerics were being given too much power in temporal affairs, that they were, in fact, now ruling the state.[57] Azevedo belonged to the old school of soldiers who were accustomed to running Indian matters pretty much as they pleased. He misjudged the feelings of the king in his report and openly boasted of the number of Indians he had rounded up on one of his frequent raids to the interior.[58] Even the local governor did not approve of such actions. In August, 1647, upon his arrival in Belém, Governor Carvalho freed most of the Indians who had been sold in the public square during recent months and severely rebuked Azevedo for his part in the scandalous traffic.[59]

[57] His complaint is quite bitter: ". . . me mandou o governador geral do estado Francisco Coelho de Carvalho por hũa ordem sua tirar sinco aldeas e que nelas não emtendesse em couza alguma dando duas de administração aos Reverendos frades de Sto Antonio dos Capuchos, outra ao Vigairo desta cidade, outra aos frades das merçes e outra que manda pasar para o Maranhão com que fico desmantilado para poder comseguir effeito de me fortificar nem tratar mais que de esperar que V.M. me faça merce mandarme subçesor para o hir servir a essas fronteiras com hũa pica para que não se compedeçe que aja minha cabeça de estas obrigado, a omenagem que tenho jurado a V.M. E frades e clerigos am de governar esta praça tendo o superintemdencia das melhores aldeas sem heu poder mandar nelas couza algũa no temporal nem espiritual, . . . sufro tudo com paciençia porque emtemdo V.M. mandara acudir a estas couzas como mais comvir a seu real serviço e a my fazerme merçe de capratarme [*sic*!] desta praça onde não poso esperar senão hũa total ruina de que Deus a livre e guarde." AHU, Pará, Papeis Avulsos, doc. 1 de janeiro de 1647. On May 1 of the same year he complained again of the governor who was handing, he said, all business over to the vicar general and the Franciscans. He declared that there were only a few Franciscans in Pará and they were concerned only with "de se sustentarem com os gentios que tem a cargo e fazer suas granjes para seu sustento como dizem." AHU, Pará, Papeis Avulsos, doc. 1 de maio de 1647.

[58] "Por meus modos e intelligencias e praticas tenho baixado a V. Magestade setecemtas almas do melhor gentio que tem toda esta America da nação topinambá e sinquenta cazaes da nação Pinaré." AHU, Pará, Papeis Avulsos, doc. 1 de janeiro de 1647.

[59] Azevedo, in a letter dated August 20, 1647, said that the governor "em odio de todos os que a ella fomos, dá por livres estes escravos que alguns se venderão

Both of the men appealed to the home government, which supported the governor, not Azevedo. On September 18 and October 30, 1647, the council considered the whole question raised by Azevedo and concluded that Governor Coelho de Carvalho had done well in freeing the Indians captured by Azevedo. The council suggested and the king ordered that Azevedo be relieved of his post and exiled to the captaincy of Gurupá.[60] In the middle of 1648, he was sent back to Portugal in disgrace.[61]

One of the problems facing every governor of Maranhão and every *capitão-mor* of Pará was what to do about the Indians who were not friendly, or who were more friendly with the French to the north of Cabo do Norte. Governor Coelho de Carvalho, shortly before his death in 1648, had urged kindness and gifts as a first resort and force as the last.[62] In the case of the Aroan

de V.M. por captivos em praça publica. E os que couberão aos pobres que lá fomos quer que sejão livres. E as Cafilas que vem do Gurupá resgatados e roubados em guerra enjusta contra o gentio barbaro que nos não faz mal recolhidos no remoto de sertão desta conquista os vendem em praça publice e navegão para o maranhão. E estes tomados em guerra justa a um corsairo olandez inimigo Capital do nome portuguez os tem dado por livres sem nos querer ouvir de nossa justiça. E se nos tira o nosso remedio ganhado com tanto trabalho e risco de nossas vidas V.M. seja servido mandar acudir a isto com justiça e piedade porque os despojos da guerra fazem soldados atrevidos e animão-se a qualquer perigo para emprehenderem grandes couzas do serviço de Deus e de V.M." He added that if the king did not control the imperiousness of the governors he should find a successor for him (Azevedo). He had served the king for forty years and did not want to die in a campaign commanded by Mateus de Sousa, the vicar general, who, claimed Azevedo, was the actual governor of the country. See the series of documents entitled "Sobre o procedimento de Sebastião de Luçena de Azevedo, Capitão do Pará. Tres cartas e dois pareceres, 1647-1648," *Documentos Leste-Oeste,* pp. 461-465.

[60] For the *consulta* of September 18, 1647, see AHU, Livros de registo de consultas mixtas, Num. 14, pp. 87 f. For that of October 30, see *Documentos Leste-Oeste,* pp. 475-479. The council also was of the opinion that Azevedo had exceeded his orders in seeking Indians in the *sertão,* in leaving therefore the city of Belém unguarded, and in opening an official register for the names of slaves. No *entradas,* the councilmen said, should be made without the express permission of the king. Any French and Dutch traders found in the region were to be treated well and sent to Portugal. The king agreed on October 30, 1647. Azevedo wrote again to the king on April 20, 1648, telling of his sad plight in Gurupá. He named three clerics (Manoel de Souza, Manuel Teixeira and Frei Luis da Assunção) and seven laymen as his greatest enemies. He then made the famous statement that all the former *capitães-mores* either died violent deaths, or died in prison.

[61] Azevedo, *Os Jesuítas no Grão Pará,* p. 50.

[62] AHU, Livros de registo de consultas mixtas, Num. 14, p. 103, doc. 25 de janeiro de 1648.

and Nheengaiba Indians of Marajó, kindness having failed, the council and the king agreed that war against them was necessary, but the governor was advised to wage it against them only, and not against friendly Indians in the process.[63] King John IV clarified the Crown's position by making a distinction between those who were vassals and those who were not. An Indian vassal, like a white vassal, could be punished for crimes but not enslaved; an Indian who was not a vassal could be attacked and captured as a slave only if he refused to accept pardon or baptism.[64]

The problem of enforcing Indian laws was also of interest. The *ouvidor geral*, Francisco Barradas de Mendonça, served as a sort of circuit judge in the captaincies of Maranhão and Pará during the years 1644-1648, with instructions to be especially alert for crimes against the Indians. He asserted in his report at the completion of his term that he believed, for the safety of the Indians, that the Franciscans of St. Anthony should be given their old-time jurisdiction over the Indians as soon as they were able to increase their numbers.[65] He was also in favor of appointing a traveling *procurador geral dos índios* for Maranhão and for Pará, to report to the officers of justice on the welfare of the Indians.[66]

The Overseas Council continued to receive other reports on the Indian situation. On May 22, 1648, the Chancellor of the Exchequer of Maranhão, Manuel Pita da Veiga, wrote to the king of a trip he had made through Maranhão to observe the state of the free Indians in the *aldeias*. What he observed was appalling. The free Indians, he said, were kept working continually for seven months out of the year, in the growing and curing of tobacco, for the picayune pay of two varas of cloth or one iron tool a month. So difficult was the work that seventeen Indian villages in Maran-

---

[63] AHU, Maranhão, Papeis Avulsos, doc. 28 de janeiro de 1650.

[64] AHU, Maranhão, Papeis Avulsos, doc. 2 de março de 1648, quoted in Fonseca, *op. cit.*, *The Americas*, VIII, 291.

[65] "Aos religiosos de S. Antonio deve V.M. cometter no espiritual a administração do gentio, como de antes tinhão por provizão de V.M., obriguando aos provinciais que provejão os mosteiros desta conquista, porque nella há so tres religiosos de Missa, dous neste Pará, e hu no Maranhão." This fifteen-page report is in AHU, Pará, Papeis Avulsos, doc. 4 de março de 1648.

[66] "Convem que aja hu procurador geral dos Indios nesta capitania, e outro na do Maranhão, que corre as aldeas e se informe do que lhes fazem os moradores e do modo com que os tratão os superiores, e que de tudo de conta as justiças, que conforme a cazo for se proceda na matteria." *Ibid.*

hão had been totally destroyed since 1626, but the profits for the Europeans were high, in one case 2,000 arrobas of tobacco in return for 200 knives in wages. Enslaved Indians, he felt, were better treated than the free Indians, since the slaves were a *couza propria do Senhor* and were better cared for by their masters. To give free Indians some rest, Veiga suggested that they be prohibited from working during the months of December, January, May and June, in order that they might plant and harvest their own crops. Moreover, free Indians should never be used by the settlers for the cultivation of tobacco. This report was considered by the *conselho* on August 22, 1648, and it was suggested that a general law be passed to cover the points raised.[67] The king approved on September 8, and on the following day an appropriate law, embodying most of Pita da Veiga's recommendations, was issued.[68]

One of the effective ways that had been developed in Pará and Maranhão since the Dutch war to hold the allegiance of the Indians was the awarding by the king of habits in the Order of Christ, or of special distinctive uniforms. In 1646 several Indian chiefs in Maranhão petitioned the king for habits in the Order of Christ as rewards for their services in fighting the Dutch. The king agreed to authorize the governor to distribute four habits in the three military orders to the most worthy Indians.[69] In 1648, the Indian chief António da Costa asked for a *mercê* for his services against the Dutch and was given a habit of the Order of Christ, the administration of the *aldeia* of Cujupe, a special uniform for

---

[67] The original letter of Pita da Veiga was not found, but the *consulta*, which repeated the terms of the letter, is in AHU, Maranhão, Papeis Avulsos, doc. 22 de agosto de 1648. With the *consulta* is a *certidão*, or sworn statement, of Fr. Francisco Pires, attesting to the good intentions and activities of the *ouvidor*. *Ibid.*, doc. 22 de maio de 1648.

[68] The text of the law of September 9, 1648, is in *Livro Grosso*, I, 19. The pertinent parts are these: "hei por bem e mando ao Governador do Estado do Maranhão que hora he ao diante for que em nenhua maneira ocupe os Indios forros, nem consinta que outrem o faça nos mezes de Dezembro, Janeiro, Maio e Junho, que são os quatro do anno em que fazem suas lavouras, e que tambem não consintão que naquelle estado se faça tabaco com Indios forros, sob pena de que quem o contrario fizer perderá seus bens para a despeza dos soldados." There is a MS copy of the *alvará* of September 9 in AHU, Maranhão, Papeis Avulsos, doc. 24 de outubro de 1648.

[69] AHU, Maranhão, Papeis Avulsos, doc. 22 de março de 1646.

his wife and gifts valued at thirty milreis.[70] On October 11 of the
same year, the new governor of Maranhão, Luis de Magalhães,
who was then about to leave for São Luiz, was authorized to grant
twelve habits in the military orders to deserving Indians and to
distribute twelve special suits or uniforms among as many Indian
men and twelve special dresses among the Indian women.[71]

The perennial problem of controlling the labor of the Indians
occupied the court also in 1649. A *provisão* controlling the type
of labor to which a free Indian, working for a salary, could be
subjected was decreed on May 29, 1649. It provided that no
Indian could be obliged to serve without salary or at very hard
labor, such as in tobacco-curing sheds. Any settler could go to
the *aldeias* to arrange the terms of the wages to be paid the Indians.
The colonists who violated this law were subject to the punishment of four-year exile in Africa and a fine of 500 *cruzados*, half
of which would go to the informer.[72]

All these provisions were well intentioned, but the lack of organized care for the Indians was recognized again and again during
these interim years as the most glaring deficiency. On March 2,
1649, the Town Council of Belém do Pará petitioned the Crown
for the return of the Franciscans as administrators of the Indians.
This represented a remarkable change from the position taken
by the *Câmara* of Belém in 1625 when it did not permit Frei Cristóvão de Lisboa to promulgate the law of 1624 in the captaincy.[73]
The town councillors now admitted that the state was better off
in regard to Indians when the Franciscans controlled them; after
the Franciscans left the *aldeias*, the Indians became so reduced in
numbers that there were not enough for the needs of the colonists.

[70] *Ibid.*, doc. 3 de outubro de 1648. The king agreed with the decision of the
council, but raised the twenty milreis proposed by the council to thirty.
[71] Studart, *Documentos Brasil*, III, 180.
[72] I could not find the text of this law. For a résumé see Azevedo, *Os Jesuitas
no Grão Pará*, p. 57, or Manoel Guedes Aranha, "Papel politico sobre o estado do
Maranhão apresentado em nome da camara ao Senhor Rei dom Pedro Segundo
por seu procurador Manoel Guedes Aranha, anno de 1685," *RIGHB*, XLVI, Parte
I, p. 25. The original of the above is found, with the same title, in BNL, Fundo
Geral, Cód. 1570, fls. 221-297. The same document, with a different title, "Noticias
do Maranhão, situazão e costumes de seus naturais, mandado pella camara do dito
estado por seu procurador Manoel Guedes de Aranha anno de 1685," is found in
BA, 51-VI-46, Num. 5.
[73] See above, pp. 33 f.

The council agreed that the Franciscans should return.   It further decided that peaceful *descimentos* should be allowed, but only under the direction of the Franciscans and the vicar general.   The king put these recommendations into practice by his letter of September 28, 1649.[74]

On September 2 and 6, 1649, several Indian chiefs of Maranhão and Pará complained to the king of the treatment they received at the hands of the settlers, and asked for officials who could speak their language.   They also asked for Jesuits as missionaries, and complained against Vicar General Mateus de Sousa who, they said, harshly used the Indians of two *aldeias* for his own ends.   The king at this time did no more than to promise to write to the governor on their behalf and tell the officials of government to observe the laws concerning the liberty of the Indians.[75]

The request for Jesuits as missionaries could hardly have been granted because the Jesuits, like the Franciscans, were then suffering from a lack of men in the colony.   Leite says that there were then four Jesuits, at the most, in the colony: two priests and two lay brothers,[76] but three of them were soon to become the victims of an Indian attack.   Some years before, António Moniz Barreiros, who had served as *capitão-mor* of Maranhão from 1622 to 1626, bequeathed to the Jesuits the profits from a sugar plantation and mill on the Rio Itapicuru, for a period of time necessary to educate his son.   In 1649 Fathers Francisco Pires and Manuel Moniz and

---

[74] The petition of the *câmara* read in part: "No espiritual tinha V.M. consentido por provizão sua aos religiozos de Santo Antonio administração do Gentio.   Emquanto a tiverão não enfraqueceu tanto este povo, antes davam mostras de florear muito na fée.   Depois que os Superiores por suas conveniencias lha impedirão veio a estar tão necessitado que apennas chegão os moradores della a ter um indio por seu pagamento para se alimentarem."   The *parecer* of the council was given on September 19, 1649: ". . . no que toqua a administração dos Indios que pedem para os religiosos de Santo Antonio daquelle Estado se lhe consede na forma que pedem nesta sua carta, e que asim mais se lhe consede que possa deser este gentio por sua vontade na forma do que se consedeo a Antonio Coelho de Carvalho e Alvaro de Sousa.   E que lhe assistão os ditos frades de S. Antonio juntamente com o vigairo geral. . . ."   See AHU, Maranhão, Papeis Avulsos, doc. 19 de setembro de 1649.   The king's letter is in *ibid.*, doc. 28 de setembro de 1649.

[75] AHU, Pará, Papeis Avulsos, docs. 2 and 6 de setembro de 1649.

[76] Leite, *Historia da Companhia*, III, 144: "Os Jesuítas do Maranhão eram então três ao todo, quando muito quatro."   The uncertainty is concerning a second lay brother who may have been in São Luiz at the time.   But if so, Leite says, he died at this time also.   *Ibid.*

a lay brother by name of Velho were living at the plantation, which was also the center of their activities at the time. On August 20 a group of Indians fell upon the nearby plantation of Vital Maciel, the son of Bento Maciel Parente. Father Pires, when he heard of this, paid no attention and did not seek safety elsewhere nor allow the other two Jesuits to leave, although they wished to. Eight days later the same Indians, guided by two disgruntled former slaves of the Jesuits, whom Pires had punished severely for sexual misconduct, arrived at the mill and killed the three Jesuits. They also killed twelve to fifteen of the slaves working on the plantation. A punitive expedition of forty soldiers and 250 Indians later set out from São Luiz to apprehend the guilty ones, wandered over the interior for thirty days, but could not find the culprits. The governor then abandoned the plantation and mill and suggested to the king that a new fort be built on this river with a garrison of thirty soldiers to protect the fazendas that might be established in the vicinity. The council agreed with the governor, provided he could achieve what he proposed without making new demands upon the treasury, which was in no position to bear an additional expense.[77]

One of the important determining factors in the formation of the Indian policy of Portugal in the Amazon region was money. The royal treasury at home and in Maranhão was always in a precarious state. Funds were often not available to pay the various officials on time, and sometimes salaries were paid in installments or simply in part.[78] In 1649 Governor Luis de Magalhães, faced with the necessity of raising enough money to take care of salaries, levied a tax on wine, aguardente, tobacco and slaves brought from the interior. Clearly, under such conditions, the temptation for the governor must have been great to close his eyes to illegal enslavement of the Indians, in order to raise more money from the tax. The governor's action was allowed by the home government until something better could be arranged.[79]

[77] These details, many of which are not in Leite, História da Companhia, III, 143-145, are taken from the official report concerning this incident sent by Governor Luis de Magalhães on January 28, 1650. See AHU, Maranhão, Papeis Avulsos, doc. 28 de janeiro de 1650.

[78] Thus Sebastião de Lucena de Azevedo in 1648 tells how the foot soldiers were not paid at all, and the higher officials received only part of their salaries. He himself, for instance, received only seventy milreis of his 200 milreis salary. See Documentos Leste-Oeste, pp. 465-475.

[79] See AHU, Livros de registo de consultas mixtas, Num. 14, pp. 205v-206. The

The economic situation, with its constantly recurring crises, finally caused Governor Luis de Magalhães in 1649 to complain against the control of the religious and secular priests over the Indians. Only through the exploitation of the Indians, he thought, could the budget be balanced. The administration of the Indians, he said, ought to be taken away from the clergy, who used the Indians only for their own profit, and not for the good of the state. He named three religious who should be recalled to Portugal—two Franciscans, Father Francisco de Presepio in São Luiz and Father Agostinho in Pará; and one Carmelite, Frei Elizeu. Others could come in their place, he insisted, but these must go.[80] In November of 1650 the same governor complained about other people in the captaincy. Available Indians, he said, were so scarce that he was not able to get even one to work on the forts and other public buildings.[81]

The situation in Maranhão and Pará, already complicated by poverty of resources and Indian matters, was thrown into still more confusion by the struggle for independent power between the *capitães-mores* and the governors-general, a struggle which was to cause the home government to make two independent captaincies out of Pará and Maranhão (an arrangement, however, which lasted less than three years). We can study this struggle by analyzing the two lawsuits held in 1650 and 1651. The first was taken at the instance of Governor-General Luis de Magalhães against Inácio do Rego Barreto, *capitão-mor* of Pará. Initiated by the Provedor da Fazenda, at the request of the governor, on September 22, 1649, the investigation was closed on May 28, 1650. Barreto was accused of showing contempt for the people of the colony, but the principal accusations against him involved his treatment of the Indians. He was accused of making illegal and forced *resgates* to obtain Indians to work in his tobacco fields, and of putting Indians to work in the salt flats and in the fisheries. The prosecution argued that his forays left the colony defenseless,

---

governor had written on June 20, 1649. The council's *parecer* was given on December 17; that of the king on August 13, 1650.

[80] AHU, Maranhão, Papeis Avulsos, doc. 28 de janeiro de 1650. This is the date of the *consulta*. The *parecer* merely mentioned that the complaint had been seen. Nothing was done about it.

[81] "Carta do Governador Luiz de Magalhães a El Rey de 30 de novembro de 1650," Studart, *Documentos Brasil*, III, 185-189.

since he always took many soldiers with him. The Crown, however, obviously was not impressed by the charges preferred against him because it appointed Barreto independent captain-major of Pará upon its separation from Maranhão in 1652, a position he held until his death in 1654. [82]

Barreto lost no time in defending himself or in incriminating the governor. On May 19, 1650, he and the Town Council of Belém lodged a formal complaint against the governor. [83] On October 18, 1650, *Ouvidor* Manoel Gameiro de Barros held a *devassa* in Belém which looked into the governor's administration, but the governor was not asked to testify. [84] Magalhães was accused of setting out within six months after his arrival on February 17, 1649, at the head of an expedition of twenty-six canoes, eighty soldiers, and 500 Indians ostensibly to search for gold, but actually, as everybody knew, to capture Indians. He had made this trip even before he had repaired the fort, which was in a sorry condition. He was reputed to have given the administration of two Indian *aldeias* to João Ribeiro and Sebastião Pestama, two citizens of Maranhão, and of having imprisoned some eighty Indians who had settled in Maranhão. On May 15, 1651, the Conselho Ultramarino met to discuss the *devassa*. Councilman Francisco de Vasconcelos da Cunha insisted that the governor could not be judged without being heard, nor could his goods be confiscated until his side of the story was known. He observed that while the *capitão-mor* of Pará and the Town Council of Belém subjected the governor to these indignities, the citizens of Maranhão wanted Magalhães for another three-year term as governor. No details, Cunha said, were given by the accusers as to the Indians captured on the gold-hunting trip. As regards the eighty Indians he imprisoned, Cunha pointed out that the governor was trying thereby to obtain the release of some Portuguese being held by these same Indians. Cunha believed that the governor should be allowed to finish out

---

[82] "Treslado de hus autos que mandou fazer a provedor da fazenda Marcos Gomez Correa a requerimento do Almoxarife Francisco da Costa Tristão contra o cappitão mor Inassio do Reguo Barreto e imquizisão junta, 22 de setembro de 1649—28 de maio de 1650." AHU, Pará, Papeis, Avulsos, doc. 29 de maio de 1650. The royal letter telling the Town Council of Pará of Barreto's reappointment, dated April 27, 1652, is in AHU, Cód. 1275: Ordens régias da camara do Pará, fl. 6.

[83] AHU, Maranhão, Papeis Avulsos, doc. 19 de maio de 1650.

[84] *Ibid.*, doc. 18 de outubro de 1650.

his term of office, and in this the king concurred on July 1, 1651.[85] The Conde de Odemira, the president of the *conselho*, also suggested the separation of the two captaincies, to put an end to the friction that always existed between them, and this too the king did, by the royal order of April 27, 1652.[86]

Other matters concerned with the perennial Indian problem were considered by the council, as, for example, the office of *pai dos cristãos*. Ever since 1646, when the vicar general of Belém was given the control of an *aldeia*,[87] this ecclesiastic had had something to do with the Indians. As time went on, however, he seems to have lost some of his authority, and he eventually petitioned the Crown for its renewal. He also suggested that the office of *pai dos cristãos*, or Defender of the Indians, be re-established, a suggestion which the council approved. The council believed that either a Jesuit or a Franciscan should be appointed to the office for a three-year term. The king decided that the Franciscan superior of São Luiz should be given preference. If he was not available, the Jesuit superior of São Luiz would take his place.[88] This appointment had little effect on the situation of the Indians, for the question of the protection of the Indians would soon take another direction. Already in March of 1652 the Jesuits were preparing for the second great effort of their Order to set up a workable system to deal with the Indians. With the arrival of Fr. António Vieira in the state of Maranhão shortly thereafter, the office of *pai dos cristãos* was never made a reality.

The Franciscans, meanwhile, received permission from the Crown and were encouraged to replenish their depleted ranks in Maranhão and Pará, over the protests, it should be added, of the Jesuits. From their petition to the king for the usual financial aid, a number of interesting facts may be gleaned. Eight friars, they said, sent in 1636 with Governor Bento Maciel Parente to Maranhão, were captured by pirates. Most of them died in captivity.[89] When the Dutch captured Maranhão in 1641, they forced the friars in the city to leave for Portugal. These two blows, accord-

---

[85] *Ibid.*, doc. 15 de maio de 1651.

[86] AHU, Cód. 1275: Ordens regias . . . da camara do Pará, fl. 6, doc. 27 de abril de 1652.

[87] See *supra*, p. 67.

[88] AHU, Maranhão, Papeis, Avulsos, doc. 28 de setembro de 1652.

[89] This fact is mentioned nowhere else in the documents I was able to consult.

ing to the petition, accounted for the lack of Franciscans in the
state. They now hoped, of course, to remedy the situation. The
new custos, Frei Francisco de Alcântara, and seven other religious[90]
were ready to leave as soon as they received the royal alms custo-
marily given to departing missionaries. This initial support, however, the friars felt, would not be enough. They asked for an
annual salary as the king had promised to them years before.
This subsidy in their mind was indispensable. Without its faithful payment each year they would be obliged, they said, to abandon their convents in Maranhão and Pará and return to Portugal.

The Jesuits, through Father António Vieira, protested against
the sending of Franciscans to Maranhão on the grounds that the
missions of that state had already been confided to the Jesuits.[91]
But the Overseas Council believed that there was room enough
for both Orders in the vast reaches of Maranhão and Pará and so
advised the king.[92]

[90] According to "Relação dos religiosos mais qualificados em ciencia e virtudes
que por ordem dos Senhores Reys Felipes 3 e 4 de Castella reynando em Portugal
forão mandados a Conquista do Maranhão e Grão Pará," ANTT, St. António dos
Capuchos, maço 6, the names of the seven were: Fr. Francisco da Ilha, António
da Madre de Deus, Bento da Ascenção, Boaventura de S. Francisco, João de Neves,
Melchior da Barca and Francisco de Alcântara, the superior.

[91] Vieira wrote to the *cappelão mor* of the royal palace, who was in charge of dis-
bursements to religious going overseas as missionaries. The *consulta* refers to
Vieira's letter in these words: "Tendo disto noticia o P. António Vieira, lhe [i.e.,
the cappelão mor] disera que a missão do Maranhão estava cometida por V.M.
aos religiozos da Companhia da Provincia do Brazil, o que tambem se vio de hu
escrito seu que invio ao dito Bispo." AHU, Maranhão, Papeis, Avulsos, doc. 7
de março de 1652.

[92] The petition of the friars, addressed to the king, was made shortly before
February 22, 1652. It was later discussed by the Overseas Council. The *consulta*
of the council, after telling of the early days of the conquest, and the coming of
Frei Cristóvão de Lisboa, "que assistio naquelle estado mais de doze anos por
Custodio," continues: "achandose no discurso de todo espaço os ditos religiozos
em todas as guerras que se offereçerão não so com os Indios naturaes, mas ainda
com os olandezes e outras nações em que derramarão muito sangue, e que passando
ultimamente oito religiozos com novo custodio ao dito estado em companhia do
governador Bento Maciel Parente, forão cativos e morrerão os mais deles no cativeiro, e alem disso com a entrada que os olandezes fizerão no Maranhão forão
roubados e prizioneiros os que então se acharão naquelle estado e embarcados para
este Reyno os mais delles, por cuja cauza ficarão os dous conventos que tem naquelle
estado muy faltos de religiozos, e de tudo o necessario e de proximo ordenando V.
M. aos prellados que mandassem religiozos as conquistas deste reyno, elegerão ao
Custodio Frei Francisco de Alcantara, com sete religiozos mais, para haverem de

On July 1, 1652, the *conselho* considered a petition of the same
Franciscans for an increase in their *ordinária*, or salary, which
consisted of two arrobas of wax, a jar of olive oil, another of flour,
a barrel of wine, and sixty varas of *burel* (a rough cloth used for
habits). The friars pointed out that this salary had been given
for four friars in 1617, and that it should be increased since more
than four were now involved. The council agreed to double the
salary, but for one time only, and the decision was approved by
the king on July 15.[93]

The years 1643-1652, by way of conclusion, witnessed little
organized effort to set up *aldeias* and expand mission activity.
The lack of missionaries was the insurmountable difficulty in
achieving these ends. Only a single Franciscan was left in the
entire state of Maranhão and Pará in 1652;[94] the Jesuits were not
represented in that state at all from 1649 to 1652. The ensuing
period, however, was considerably livelier. In 1652 and 1653[95]
the Franciscans sent eight and eleven men, respectively. The
Jesuits were even more active. They now made a supreme effort
to assume control of the Indians in a comprehensive way, under
the leadership of Fr. António Vieira.

passar aquelle estado a tratar da salvação e fructo das almas; e porque são muito
pobres pedem a V.M. lhes faça merce mandar que se lhe de o viatico e passagem
custumada . . . e quando V.M. não seja servido de lhes fazer esta esmola, por os
religiozos que assistem naquelle estado estarem faltos de socorro ha muitos anos,
e não poderem por essa cauza assistir nelle, pedem com todo o [one word illegible]
lhes conçeda V.M. licença para se virem para esta reyno, por lhes não ser posivel
sustentarem se naquelle estado sem serem socorridos e dos conventos que nelle tem
poderá V.M. então dispor como for servido." The council concluded, after considering Vieira's protest, that there would be room for both Orders: "e pode suceder
que com o exemplo e emulação de hus fação ambas as religiões sua obrigação como
se espera, deve V.M. mandar que ambas vão fazer o officio de missionarios naquelle
estado. . . ." AHU, Maranhão, Papeis Avulsos, doc. 7 de março de 1652.

[93] AHU, Maranhão, Papeis Avulsos, doc. 1 de julho de 1652. According to the
Franciscan vow of poverty, the friars were not allowed to accept money in payment
for their services. That is why their salary is listed in products necessary for their
work, instead of in money.

[94] So we gather from the *consulta* of March 7, 1652, which quotes a remark of
the *cappelão-mor* to that effect. See AHU, Maranhão, Papeis Avulsos, doc. 7 de
março de 1652.

[95] See Luis da Assunção, "Relação dos religiosos mais qualificados . . . ," ANTT,
Santo António dos Capuchos, maço 6. Of the eleven friars sent in 1653, the most
outstanding were Fr. Lourenço de S. Pedro, who was later named major prelate
of the custody, Fr. Gaspar da Madre de Deos and Fr. Manoel de Espirito Santo.

CHAPTER IV

THE JESUITS AND THE INDIANS, 1652-1662

The Jesuit effort on behalf of the Indians of Maranhão and Pará was intensified during the years 1652-1662 largely through activities of Father António Vieira.[1]

António Vieira, whom many consider the most celebrated sacred orator in the Portuguese language, was born in Lisbon on February 6, 1608, of parents of moderate means. The family moved to Bahia when he was six years old. He attended the Jesuit College in Bahia, and in 1623 entered the Jesuit Order. In 1641 he returned to Portugal where he soon gained the confidence of King John IV. He was named Royal Preacher in 1644. The king made use of his services as counsellor in matters of war and peace, entrusting to him important diplomatic missions. From 1652, when he was sent to Maranhão with royal authority to organize the Indian missions, until the day of his death in Bahia in 1697, he was intimately connected with the legislation passed in favor of the Indians.

Father Vieira began his work on behalf of the Indians in the Amazon region in 1652 with every advantage of prestige and power. His position at Court enabled him to wield an influence never before experienced in the affairs of Maranhão.[2] His energy was remarkable and he planned the missionary enterprise with even greater care than had Fr. Luiz Figueira in 1637-1643. Through his efforts, adequate financial support for the missions was assured. By the *alvará* of February 16, 1652, each member of the Jesuit

[1] For a completely sympathetic biographical treatment, see Hernani Cidade, *Padre António Vieira* (4 vols.; Lisboa, 1940). A slightly more acrid study is that by J. Lúcio de Azevedo, *História de António Vieira* (2nd. ed.; 2 vols.; Lisboa, 1931). The standard Jesuit biography is by André de Barros, *Vida do apostolico Padre António Vieyra da Companhia de Jesus chamado por antonomasia o grande* (Lisboa, 1746). Leite, *História da Companhia*, IV, xvii-xx, says that the definitive biography of Vieira still remains to be written.

[2] It is not pertinent to my study to trace the beginning of his missionary interest, nor the political machinations that went on both within and without the Jesuit Order when he announced his intention of missionizing Maranhão. Those biographical details may be found in the standard biographies of Vieira.

College, to the number of ten, was granted thirty-five milreis annually, to be paid half from the tithes of Bahia, and half from the tithes of Rio de Janeiro.[3] Two royal orders dated June 7 and July 7, 1652, reinforced the Jesuits' claims to the tithes of Bahia by providing that they would be paid at the same time as the bishop and the cathedral chapter.[4] Besides the salary mentioned above, Vieira and his group received 420 milreis for traveling expenses (viático), 750 milreis to outfit their future churches, and 1,000 cruzados for the same purpose, all from the king.[5] The Jesuits also received other royal favors in 1652. The governors and captains were commanded by the Crown to assist the fathers in selecting favorable sites for their churches and houses and to aid them in general.[6] On September 20 the king granted the Jesuits a private aldeia of Indians in Maranhão and in Pará, with the stipulation that they should pay the Indians for their work and should not capture Indians for their villages.[7] Two days later they were granted an aldeia in Gurupá under the same conditions.[8] This latter aldeia was particularly important to Vieira's plans, since he looked upon Gurupá as the gateway to the Amazon Valley.

---

[3] The process of payment was rather complicated: the Jesuit procurators in Bahia and Rio de Janeiro would receive products to the amount indicated and would send them to Lisbon, where the Jesuit procurator would sell them, and with the proceeds buy the articles necessary for the missions of Maranhão, and send them to São Luiz on the first available vessel. See ANTT, Chancelaria de João IV, Liv, 25, fl. 4v: "Alvará de assentamento de ordinarias de collegio de Companhia de Jesus no Maranhão, 12 de fevereiro de 1652." This system of payment, however, had been ordered as early as November 27, 1651, when the council considered a petition of the Jesuits for salary for four men ready to go to Maranhão. They were Jesuits from the province of Brazil, who had come to Lisbon in response to a royal order of October, 1649, that the Brazilian province send twelve, or if this were not possible at least six, missionaries to Maranhão at once. Four were sent to Lisbon and were apparently still there in 1651. See AHU, Maranhão, Papeis Avulsos, doc. 27 de novembro de 1651. The king agreed to the decision of the council on December 19, 1651.

[4] AHU, Maranhão, Papeis Avulsos, docs. 5 de junho and 6 de julho de 1652. From the early date of the royal letter in each case, it is possible to gauge the influence of Fr. Vieira.

[5] This information is contained in a letter Vieira wrote to Fr. Francisco Gonçalves, the Jesuit provincial of Brazil. For text, see J. Lúcio d'Azevedo, Cartas do Padre António Vieira (2 vols.; Coimbra, 1925-1926), I, 274-290.

[6] AHU, Maranhão, Papeis Avulsos, doc. 20 de setembro de 1652.

[7] Ibid.

[8] AHU, Maranhão, Papeis Avulsos, doc. 22 de setembro de 1652.

On September 23, 1652, a royal letter was addressed to the Town Council of Belém do Para, commanding them to welcome the Jesuits upon their arrival.[9] Finally, on October 21 of the same year, King John IV, by a special provision, authorized Father Vieira to found missions wherever he saw fit, and to organize and direct the *entradas* into the interior to gather more Indians. Vieira was given, in effect, a free hand to do whatever he thought best in practically every way.[10] Such support had never before been given a religious order in the Maranhão-Pará region, and it remained now to be seen what the Jesuits would do.

On September 23, 1652, the first contingent of eleven Jesuits left Lisbon for Maranhão.[11] Vieira did not leave at this time; the king was unwilling to lose his favorite. Vieira, however, was determined to go. On October 21 he finally secured the king's permission. The king soon thereafter revoked it, but Vieira left anyway on November 22.[12] The first group arrived in Maranhão probably on November 17; Vieira and his group of three Jesuits arrived on January 16, 1653.[13]

Fr. Manoel da Lima, who sailed with Vieira, had been given the powers of Inquisitor for Maranhão. The Overseas Council had also wanted to make him *repartidor dos índios* and *pai dos cristãos* so that the Indians could turn to him as their protector against

---

[9] AHU, Cód. 1275: Ordens regias . . . da camara do Pará, fl. 6, doc. 23 de setembro de 1652.

[10] For text, see *Collecção chronológica (1648-1656)*, p. 293, where, however, it is erroneously dated October 21, 1653. Leite, *História de Companhia*, IV, 36 f. and Berredo, *Annaes históricos*, II, No. 974, date it correctly as 1652. The pertinent part of the text reads: ". . . e levanteis as igrejas, que vos parecer, nos logares que para isso escolheres, e façaes as Missões, pelo sertão, e paragens que tiveres por mais convenientes, ou por mar, ou por terra, ou levando indios comvosco, descendo-os do sertão ou deixando-os em suas aldeas, como então julgares por mais necessario á sua conservação, que de tudo terei grande contentamento . . . E para melhor o conseguirdes, ordeno aos governadores, capitães mores, ministros de justiça e guerra, capitães das fortalezas, camaras e povos vos dêem toda a ajuda, e favor, que pedirdes, assim de indios, canôas, pessoas praticas na terra, e linguas, como do mais que vos fôr necessario; para o que lhe mostrareis esta, ou a copia della, que guardarão inviolavelmente, como nella se contem; e fazendo o contrario, me dareis conta, para mandar proceder contra os que assim o não fizerem, como me parecer justiça."

[11] Leite, *História da Companhia*, IV, 336.

[12] *Ibid.*; Azevedo, *Cartas de Vieira*, I, 279-286.

[13] Leite, *História da Companhia*, IV, 336.

Portuguese vexations, but the Jesuits opposed these additional responsibilities. They felt that these offices would be too onerous for them at a time when they were establishing themselves.[14]

Vieira had intended to leave for the captaincy of Pará shortly after his arrival in Maranhão, but he soon became involved in local affairs, and he had perforce to postpone his departure. In the very month of his arrival he did, however, send Fr. João de Sotomayor in his place, together with several other Jesuits, to found the first Jesuit house in Pará.[15] The same Belém that had repulsed the Jesuits in 1622 and Frei Cristóvão and the Franciscans in 1624, that had always stubbornly resisted any innovation in Indian policy, now received the Jesuits, but only with reservations. Not until the fathers had signed, on January 26, 1653, a *termo*, or statement, to the effect that their purpose in coming was to open a school for Portuguese scholars, and not to protect the Indians, were they accepted.[16] With these assurances in writing, the fathers were allowed to begin the building of their college of St. Alexander. Here they were destined to remain until they were expelled by the law of 1759.

Meanwhile, Fr. Vieira was having very different difficulties in Maranhão. When Vieira arrived, the Jesuits already had a residence and some property in São Luiz, theirs since it was deeded to them by António Moniz Barreiros in 1622.[17] The difficulties were of another kind; they involved the Indians.

On February 23, 1652, by decree of the king, Maranhão and Pará became separate captaincies, independent of each other.[18]

[14] Azevedo, *Cartas de Vieira*, I, 286.

[15] Leite, *História da Companhia*, III, 208.

[16] *Ibid.*, pp. 208 f.; Azevedo, *Os Jesuitas no Grão Pará*, pp. 37 f.; Berredo, *Annaes históricos*, II, No. 972. Both Leite and Berredo give the text of the *termo* signed by Sotomayor. The signing was considered as null in binding force by Vieira, since the town council could not oblige the king.

[17] See above, p. 33n.

[18] António Ladislau Monteiro Baena, *Ensaio corografico sobre a provincia do Pará* (Pará, 1839), p. 132. On April 27, 1652, the king wrote to the Town Council of Pará, acquainting them of the separation and of the nomination of Barreto for the captaincy. See AHU, Cód. 1275: Ordens regias . . . da camara do Pará, fl. 6. The struggle for power between the governor and the *capitão-mor* of Pará in 1650 and 1651 brought about this legal separation in 1652. See above pp. 74-76. But the matter of separation of the two captaincies had been mentioned earlier. See AHU, Maranhão, Papeis Avulsos, doc. n.d. [but after 1637], which proposed this. See also BNL, Fundo Geral, Cód. 7627, fl. 131, printed by Studart, *Documentos Brasil*, II, 270.

Each was now to have a *capitão-mor* who would exercise the highest civil authority. In accordance with the new law, Inacio do Rego Barreto on March 3, 1652,[19] was appointed for Pará, and Baltasar de Sousa Pereira on April 16, 1652, for Maranhão.[20] Pereira arrived in São Luiz in November or December of 1652, provided with a *regimento* which obliged him, among other things, to free the Indians who had been enslaved up to that time. Unfortunately for Vieira, Pereira published this part of his *regimento* only fifteen days after Vieira's arrival, and this led many of the people who were in favor of the *status quo* to blame the Jesuit for Pereira's action. A riot eventually broke out, during which people shouted, "Away with the Jesuits," but nothing more was accomplished. On March 2, 1653, the following Sunday, Vieira told the faithful from the pulpit that those who held slaves unjustly were on the road to eternal damnation. After the Mass, while excitement was still high, at a meeting of the ecclesiastical and civil officials, it was decided to institute proceedings in order to secure the release of Indians held in illegal captivity.[21]

On May 20 Fr. António Vieira wrote a long letter to the Portuguese monarch. He spoke of the lack of secular clergy for the Portuguese settlers; of the difficulty in referring ecclesiastical matters to the Archbishop of Bahia, 500 leagues away; of the need for an ecclesiastical administrator; of the miserable lot of the Indians, both free and slave, especially of those who lived with the Portuguese. The cause of the misfortune of the Indians, he said, was avarice. They were often unjustly captured by the *entradas* into the interior. Vieira thought that *resgates* and *entradas*, as they were carried out by the colonists, should be prohibited. There was no other morally sound solution. Yet he realized the impossibility of putting a stop to these practices; the economic well-being of the Europeans depended on Indians. In view of this problem, he suggested a milder solution, the one adopted at the meeting of town notables on March 2. This involved an examination concerning the legality of the captivity of the existing Indian slaves with the end in view of freeing those who had been captured illegally. From a practical point of view, Vieira believed that

---

[19] ANTT, Chancelaria de João IV, Liv. 24, fl. 168.

[20] *Ibid.*, Liv. 22, fl. 75.

[21] Vieira's firsthand account of this is contained in his letter to the Jesuit provincial in Brazil, of May 22, 1653. See Azevedo, *Cartas do Vieira*, I, 316-355.

entradas were necessary, but he thought that in the future *entradas* should be made only for the purpose of converting the pagans and reducing them to obedience. On these occasions *índios em cordas*, or legitimate Indian slaves, might, at the same time, be ransomed and bought. As to the free Indians of the villages, they fared even worse than the slaves; the only legal difference between them was that the free Indians received a new master every three years with each change of administration. The free Indians worked for the governors and captains, especially in the growing and curing of tobacco, and they treated them as though they were actually slaves. Many of them died under the heavy yoke. Under the circumstances, the governors and captains, Vieira believed, should be forbidden to grow tobacco or any other product, or from using or distributing Indians in any way, except for public projects, such as the building of fortifications. Nor should they be permitted to place the *aldeias* in the hands of laymen. On the contrary, no white man should be allowed in the *aldeias* except the missionary who lived there. Because of the long history of abuses, the Indians deep in the interior mistrusted the Portuguese. Vieira insisted that the laws on the statute books in favor of the Indians be rigorously executed. If this were done, the Indians who were unjustly captured would be freed, the free Indians of the villages would serve only those who paid them, and the Indians of the interior would be at peace with the Portuguese. Such a situation, he felt, would encourage large numbers of Indians to come down the Amazon to be converted to Christianity and serve as an added bulwark against foreign attack.[22]

While Vieira was thus trying to influence the Crown, the settlers of the two captaincies were alert to the threat to the *status quo*. They therefore sent delegates (*procuradores*) to plead their case and obtain legislation favorable to their interests. In rebuttal to the observations of Vieira, the procurators alleged that

> . . . it would be a deplorable mistake to compare the situation of this captaincy [Maranhão] with that of the state of Brazil, where every month large numbers of Negro slaves enter. Here the only help is the Indian; and the new settlements, scattered

---

[22] Letter of Vieira to King John IV, May 20, 1653, *ibid.*, pp. 306-315. Strikingly similar observations and remedies were voiced much earlier by the Franciscans, especially by Frei Cristóvão de Lisboa (See above, pp. 29 f.; 61-64), and by Fr. Luiz Figueira (See above, pp. 50 f.).

on the islands and the shores of rivers, at great distance, cannot dispense with the services of that people, as rowers, on trips. Neither can they do without Indians in the work of the fields, where they grew sugar, tobacco and so many other products that made up the wealth of the community. And the Indians were not exclusively slaves: as soldiers they helped to defend the territory against the attacks of savage hordes and foreign intruders. To these reasons of usefulness were added those of law and religion combined: there existed no law, divine or human, which forbade the possession of slaves obtained justly; on the other hand, it was a benefit for the latter, for their entering in any manner into the body of the Christian Church compensated for everything.[23]

Vieira's letter of May 20 was sent by the king to the Conselho Ultramarino on July 30, 1653, which considered it on August 21. The president of the council, the Conde de Odemira, son of Jácome Raimundo de Noronha, sometime *ouvidor* and interim-governor of Maranhão, pointed out that Vieira's proposals concerning the Indians were inadequate. Odemira believed that there were six legal reasons for a just war against (and therefore legal enslavement of) the Indians. They were:

1) if the Indians impede the preaching of the Gospel;

2) if they leave off defending the lives and property of vassals of the king;

3) if they throw in their lot with enemies of the king;

4) if they commit robberies or assaults or impede the commerce of men in the country;

5) if the Indians fail in the obligations they solemnly took upon themselves at the time of their initial conquest;

6) if they eat human flesh.

---

[23] "Erro lastimavel seria comparar a situação desta capitania á do Estado do Brasil, onde cada mez entram em grande numero negros africanos. Por aqui, o unico soccorro é os indios; e os povoados novos, espalhados pelas ilhas e margens dos rios, á grande distancia não podem dispensar dos serviços dessa gente, como remeiros, para viagens. Tão pouco para o trabalho das roças onde fabricavam o açucar, o tabaco, e tantos outros géneros que faziam a riqueza da república. E não eram os indios exclusivamente servos: como soldados ajudavam a defender o território contra os ataques das hordas selvagens e de invasores estranhos. A estas razões de utilidade acresciam as do direito e da religião conjugadas: não existia nenhuma lei, divina ou humana, que vedasse a posse de escravos, sendo feitos com justiça; e, por outro lado, beneficio era para estes, que tudo compensava o entrarem de qualquer forma no grémio da igreja cristã." *Memorial* quoted by Azevedo, *Os Jesuítas no Grão Pará*, p. 61.

Indians, Odemira added, could also be legitimately captured, in his estimation, when they were *índios atados a corda* and when they had been the lawful slaves of other Indians. It was in this connection that the conditions set up by Fr. Vieira for *resgates* could be used to advantage, he thought. He agreed with Vieira that the governors should not be allowed to use or distribute Indians in any way. Odemira's point of view prevailed in the council[24] and the king made it his own on September 30, 1653.[25] Neither Odemira nor the council paid much attention to the arguments of the procurators, whose reports were considered at the same time.[26] The case, as presented by Vieira and the procurators, was resolved in Lisbon by the law of October 17, 1653, an attempt at a compromise solution.

In its preamble the king admitted that the prohibition against capturing Indians as incorporated in the 1652 *regimentos* of Captains Baltasar de Sousa Pereira and Inácio do Rego Barreto had not benefited Maranhão and Pará, but had, on the contrary, disturbed the colonists and raised problems for the future. He therefore revoked the previous legislation, and ordered a general examination of all the slaves held by the colonists, according to the ideas suggested by Vieira.[27] In this examination the judges were

[24] "Consulta sobre o Papel do P. António Vieira sobre o spiritual e temporal do estado do Maranhão, e sobre do que pareçe do cattiveiro do gentio a que as Camaras mandarão seus procuradores," AHU, Livros de registo de consultas mixtas, Num. 15, pp. 60v-61v.

[25] The resolution of the king on September 30 was as follows: "A Mesa da Consciencia e Ordens mando me proponha sogeitos para escolher administrador que governe o ecclesiastico no Maranhão. E escolher os citios para as igrejas conciderando o numero que serão. E as funde o Sr. Capellão mor que nomee comissarios e os faça partir. No mais como pareçe ao Conselho e nesta conformidade se passe por elle os despachos necessarios. Lisboa a 30 de setembro de 1653. Rey." *Ibid.*

[26] Concerning the procurators of Maranhão, sent by the town council the *consulta* merely says: "E com o que fica referido, se differe tambem aos requerimentos a que do Maranhão e Pará forão enviados dois procuradores que andão nesta Cidade, e cujos papeis se enviarião a V. Magestade sendo servido que são largos."

[27] The text concerning this examination is the following: "Hei por bem e mando que os officiaes da camara do Maranhão e Pará, examinem, em presença do Desembargador João Cabral de Barros, Syndicante que anda no dito Estado, e em sua falta com os Ouvidores dellas, quaes dos gentios captivos, que já o forem, o são legitimamente com boa consciencia, e quaes não, e que os taes exames, sejam approvados pelo dito Desembargador ou Ouvidores, e julgados por elle, e por este modo possa dar e dê por livres os que o forem, e por captivos os que legitimamente o forão. . . ." *Collecção chronológica (1648-1656)*, p. 292.

to keep in mind the rest of this law which stated in which cases capturing of Indians was lawful. The king continued the law by quoting almost verbatim the conditions laid down by the Conde de Odemira.[28] Under the given conditions, the king allowed Indians to be captured as slaves. He added that captivity by the Portuguese was legal also for "Indians of the cord" and for those already slaves of other Indians.[29] *Entradas* were permitted, with the choice of the leader up to the captain or governor, in conference with the members of the town council, and the prelates of religious orders and the vicar general. Religious must accompany these expeditions, and the decision as to the legality of enslavement was up to this accompanying religious.[30] The last part of the law absolutely forbade to the governor or captain-major the use of Indians in any way at all, except for public causes, such as building fortifications.[31]

[28] All the italicized words in this text of the law are the words of the Conde de Odemira, as he suggested them in the council. See above, p. 85. "... e resolvi que pode e deve haver captiveiro d'aqui em diante, as quaes são as seguintes: *Preceder guerra justa*: e para se saber se o é, ha de constar que o dito gentio livre, ou vassallo meu, *impedio a pregação do Sagrado Evangelho, e deixou de defender as vidas e fazendas de meus vassallos em qualquer parte; Haver-se lançado com os inimigos da minha Corôa e dado ajuda contra os meus vassallos. Exercitar latrocinios por mar e por terra, infestando os caminhos salteando, ou impedindo o commercio e trato dos homens para suas fazendas e lavouras. Se os Indios meus subditos faltarem ás obrigações que lhes forão postas e aceitados nos principios das suas conquistas, negando os tributos, e não obedecendo quando forem chamados para trabalharem em meu serviço, ou para pelejarem com os meus inimigos. Se comerem carne humana, sendo meus subditos.* Ibid.*, pp. 292 f.

[29] "... como o poderão ser tambem aquelles gentios que *estiverem em poder de seus inimigos atados á corda para serem comidos,* e meus vassallos *os remirem d'aquelle perigo com as armas, ou por outra via, e os que forem escravos legitimamente dos senhores, a quem se tomaram por guerra justa, ou por via de commercio e resgate. Ibid.,* p. 293. Again, the italicized words are those of Odemira.

[30] "... se poderão fazer entradas ... com religiosos que vão a tratar da conversão do gentio; e as pessoas a que se encarregarem as taes entradas, serão eleitas ... pelos capitães-mores ... pelos Officiaes da camara dellas, e pelos prelados das religiões e Vigario Geral ... offerecendose ... alguma das sobreditas clausulas de captiveiro licito, se possa usar della como açima se refere; cuja justificação se fará pelos religiosos. ... *Ibid.* The ideas are Vieira's.

[31] This part of the law is in the words of Odemira, but the ideas are those of Vieira's as expressed in his letter of May 20, 1653. "... nenhum governador ou ministro que tiver supremo logar ... possa mandar lavrar tabaco ... nem outro fructo algum, nem o mandem para nenhuma parte, nem occupem ou repartam indios, senão por causa publica. ..." *Ibid.* The complete text of this law is also found in *Livro Grosso,* I, 19-21.

Such was the law of October 17, 1653. It was not entirely pleasing to Vieira, and he left for Lisbon in 1654, hoping to be able to improve it; but before we continue with our story, we must speak of Vieira's activities before he received word of the king's solution to the Indian problem.

Vieira remained almost a year in São Luiz after his arrival before setting out for Pará. After the short-lived revolt upon their arrival, the Jesuits, as a conciliatory gesture, abandoned their claims to their property in Itapicurú. Since 1649, after the murder of the three Jesuits there by the Indians, the Jesuit's sugar mill and plantation had been deserted, and their slaves and cattle had been appropriated by others.[32] During the same year, five more Brazilian Jesuits arrived. Vieira was especially pleased with them, since they, unlike the Jesuits from Portugal, knew the *lingua geral*.[33]

During this first year, Vieira occupied part of his time in writing letters and part in learning the Indian language necessary for missionary work. Vieira and the other Jesuits attended daily class in the *lingua geral*. They also discussed various moral questions that were bound to come up in their work. One such question, or *casus conscientiae*, was: What were confessors obliged to do about the habitual sin of the unjust enslavement of Indians? The priests were of the opinion that they had no obligation to speak of this sin to those who did not confess it. In this connection they also decided to follow three practical rules: 1) they would never speak of Indians in their conversations with lay people; 2) they would not speak of unjust enslavement even in confession unless they thought that the penitent's disposition was such that speaking about it might be fruitful, especially at the time of death; 3) if anyone in the confessional or elsewhere asked them about it, they would declare the obligation of Christians in this regard sincerely and freely. As a reminder to their colleagues in Belém to support this view equally strongly, they sent them word of their resolutions.[34]

Vieira also occupied himself during this time with preaching and examining the validity of the baptisms of the Indians who had been converted earlier. He as well as the other fathers heard

[32] See letter of Vieira to the provincial of the Jesuit province of Brazil, May 22, 1653, in Azevedo, *Cartas do Vieira*, I, 343 f. See also above, pp. 72 f.

[33] *Ibid.*, pp. 345-347.   [34] *Ibid.*, pp. 327 f.

confessions, especially during the season of Lent.[35] During Lent
the fathers also held daily catechism classes for the Indians in the
Igreja Matriz.   Vieira gave a graphic description of these classes
to his Jesuit superior in Brazil.   He told of the procession through
the streets which preceded the class, made up of Indian men and
women and children.   In the church a priest gave a doctrinal
sermon to the assembled crowd, teaching them first the necessary
prayers and then the mysteries of faith.   He told of the special
shortened catechism they used, since these people were so simple,
and of the proficiency of some of the Indians in answering questions.[36]

Vieira finally left for Belém in September, where he arrived
thirty days later, on October 5, 1653.   A short time later he was
invited by the *capitão-mor*, Inácio do Rego Barreto, to take part
in an expedition to the interior.   Barreto expected to go up the
Tocantins River by way of Gurupá.   Vieira was delighted at the
opportunity to visit the country thus offered him, and he gladly
accepted.   His primary intent in coming to Pará had been to establish a base at Gurupá and proceed to the pacification of the
Amazon River and its environs.   But this trip to the Tocantins
was also welcome, since everyone knew that there were many Indians along this river who spoke the *língua geral*.   Perhaps, he
thought, some of them could be persuaded to accompany the
fathers up the Amazon River.[37]

The intentions of the captain-major were quite different, however, from those of Vieira.   What Barreto had in mind was a
regular expedition of *resgate*: Indians would be persuaded to settle
near the Portuguese settlements by means of gifts and kind works,
and if these blandishments failed, by force.   The Indians thus obtained would then be divided among the various settlers and the
religious orders, on the basis of the amount of *resgate*, or trade
goods, which each person or Order contributed to the expedition.
Barreto now offered the Jesuits some of the prospective Indian
captives for their *aldeias* in Pará and Maranhão.[38]   Vieira, of
course, was aghast; this was his first contact with the naked reality

[35] *Ibid.*, p. 348.

[36] *Ibid.*, pp. 350 f.

[37] Letter of Vieira to the provincial of the Jesuit province of Brazil, 1654, *Ibid.*,
p. 356.

[38] See above, p. 80.

of the situation in Pará. He saw now that Barreto's intentions were entirely opposed to those of the Jesuits.[39] Despite their disappointment, Vieira and his single Jesuit companion made up their minds to take part in the expedition, in order to take care of the dying and the wounded and to make certain they would "not lose possession of this river [the Amazon], which we hold to be of such great importance for our holy intentions."[40] Barreto now wanted to leave the Jesuits behind, but Vieira, backed by the authority that the king had given him, insisted upon accompanying the expedition. The captain had no alternative but to promise to take them along. He also agreed to assign the Indians taken on the expedition to four *aldeias* in locations that were convenient for the Jesuits already working in the missions.[41]

At this juncture, Vieira was informed that the Franciscans of St. Anthony intended to send some of their men on the expedition. They alleged that they were the first missionaries in the captaincy and that the king, moreover, had also sent them to Pará and Maranhão as missionaries the year before.[42] Vieira was opposed to a joint enterprise. He admitted that the Franciscans had a right to work in the missions, but he felt that it would not be practicable for the two Orders to work together. The Franciscans, when they saw how determined Vieira was, then agreed to withdraw from the expedition, if they were permitted to send a canoe to bring back the Indians assigned to their *aldeias*. Vieira grudgingly accepted this offer, and the incident was closed.[43]

The controversial expedition was composed of twenty canoes, including four that belonged to the Jesuits. The party consisted of Captain Gaspar Cardoso, eight other officers, the two Jesuits, 200 Indian rowers, forty Indian *cavaleiros*[44] and sixty Indian servants. The small fleet of canoes made its way up the Rio Tocantins for more than 130 leagues, through a region supposedly

[39] Letter of Vieira to the provincial of the Jesuit province of Brazil, 1654, Azevedo, *Cartas do Vieira*, I, 357.

[40] ". . . para não perdermos a posse dêste rio, que tinhamos por uma grande importância para nossos santos intentos." *Ibid.*, p. 358.

[41] *Ibid.*, pp. 358 f.

[42] See above, pp. 76, 78.

[43] Azevedo, *Cartas do Vieira*, pp. 359 f.

[44] Higher class Indians, trained only for fighting, who did no work, and were treated better than the *índios do serviço*.

filled with Indian *aldeias*, before sighting the first canoe of Indians. The Jesuits were roughly treated by the soldiers, and little attention was paid to them, although according to law, Vieira was supposed to be in charge of all *entradas*.[45] Saddened by the cruelties practiced against the Indians, and especially by the announced intention of the captain to make unjust war on four *aldeias* whose Indians had refused to come down the river to live near the Portuguese, Vieira turned back from the expedition with his four canoes and returned to Pará, and thence to Maranhão.[46]

Upon his return from the Tocantins, Vieira devoted himself with characteristic enthusiasm to his correspondence. The Indian problem was uppermost in his mind. In a letter to the Jesuit provincial in Brazil, written before March 22, 1654, Vieira painted a somber picture of his experiences in Maranhão. He had intended to make an official visit to Itapicurú in May, 1653, but the governor and the Indian chiefs, with one excuse after another, made this impossible. He had no better luck the following year. In the interval he took three short missionary trips to the *aldeias* of converted Indians on the island of São Luiz. The system of catechetical instruction used there was substantially that of the cities. In the *aldeias* the missionaries concentrated especially on preparing the more intelligent adults to teach others. These local Indians had been converted for some time, but they showed an eagerness to learn more of their religion. Some of them even recited their lessons at night, while lying in their hammocks. They complained bitterly, however, against the settlers; their lot had not perceptibly bettered since the advent of the Jesuits. The labor in the tobacco fields and the fisheries was almost constant.[47]

On April 4, 1654, Vieira answered a request for information from the Court on the feasibility of the system of two independent captaincies as established in 1652. Vieira was in favor of the older system of having one governor. He said, "It will be less evil to have one robber than two."[48] In so far as Indian affairs were concerned, he felt, the governorship was of crucial importance. If

---

[45] Azevedo, *Cartas do Vieira*, I, 379-383.

[46] Azevedo, *Os Jesuítas no Grão Pará*, pp. 66 f.

[47] Azevedo, *Cartas de Vieira*, I, 383-416.

[48] ". . . que menos mal será um ladrão que dois." Vieira characterized the incumbent captains as follows: "Baltasar de Sousa Pereira não tem nada; Inácio do Rego Barreto não lhe basta nada." *Ibid.*, pp. 416 f.

the governor's control of the Indians could be broken, the situation would improve immediately. It would be better, he thought, to appoint a local man as governor instead of bringing one from Portugal. This would be no guarantee of honesty in government, but at least the ill-gotten wealth of a local man would remain in the country. Inácio do Rego Barreto, for example, declared Vieira, had already sent over 100,000 *cruzados* to Portugal. In addition to a conscientious governor, the civil administration should be provided with an honest judge and a capable sergeant-major. The latter should preferably be a soldier trained in America, not in Europe. Such a man would have to know how to handle canoes and Indians, without which a successful campaign could not be waged. The evil in high places, he added, had made it difficult for the Jesuits to operate in Maranhão and Pará. Unless the king settled the Indian problem once and for all, the Jesuits might better abandon their efforts to help the natives.[49]

In his letter to King John IV of April 4, 1654, Fr. António Vieira spoke of the outcome of the expedition of 1653 up the Tocantins. He had been told that Barreto's captain, Gaspar Cardoso, had managed to round up some 500 Indians. A few of the Indians were assigned to the soldiers, but most of them were settled in inadequate quarters near a tobacco field which belonged to Captain Barreto. At the end of the letter, Vieira requested the king to apply a more immediate sanction to his Indian laws than the sanction of royal displeasure for evildoers, since this latter penalty meant nothing to the colonists, who had heard it so often and had never seen it put into effect. He ended with the plea that missionary activity be freed from all outside jurisdiction and intervention, which was so often unjust, and which hindered the missionaries in their all-important task of saving souls.[50]

Vieira told the king quite specifically what should be done for the missions and the Indians in his letter of April 16, 1654. He outlined his ideas in nineteen paragraphs.

1) The governors and captains-major should have no jurisdiction over the Indians, Christian or pagan, except in time of war. A number of Indians should be assigned to the governor for his use.

2) The Indians should have a *procurador geral* in each of the two captaincies, for their protection. He should be elected by

---

[49] *Ibid.*, pp. 416-421.   [50] *Ibid.*, pp. 421-431.

the people[51] at the beginning of each year, to serve with absolute independence of the governor or captain.

3) The Indians should be ruled and controlled only by the religious.

4) At the beginning of each year a list of *indios de serviço* should be made in the *aldeias* near the Portuguese towns, and a division of the available Indians should then be made, the poor receiving their Indians first. This list and distribution of Indians should be the exclusive responsibility of the prelate of the religious in charge of the Indians, and the procurator. No interference on the part of the governor or the town council should be tolerated.

5) Since the number of Indian villages had notably diminished, the people of the remaining villages should be regrouped to form larger *aldeias*, to be located in places more convenient for catechization and the needs of the commonwealth.

6) Since the Indians must have time to work their own fields, no Indian should be absent from his *aldeia* more than four months out of each year, and not for more than two months at a time.

7) No Indian should be forced to work for the state or for private individuals unless an amount thought sufficient to cover his salary was deposited in his *aldeia*. Upon his return, he should be paid according to what he has actually done. This money should be kept in a chest locked with two keys. One key would be in the hands of the missionary; the other in those of the village chief.

8) Every week or every two weeks a fair should be held to permit the Indians to sell their goods or produce. The procurator or his delegate should preside at these fairs to make sure that the Indians would not be cheated by the whites. In settling disputes he would act jointly with the missionary of the village.

9) *Entradas* should be made only by the ecclesiastics, who have control of the Indians.

10) The control, or *cargo*, of the Indians should be given to a single religious order.

11) Indians should not be brought from the interior before villages and fields were ready for their occupancy and use. No Indian should be put on the list of *indios de serviço* until he was well rested from the trip made from the interior, and had been catechized and domesticated.

---

[51] The text reads: "ao qual elegerá o povo no principio de cada ano." *Ibid* p. 432. It is not clear just whom Vieira had in mind with this term.

12) On *entradas* the redemption of *índios de corda* and other captives should be permitted provided that the original captivity of such Indians should be found to be just. This should be judged by a religious properly trained in theology and the Indian languages, with the assistance of the military leader of the *entrada*.

13) The division of ransomed Indians among the colonists should be on a pro rata basis, beginning with the poorest, under the supervision of the Procurator of the Indians and the prelate of the religious order in charge of the *aldeias*.

14) A permanent "Company of the Propagation of the Faith," made up of white soldiers, should be created to protect the missionaries from unfriendly Indians on their trips to the interior. The captain and soldiers should be recruited from among the more pious men of the community, and the king should honor them in a special way for their service. The company should be under the command of the governor only in time of war. Ordinarily it should be at the disposition of the major prelate of the Order in charge of the missions.

15) The merchandise transported on an *entrada* for ransoming purposes should be in the charge of the *cabo da escolta*, or some other trusted person, and he should be obliged to give an account of dealings to the town council.

16) The Indians brought from the interior should be settled in locations conveniently placed for the conservation and growth of the state. No violence should be used. The expenses of the *entradas* should be borne by the captaincy receiving the Indians.

17) In order to assure the greatest possible number of *gente do serviço*, very few Indians should be given a military title, with its consequent exemption from the labor corps.

18) Titles of the Indian leaders should not be given by the governors, but rather by the Indian chiefs of the *aldeias*, with the consent of the local missionary. By this means would be avoided the practice of giving the Indians fictitious titles in return for their work.

19) The religious in control of the *aldeias* should not be permitted to own plantations or any other kind of agricultural property which might require the use of Indians. The Indians necessary for the operation of their convents, as well as of the convents of other Orders, should be allocated in the manner prescribed for the colonists. The king, Vieira insisted, should place the missions in the

hands of a single Order. Not every Order in his opinion, would do. The work should be entrusted to an Order known for the virtue, disinterestedness, zeal and learning of its members. Moreover, the Indians should be independent of the authority of the governor. To do anything else would be to invite failure.[52]

Actually the Court of Lisbon had been acting too erratically on the Indian question to please Vieira. While Vieira in 1651-1652 was arranging what he had hoped would be a monopoly of the missions for the Jesuits, the Court had at the same time given permission for two large groups of Franciscans to go to Maranhão to engage in missionary work. In 1653, when the Vicar General of Maranhão, José Machado, requested royal permission to make *entradas* for Indians in order to convert them, the king denied it on September 4, 1653, on the grounds that the task of converting the Indians had been given to the religious, but he did not specify the Order.[53]

The law of October 17, 1653, concerning treatment of the Indians had also displeased Vieira. When he received news of it in São Luiz, he decided to abandon his mission post for the time being and to return to Lisbon. He was hopeful that his presence at Court might convince the king of the necessity for even stronger legislation on Indian missions and slavery.[54]

Vieira left São Luiz in June, 1654, and arrived in Lisbon after a perilous voyage in November of the same year. There was much for him to do. The two procurators of the Town Councils of Belém and São Luiz were already active at Court, protecting the interests of the colonists. The new governor of Maranhão-Pará, André de Vidal Negreiros, appointed on August 11, 1654,[55] was ready to depart for his post. The king, however, anxious to settle this Indian question once for all, called a full-dress junta of the most prominent theologians in the country to decide the thorny question of Indian enslavement. The king first of all sent out, on March 15, 1655, copies of the older laws on the subject to a group of theologians, asking them for their opinions on the matter.[56]

---

[52] *Ibid.*, pp. 431-441.

[53] AHU, Maranhão, Papeis Avulsos, doc. 23 de agosto de 1653.

[54] Azevedo, *Os Jesuítas no Grão Pará*, p. 67.

[55] ANTT, Chancelaria de João IV, Liv. 17, fl. 63 v.

[56] According to a document published by Studart, *Documentos Brasil*, IV, 70 f., the following theologians were asked for their opinion: two members of the king's

After giving the theologians time to form their opinions the king ordered the junta to meet, probably in early April. The meeting was presided over by the Archbishop of Braga, Dom Pedro de Alemcastre. Also present were the Bishop-elect of Elvas and the Bishop-elect of Lamego: the three teachers of theology at the University of Coimbra, Dr. Marçal Casado, Dr. Gonçalo Alvo and Frei Ricardo; Dr. Miguel Tinoco of the Society of Jesus, Dr. Frei João de Andrade of the Order of the Most Holy Trinity and Fr. António Vieira. The last-named, who gives us this list, also mentioned that he asked the king that the provincials of the Carmelites and the Franciscans of St. Anthony be present, since they had representatives in Maranhão. The two procurators of São Luiz and Belém were not invited to be present. However, according to Vieira, they were given beforehand lists of those present. Also they were allowed to present a *papel largo* to be read at the junta.[57] Coincidental with this meeting, a smaller meeting was held to discuss practical details. It was attended by the new governor, Fr. Vieira himself, and the two procurators.[58]

The result of the deliberations of these two juntas was the law of April 9, 1655, which regulated Indian enslavement.[59] In the preamble the king mentioned how he had tried this time to end this matter definitively, so that there be no further discussion.

council, all the *Desembargadores do Paço*, Gonçalo Alves, deputy of the Mesa da Consciência e Ordens; Nicolão Monteiro, Bishop-elect of Portalegre; Frei Ricardo de Santo Victor, teacher of theology; António Vieira, the royal preacher; Miguel Tinoco of the Society of Jesus; Frei Fernando Soeiro of the Order of St. Dominic; Frei João de Andrade of the Order of the Most Holy Trinity; the Fathers Provincial of the Order of Carmelites and of the Franciscan Order of St. Anthony. The instructions to them read: "vejão com a consideração que pede materia tão grande, as leis antigas e a moderna, que se passarão sobre os cazos, em que se podem captivar legitimamente os Indios em minhas conquistas. E vejão tambem o papel em que se apontão alguns casus que não estão expressos naquellas leis, e me digão se devo e posso estar pela que ultimamente passei; ou se devo estar pelas antigas, e a moderação e forma em que devo mandar uzar dellas: advertindo que em tudo o que não encontrar a consciencia folgarei de favorecer os vassallos que tenho no Estado do Maranhão, cuja conservação e augmento depende de haver escravos . . . Lisboa a 15 de março de 1655."

[57] See Vieira's "Resposta aos capitulos que deu contra os religiosos da Companhia em 1662 o procurador do Maranhão, Jorge de Sampaio," in Melo Morais, *Corographia*, IV, 187 f.

[58] *Ibid.*

[59] For the text, see *Livro Grosso*, I, 25-28.

The body of the law began with a prohibition against capturing Indians except in the cases to be enumerated. The first is in a just offensive war against the Indians, which is defined as a war fought with the written authority of the king, after he had asked the opinion of all the civil and religious officials in the state. This effectively took away the power to wage offensive war from the governor. The same official, however, could wage a defensive war to free the state of enemies, but only after hearing the opinions of all the major civil and religious officials in the state. Any Indians taken in a legal offensive or defensive war would be considered and treated as slaves. A defensive war was understood as one begun unjustly by any Indian chief or community against the state.

The second case in which the Indians could be captured as slaves would be one in which they impeded the preaching of the Holy Gospel, for they were obliged to allow it to be preached, even though they could not be forced with arms to accept it and believe it. The king noted, however, that if the Indians' principal intent was not to impede the preaching of the Faith, but to avenge some oppression done to them, the war against them in this case would not be just, nor would the enslavement following it be legitimate.

The third case would be if the Indians were ransomed while being *presos a corda para serem comidos.*

The fourth case in which Indians could be legally enslaved would be if they were purchased from other Indians, whose legitimate slaves they were, having been taken in a just war of the Indians among themselves. The justness of this war would be judged by the missionary, together with the leader of the armed party of Portuguese. However, even though the internecine Indian war was not just, the king allowed the Portuguese to ransom an enslaved Indian, who would then serve the ransomer for five years, after which he would be placed in the *aldeias* of the free Indians.

The next section of the law was concerned with the judging of the Indians already captured. The king ordered that the legality of the enslavement be judged by the laws in force at the time of the Indians' capture, with the Indians in all cases defended by the Procurator of the Indians. In order to make sure that the governor would not be influenced in his judgments concerning the Indians, the king forbade all governors to work tobacco, or to use or distribute the Indians in any way at all, nor could the governor place lay captains in the *aldeias*, since these villages were to be ruled by their pastors and the Indian chiefs. Finally, as was the custom, the king abrogated all the previous laws on the subject. It can easily be seen that the law of April 9 was concerned with only one facet of the Indian problem. It was supplemented in many practical details by the *regimento* given to André Vidal de Negreiros on April 14, 1655.[60] In the course of the long document, Negreiros was admonished to keep the spread of the Catholic Faith uppermost in his mind at all times, and to favor in every way the religious, especially the missionaries, besides seeing that all the churches constructed or already existing be kept in a state of good repair.[61] He was commanded to treat newly converted Indians kindly and see that others treated them the same way.[62] Foreign trade in the Amazon Valley, he was told, must be stopped. For this purpose he should use missionaries to gain the friendship of Indians working with the foreigners.[63] Chapter 43 of the *regimento* confided the entire mission work to the Jesuits exclusively:

It pertains to the same divine and kingly service that the Indians of all the *aldeias*, both in the royal captaincies and those of the donataries, be administered by religious pastors of only one Order, and not of many Orders, because of certain reasons most necessary, and that this Order be the Society of Jesus. This I do because of the knowledge I have of their zeal, application and industry in converting souls and because of their acceptance by the Indians of that state. Let this rule also be observed in the missions [i.e. *entradas*] set up for the propagation of the Faith: that only Jesuits go to them.[64]

The vital point of the distribution of the Indians was, according to the *regimento*, to be taken care of by two judges, one of them

---

[60] For the text, see *Annaes da Bibliotheca e Archivo Publico do Pará*, I (1902), 25-45.

[61] *Ibid.*, pp. 25 f.

[62] *Ibid.*, p. 29.

[63] *Ibid.*, p. 33.

[64] "Ao mesmo serviço de Deus e Meu convem (como tenho rezoluto) que os Indios de todas as aldeyas, assim das Capitanias que me pertencem, e das de Donatarios, sejam administradas por Parrochos Regulares de huma só religião, e não de muitas, pelas particulares razões que a isso obrigão, e que esta seja da Companhia de Jesus, pela muita experiencia que se tem de seu zello, muita applicação e industria para a converção das almas, e pelo muito que estão acceitos aos Indios desse Estado; e nas Missões para a propagação da Fée se observará o mesmo estilo de hir a élas só a religião da Companhia pelas sobreditas razões." *Ibid.*, pp. 40 f.

the Indians' pastor and the other a man named by the town council of the locality. The distribution, the *regimento* insisted, must be carried out with complete equity to satisfy the needs of all. Each year a list was to be made of all the available Indians and of the Portuguese who needed Indians.

The Indians were to serve six months of each year, divided into terms of two months at a time, after which they must spend two months at home. The payment for the two-month service must be made before the Indians left for the work. This money was to be kept in the *aldeia* in a box with two keys, one in the possession of the missionary and the other in the possession of the chief of the village.[65] The *regimento* decreed concerning *entradas* that on the years when these were undertaken, the Indians of service would serve proportionately less time in working for the colonists. *Entradas* were to be made only for the purpose of the propagation of the Faith. The Prelate of the Missions would give the order for the entrada, and the governor was commanded to furnish him with the soldiers necessary and a suitable leader, who, however, should have nothing to do with the religious side of the expedition, only caring for the military preparations. The Jesuit prelate shall decide the time and place of the *entradas*.[66] The *regimento* also suggested to the governor that he consolidate some of the smaller Indian villages, to form, as far as possible, villages with not less than 150 families. The governor was also told to see to it that the Order in charge of the missions did not work the Indians in sugar cane or tobacco or in mills.[67] The governor must assist the missionaries to make contact with as many Indian tribes of the interior as possible. If these remote Indians did not care to be vassals of the king of Portugal, but were willing to sign papers of friendship, let that suffice. If they did not care to sign even papers of friendship, let no harm be done to them, unless they harm the Portuguese or impede the preaching of the Gospel. The governor was commanded to punish Indians who committed robberies or other insults, according to Portuguese law. Only if the insults were committed by some tribe or some pagan chiefs who acknowledged no superior could the rules of the law of 1653 be invoked.[68] Since the Indians of service were so few, Negreiros was admonished

---

[65] *Ibid.*, pp. 41 f.   [66] *Ibid.*, pp. 42 f.   [67] *Ibid.*, p. 43.

[68] *Ibid.*, pp. 43 f. According to the rules of the law of 1653, such Indians could be enslaved. See above, pp. 86 f.

to bring from the interior just as many Indians as he could, within the law. In case of emergency of any kind, the governor was told to ask the advice of all the more important royal officials in the state; while if the case involved the Church or the missions in any way, he was told to call a junta of all the prelates of religious orders to decide these matters.[69] The majority of votes would decide in both types of meeting, secular or ecclesiastical.[70]

It can be seen from a perusal of the law of April 9 and the *regimento* of April 14 that many of the ideas suggested by Vieira the year before had been followed by the king. Another suggestion of the Jesuit which was followed was the restoration of the state of Maranhão and Pará in the place of the two separate captaincies of the past three years. The governmental set-up became once again that of one governor with a subaltern *capitão-mor* for Pará.[71]

These two documents of 1655, together with the inevitable appointment of Fr. Vieira as Superior of the Missions, were to be the foundation upon which the Jesuits attempted to build control of the Indians. Vieira left Lisbon on April 16.[72] When he arrived in São Luiz, Negreiros was already there. Largely because of the governor's interest, the law and the *regimento* were immediately put into practice. The choice of governors had been a wise one. Negreiros knew the country well, being a Brazilian by birth. He was, moreover, openly in favor of missionary activities. The discontent of the colonists at the arrival of Negreiros and Vieira with such a strong law was general. It was hard for the settlers to realize that the Indians, the great source of wealth in the colony, were now completely entrusted to the Jesuits. Yet they had no

---

[69] *Ibid.*, p. 44. The lay officials whose opinions were required were: the *ouvidor geral*, the *provedor da fazenda*, the oldest *vereador* of the *câmara*, and the *sargento-mor*. According to the majority of their votes, the governor was allowed to act in any way not contrary to the laws of the realm or to the present law on Indian enslavement.

[70] There were, therefore, two *Juntas das Missões*, the one in Lisbon, which met only occasionally, when called by the king, and which decided matters of mission and Indian policy; the other in Maranhão or Pará, which was more or less of a standing committee, since it could be called at any time to decide matters of pressing urgency concerning local problems of the Indians or the missions.

[71] The governor's nomination made this clear. See ANTT, Chancelaria de João IV, Liv. 17, fl. 63 v.

[72] Azevedo, *Cartas de Vieira*, I, 443.

alternative. The presence and prestige and determination of Negreiros were sufficient to ensure the carrying out of the royal will in both Maranhão and Pará.[73]

Vieira, on the other hand, was not satisfied with the provisions of the latest law concerning the Indians. That the Jesuit missionaries were placed in a privileged position in mission matters was evident enough; they now had a monopoly of the missions of the state. The Franciscans as well as the Mercedarians were excluded from this work.[74] Moreover, they were able to control the free Indians of the *aldeias* at least so long as the governor let them do it. But in some respects the law was still a compromise. Vieira would have preferred to close the door entirely upon the enslaving of Indians. He knew that any loophole would be used by the labor-hungry colonists, and there were several loopholes in the present law. For instance, offensive warfare was practically outlawed, but not so defensive warfare. Who would stop the colonists from creating incidents which would lead to the declaration of a defensive war? Another weakness stemmed from the fact that the Jesuit prelate did not have the power to locate the *aldeias* where he wanted them. This was left to the discretion of the governor.[75] It must be admitted, though, that Vieira and the Jesuits gave the benefit of the doubt in Indian matters to the colonists wherever they could. Thus, in the case of a war between two tribes of Indians of which no one knew the beginning, the captives of such a war were considered by the Jesuits as legal captives for the Portuguese. Also, if an Indian slave was sold from his nation to other tribes, so that one could not verify the origin of his captivity, he was judged as a legitimate slave.[76]

---

[73] A royal gesture designed to placate the colonists was the grant, on April 15, 1655, of the privileges of the citizens of Pôrto to the citizens of Belém. See ANTT, Chancelaria de João IV, Liv. 27, fls. 118 ff. This privilege had already been given to the citizens of São Luiz in payment for their heroic action against the Dutch from 1641 to 1644. See Studart, *Documentos Brasil*, III, 122-137, for the request, dated August 3, 1644. The main privilege in which the citizens of Belém and São Luiz were interested was that which prohibited their being put in chains or in prison, except in cases in which *fidalgos* were so punished. See Azevedo, *Os Jesuítas no Grão Pará*, p. 181.

[74] See above, p. 98.

[75] In the introduction to Betendorf's "Chronica da missão dos padres da Companhia de Jesus no estado do Maranhão," *loc. cit.*, p. xviii, it is erroneously stated that the prelate had this power, but this does not appear in the law or *regimento*.

[76] See "Resoluções que os Padres da Missão tomaram da Ley de 9 de abril de

However, even though the new law had its weaknesses, Vieira was determined to make the best of the situation. He worked indefatigably to achieve his ends. He sent out his men to the existing *aldeias* and founded others, so that by the end of 1656 the Jesuits controlled some fifty-four *aldeias* in Maranhão and Pará.[77] He issued numerous regulations, besides his famous *Regulamento das Aldeias*,[78] as, for instance, the rules to be followed by the missionaries in examining Indians acquired on the *resgate* expeditions.[79] He even prescribed the form to be used in registering slaves.[80]

Many were the reports written by Father Vieira concerning the way in which the new law was carried out. Such a report was the detailed *informacão* he sent to the Court on the trial of captured Indians held in Belém by Negreiros three months after his arrival. The object of the trial was to judge the legality of the slaves taken since 1653. The cases of 762 Indians who had been declared slaves were now examined in proceedings that took about sixty days. As a result of the investigation a great number of Indians, Vieira said, were given their freedom. The judges found that some of the Indians had been forced through fear of punishment to declare themselves slaves or *índios de corda*.[81]

The best account of the Jesuit mission activity during these

1655," in ADE, Ordens MSS annexos de Regimento e leys sobre as missões, pp. 100 f.

[77] Roberto C. Simonsen, *História económica do Brasil, 1500-1820* (2 vols.; São Paulo, 1938), II, 128.

[78] According to Leite, *História da Companhia*, IV, 106, who gives on this and the following pages the text of the Regulamento, Vieira composed it between the years 1658-1661. It consists of rules for the spiritual and missionary life of the Jesuits in Maranhão.

[79] ADE, Ordens MSS. annexos de Regimento e leys sobre as missões, pp. 101 f.: "Modo de examinar os Indios captivos."

[80] The registry should read: "NOME principal ou cavalheiro etc. de tal aldea vendeo hum Indio ou India de tal nação por nome . . . de tanta idade pouco mais ou menos, com tais signais, etc. E disse o ditto vendedor que elle e suo escravo por taes razões. E o mesmo escravo confesseu ser assim. Pello que foi havido por escravo para o cabo da tropa e R.P. Missionario, e se deo a NOME. E por tudo assim passar na verdade. Ao NOME escrivão da tropa passei a prezente rezeyto, que assignei com o ditto cabo, e o R.P. Missionario nesta aldea, etc. de tantas de tal mes, etc. *Ibid.*, no pagination.

[81] "Informação do modo com que forão tomados e sentenciados por cativos os indios do anno de 1655, feita pello P. António Vieira de Companhia de Jesus," BA, Cód. 49-IV-23, fls. 115-136.

years is given in the letters of Vieira to King John IV. In his letter of December 6, 1655, he praised Governor Vidal de Negreiros for having carried out the king's orders without hesitation in all fairness. Negreiros, said Vieira, is:

very Christian, very zealous of the service of Your Majesty, and observant of the royal orders, and above all he is very disinterested, and understands all matters very well.[82]

Other ecclesiastics in Pará and Maranhão, Vieira confessed, did not share the governor's enthusiasm; people were already saying that when Governor Negreiros left, things would be as they were before. Vieira held Negreiros in the highest respect, and felt that his present post was not important enough for a man of his abilities. India itself, he thought, would not be too much for him to govern.[83]

Vieira's letter of December 8, 1655, to the king contained much information on the missions, largely of Pará, whither he went almost immediately after his return to Maranhão from Lisbon. He reported that the *aldeias* of the Indians were far from the European settlements and sparsely settled. He therefore instituted three teams of two missionaries each to visit these smaller *aldeias* and at the same time tried to persuade the Indians to move to more central locations. He left two priests in the captaincy of Caité, midway between São Luiz and Belém. He also sent two priests to Gurupá, accompanied by 100 liberated slaves. He sent another mission of two priests to the island of Marajó, but the Indians there would have nothing to do with them, since they mistrusted all Portuguese. Vieira had high hopes for the future. The Jesuits were already twenty strong, and were working in pairs in the various missions. Vieira realized, of course, that more Jesuits were necessary for so large a territory, and if Portuguese were not available, then Jesuits from other European countries should be encouraged to come. Foreign missionaries worked in China

---

[82] ". . . muito cristão, muito executivo, muito amigo da justiça e da razão, muito zeloso do serviço de V.M. e observador das suas reais ordens, e sobretudo muito desinteressado, e que entende mui bem todas as materias." Azevedo, *Cartas de Vieira*, I, 445-447.

[83] Negreiros was, in fact, named *capitão-mor* of Angola on November 2, 1654, but this was never put into effect. See ANTT, Chancelaria de João IV, Liv. 26, f. 202v. He left Maranhão to take over the government of Pernambuco on September 23, 1656. See "Memoria dos governadores."

and India, he reasoned; why not in Maranhão and Pará? But the Jesuits of this state, if their work was to be successful, also had to be assured that they would not be molested. He realized that the resistance to the Jesuit plans was deep-seated and constant, and was only kept under control by the presence of a strong, forceful governor. He told the king:

> . . . we have against us the people, the religious orders, the donataries of the captaincies, and also all those in Portugal and this state who are interested in the blood and sweat of the Indians, whose *menoridade* we alone defend.[84]

Exactly what form the resistance was taking in 1655 we are not able to say. But Vieira was certain it existed and urged the king not to listen to those who would change the new law and the *regimento* of the governor. He reminded the king that the latest legislation had been passed after careful consideration by the greatest minds in Portugal, and that it had been approved by the procurators of Maranhão and Pará afterwards, although they had no part in forming the laws. The colonists, he felt, would always complain so long as they were permitted to make *requerimentos em contrário*. He thought that this avenue should be closed to them. It was the king's duty, moreover, to see that the missionaries in Maranhão were not persecuted or molested by the whites. Otherwise the missionaries might not want to serve in this area in the future. If the king protected his royal ministers, how much more should he protect his missionaries? The governor and the Jesuits, he said, had widely publicized the new law. If it were changed, the Indians would never again obey any law made by the king.[85]

Despite the problems that he still faced, Vieira at the close of the year 1655 could easily have congratulated himself on the progress of the missions. As Lúcio d'Azevedo expressed it,

> The superior of the missions could well feel himself powerful, since Indians were so important for the colony. With a small number of companions, for in all the Jesuits did not have over twenty, his authority extended over hundreds of leagues, and

---

[84] "Temos contra nós o povo, as religiões, os donatários das capitanias mores, e igualmente todos os que nêsse Reino e nêste Estado são interessados no sangue e suor dos índios, cuja menoridade nós só defendemos." Azevedo, *Cartas de Vieira*, I, 452 f. For parallel statements made in 1626-1627, see above, pp. 36-38.

[85] *Ibid.*, pp. 448-456.

embraced an enormous number of Indians: eleven *aldeias* of pacified Indians in Maranhão and Gurupí [Caité]; six near Belém, seven on the Tocantins, twenty-eight on the Amazon— this constituted the dominion of the Jesuits. But they also were planning to take over the island of Joanes or Marajó, and dreamed of commanding the whole immense river of the Amazon, much still unknown, with so many people waiting for catechization. Besides, the Jesuits, with school, pulpit and confessional, governed not only the simple Indian, but also the European, who was often insubordinate but always devout, and of whose number a part remained faithful under all circumstances.[86]

The colonists, however, were not all resigned to the new situation. Open trouble began in 1656. In Belém and São Luiz the residents suffered in silence, because of the closeness of the seat of government. But in Gurupá, many leagues from Belém, the settlers decided to take matters into their own hands. With the support of the soldiers in the fort, the colonists put the two local Jesuits in a canoe, took them to a spot near Belém and warned them not to return. The colonists did not know the temper of Governor Negreiros. Accompanied by thirty soldiers and sixty Indians, he immediately restored the Jesuits to their former position. Two of the guilty, Captain Aires de Sousa Chichorro and António Lameira da França, were sent in chains to Lisbon to be judged there. Two other lesser culprits were exiled to Brazil. Clearly the new governor was not to be trifled with.[87]

Vieira, meanwhile, could report progress in his plan to missionize the whole Amazon area. His letter to the Jesuit provincial of Brazil, written on June 1, 1656, reflects his exultation:

The care of this whole great harvest has been given over

[86] Azevedo, *Os Jesuítas no Grão Pará*, pp. 77 f. Azevedo appears to be a little exuberant in describing the extent of the Jesuit dominions. As we have seen just above, many of the *aldeias* in the Amazon River section were taken care of by "flying squads" of missionaries. These could hardly be said to control twenty-eight villages. But of the vastness of the Jesuit undertaking, there can be no doubt.

[87] The governor wrote, telling of his action, on July 5, 1656. His letter was considered in the council on December 5 and the queen regent agreed with the council's decision on December 7. See AHU, Livros de registo de consultas mixtas, Num. 15, pp. 259 f. For Vieira's account of the revolt, see Azevedo, *Cartas de Vieira*, I, 459 f. See also ANTT, Livraria, Miscellanea Manuscrita, Cód. 168, fl. 186, for an official letter asking information concerning the imprisoned officials.

to us by His Majesty, not without great sentiment and envy on the part of the other Orders;[88] and we worked for this [i.e., having care of all the missions], and we have accepted all because thus it was supposed from the beginning, and thus did Father Luiz Figueira; thus also it appears to all our fathers in this mission, *nemine discrepante*, since experience has shown us that in any other way we cannot attain the end we have in view.

And so, in conformity with this resolution, we are today in possession of all the *aldeias* of Indians who are Christians or allies of the Portuguese from the Amazon River to . . . Camucim, which is near Ceará. . . . These *aldeias* are along a stretch of coast 400 leagues long, in eight different captaincies. Because the distances are so great and we are so few, we had to divide up immediately to take possession of all.[89]

Much of Vieira's success in the missions was due to the strong hand of Governor Negreiros, whose short time in Maranhão and Pará was incredibly active. The eighteen months of his governorship were full of trips, military expeditions, peace parleys, correspondence and other things proper to a governor of a frontier outpost. Between May, 1655, and September ,1656, Negreiros fought an indecisive battle against some Marajó Indians, sent out an expedition to the Rio Pacajá in Maranhão, tried to take Vieira to Ceará by sea, carried out a *descimento* which brought back more

---

[88] The Franciscans, for instance, probably took it very ill that they had to give up to the Jesuits some of their *aldeias* in Pará. We know of at least two Indian *aldeias* that the Franciscans had until 1655, both of them on the island of Marajó. One was the mission of São José and the other the mission of Nossa Senhora da Conceição, both on the banks of the Rio Paracuari on the island. See AHU, Cód. 1275: Ordens registadas na câmara do Pará, fl. 8. See also Manuel Barata, *A jornada de Francisco Caldeira de Castello Branco. Fundação da Cidade de Belém* (Belém, 1916), pp. 9 f. See also *Santuario Mariano*, IX, 371-373; 392-400.

[89] "A cultura de toda esta grande messe nos está encarregada por S. Majestade não sem grande sentimento e emulação de outras Religiões; e nós procuramos, e aceitamos toda, porque assim se supôs ao princípio, e assim o fez o P. Luiz Figueira, e assim pareceu a toda esta missão, nemine discrepante, depois de nos mostrar a experiencia, que doutra sorte não se podia conseguir o fim a que tinhamos vindo. Na conformidade desta resolução, estamos hoje de posse de todas as Aldeias de Indios já cristãos ou confederados com os Portugueses desde o Rio das Amazonas até. . . Camucí, que é perto do Ceará . . . . Estão estas Aldeias em distância de quatrocentas léguas por costa, em 8 capitanias diferentes, e posto que as distâncias sejam tão grandes, e nos tão poucos, foi força dividirmo-nos logo a tomar posse de tudo. . . ." Serafim Leite, *Ncvas Cartas Jesuíticas de Nóbrega a Vieira* (São Paulo, 1940), pp. 245 f.; 263.

than a thousand Indians from the Rio Tocantins region, besides carrying on correspondence with the home government concerning the progress of the colony.[90] In all things, he endeavored to carry out the law impartially. But this very impartiality caused the colonists and even Father Vieira to complain to the home government. Clearly the situation was far from satisfactory for everybody. On April 12, 1657, the Town Council of Belém addressed a formal complaint to the Crown, directed against the Jesuits who, according to the accusation, were the absolute masters of the whole government of the Indians both temporally and spiritually, a state of affairs which, in the opinion of the town council, was rapidly ruining the state.[91] Vieira did his complaining in his letter of April 20, 1657, to the young King Afonso VI.[92] He told the young prince of the progress of the missions and also of their difficulties. The free Indians of the *aldeias* were reported to have been so well grounded in the Faith that they know as much about it as the best-instructed Portuguese. The same free Indians, however, were obliged to work too long. Although they were supposed to have six months to themselves for their own work, they ordinarily served the settlers for ten months out of the year. Even so the settlers were not satisfied. In fact, continued Vieira, over the years the cruelties inflicted upon the Indians were appalling:

... the injustices and tyrannies practiced on the Indians in

[90] See Azevedo, *Os Jesuítas no Grão Pará*, pp. 83-88. For some of the correspondence of Negreiros with the home government see the following: AHU, Livros de registo de Consultas Mixtas, Num. 15, p. 233v., doc. 26 de junho de 1656; Cód. 1275: Ordens regias registadas na camara do Pará, fl. 9, doc. 2 de julho de 1656; *Livro Grosso*, I, 28; AHU, Livros de registo de Consultas Mixtas, Num. 15, pp. 236v-237, doc. 3 de julho de 1656; AHU, Pará, Papeis Avulsos, doc. 8 de julho de 1656; Studart, *Documentos Brasil*, III, 201-204, doc. 8 de julho de 1656; AHU, Livros registos de Consultas Mixtas, Num. 15, pp. 229 f., doc. (?) de julho de 1656; *Ibid.*, p. 249v., doc. 22 de setembro de 1656. This last document was written shortly before his departure for Pernambuco. His successor, Pedro de Melo, did not take possession of his office until September 19, 1658, and ruled until March 26, 1662. See "Memoria dos governadores."

[91] AHU, Pará, Papeis Avulsos, doc. 12 de abril de 1657.

[92] King John IV died on November 6, 1656. Prince Afonso was only thirteen years old at the time, but was proclaimed king irregardless of his age, mainly because of the influence of Queen Luisa, who naturally became the queen regent until Afonso came of age. Afonso was to be much less a friend of Vieira than John IV had been. See H. V. Livermore, *A History of Portugal* (Cambridge, 1947), p. 302.

these lands exceed by far those done in Africa. Within the space of forty years there were destroyed along this coast and in the interior more than two million Indians, and more than 500 Indian settlements as large as cities, and no punishments have been given for this.[93]

The recent *resgate* expeditions sent out by the governor, Vieira added, had turned out badly because the governor and the other officials in Maranhão and Pará had not listened to Vieira as to the location of the *resgate* expeditions, preferring to select places where they expected more profits.[94] Vieira also complained, finally, against the other religious and the secular clergy. Many of them preached and worked against the Jesuits and thus helped to confuse the minds of the faithful. Vieira insisted that the king should close his ears to the *requerimentos* of the colonists for redress, and, on the contrary, should punish swiftly the violators of the law of 1655, which he considered a good law worthy of being retained on the statute books.[95]

The missions continued to be a burning issue during 1657. The Overseas Council, which had never been in favor of the legislation of 1655,[96] recommended in two reports of September 28 and 29 that the Court should reconsider the Indian question because of the inconveniences that the existing law of 1655 caused the inhabitants of Maranhão and Pará.[97] The queen regent followed

---

[93] ". . . as injustiças e tiranias, que se têm executado nos naturais destas terras, excedem muito às que se fizeram na África. Em espaço de quarenta anos se mataram e se destruíram por esta costa e sertões mais de dois milhões de indios, e mais de quinhentas povoacões como grandes cidades, e disto nunca se viu castigo." Azevedo, *Cartas de Vieira*, I, 468. Modern estimates of population of the aborigenes of America are much lower than the estimates of earlier historians. A. L. Kroeber, in his *Cultural and natural areas of native North America* (Berkeley, 1939), pp. 155 f., states that the aboriginal population of South America was about 4,000,-000 with 3,000,000 of this total in the Andean Inca Empire and the remaining 1,000,000 scattered through the rest of South America. Varnhagen, *História geral*, I, 15, says the native population of Brazil was not quite one million people. This would leave considerably less than a million for the Amazon area.

[94] Azevedo, *Cartas de Vieira*, I, 464.

[95] The full text of the letter of April 20, 1657, is found in *ibid.*, pp. 460-472.

[96] The Overseas Council had, in fact, not been consulted concerning the legislation of 1655, as we can see by examining the lists of those present at the juntas of that year. See above, p. 96.

[97] AHU, Livros de registo de Consultas Mixtas, Num. 15, p. 278v, doc. 28 de setembro de 1657. This *consulta* is also printed in Studart, *Documentos Brasil.*

the advice of the council and appointed a committee of theologians to reappraise the legislation of 1653 and 1655. The decision of the theologians was embodied in the royal letter of April 10, 1658, which ordered that the law of 1655 be carried out in every particular.[98] For the time being, at any rate, Vieira could congratulate himself on the victory.

But *requerimentos* continued to be sent to Lisbon against the law. Manoel da Vide e Souto Maior, for example, a leading political figure in Belém, suggested on April 3, 1658, that all the *aldeias* without exception, including the three given the Jesuits for their maintenance, be used only for the royal service. This, he said, would be in keeping with the law of 1655. He referred specifically to the *aldeia* of Mortigura in Pará, which the Jesuits administered for their own use. He accused the Jesuits of having enlarged the *aldeia* by bringing in Indians from other villages. He felt sure that the Jesuits, who professed such love for the Indians and the colonists, did not relish the special privileges they enjoyed.[99]

The complaints of the colonists, however, would be useless as long as Father Vieira kept his influence at Court and could count on the protection of the royal family. On September 1, 1658, he implored the queen regent to continue her support of the missions of Maranhão. He suggested at the same time that the Jesuits ought to receive a little more money in salary. Since 1652 they had received no more than the 350$000 per year. But even if this increase would not be granted, he concluded, Her Majesty's con-

---

IV, 71 f. In it we find the words: ". . . a primeira ley que, precedendo consulta deste Conselho se passou no anno 653 e se enviou e recebeu bem no Maranhão foi conforme ao parecer deste Conselho, e a segunda [i.e., that of 1655] foi com intervenção e communicação do Padre Antonio Vieira que com seu zello a veio solicitar . . . e que por na execução da dita segunda lei se offerecerem a aquelles moradores os inconvenientes que avizão. . . ." For the text of the *consulta* of September 29, 1657, see *ibid.*, pp. 72 f. In this report the council complains: "Lembrando a V. M. que nunca por este Conselho se encontrou a segunda ley [i.e., of 1655] passada pela Secretaria de Estado, antes em todos os regimentos e ordens se encommendou e encarregou a guarda e observancia della."

[98] *Livro Grosso*, I, 29. The letter was signed by the queen mother in her position as regent for her son. The names of the theologians are not given.

[99] BNL, Fundo Geral, Cód. 1570, pp. 299-307. The request is entitled "Parecer sobre os successos do Maranham, feyto por Manoel da Vide e Souto Mayor, anno de 1658," in the MS copy. The text has been published in Studart, *Documentos Brasil*, IV, 86-94.

tinued firmness with the governors concerning the missions and Indian laws would be reward enough for the Jesuits.[100] Vieira's letter of September 10, 1658, to the Jesuit general in Rome is a general account of the Jesuit missions in Maranhão-Pará, and is valuable for the insight it gives into the mission system employed by the Society.[101]   All the Jesuit missions, he wrote, had a church and many also had a house for the missionary.   The entire mission field was divided into *colónias* of eight, ten or more residences, each covering about eighty leagues.   Transportation, by canoe, was easy.   Each *colónia* had a superior, who visited the other houses in his district.   Missionaries were required to assemble in this central house, where the district superior resided, every two months for a spiritual retreat, a conference of moral cases and progress reports.   Each residence had at least two Jesuits.   At the central house of each district there were to be four to six Jesuits besides the superior, and there the religious life was more perfectly observed.[102]   The problem of temporal sustenance was not difficult, Vieira assured the general, since little was needed. The Indians gladly and freely built the churches and residences. Material and dyes for clothing were grown locally.   The Indians supplied the Jesuits with fish and meat.   Only a few things had to be imported from Portugal, and these were paid for out of the 350 milreis allotted them by the king.   The Jesuits could also count on an additional sum of about 200 milreis every year, the income from an inheritance they had received in Maranhão.   For the past three years, Vieira said, the Jesuits had received nothing

---

[100] Azevedo, *Cartas de Vieira*, I, 483-486.   The new governor, who brought with him the decree of April 10, 1658, ordering the continued observance of the law of 1655, is mentioned by Leite, *História da Companhia*, IV, 54, as being a friend of Vieira, at least during the first years of his rule (1658-1662).   Before he came to Maranhão to take possession of his post on September 18, 1658, he, at Vieira's request, looked into all the complaints that had been made against the Jesuits, in order that Vieira might answer them.   Azevedo, *Cartas de Vieira*, I, 484 f.

[101] Leite, *Novas Cartas Jesuíticas*, pp. 265-276.   The general had ordered Vieira to write this letter, which would be used to foster vocations throughout the Order. This purpose somewhat lessens its historical worth; nevertheless the account has a surprising amount of information in it.

[102] Obviously, Vieira was speaking of plans for the future, since the staffing of one *colónia* as he outlined it for the general would have exhausted the supply of Jesuits available in the whole state.   On the *colónia* system, see Leite, *História da Companhia*, IV, 101 f.

from Portugal, because of lack of ships; yet the twenty-five Jesuits in the missions had not suffered. Vieira asked the general for more Jesuits, especially for Portuguese. Some he asked for by name, including an Irishman, Richard Carew. He also asked permission to accept local Portuguese boys into the Society and to begin a novitiate in São Luiz. In conclusion, Vieira told the general that the mission of Maranhão-Pará finally was firmly established, and that all the opposing forces, ecclesiastical and secular, had been vanquished through the recent commands of the king (April 10, 1658). The king had sent copies of this decree to Vieira to be distributed to the other prelates of religious orders in the state, and in these copies was the added threat of expulsion from the state for any Order that did not obey the law of 1655 or the *regimento* of the governor. With the coming of Governor Pedro de Melo, who had a brother in the Society, everything had become peaceful.[103]

Vieira's achievements were not exclusively organizational and epistolary. He was also very successful in pacifying and converting Indians. One of his outstanding exploits in this regard was the simultaneous pacification and subsequent conversion of several large tribes of Indians on Marajó Island. These Indians had been enemies of the Portuguese since the beginning. Their pacification, which Vieira described in his letter of February 11, 1660, to King Alphonse VI, is well-known and need not be told here in full detail.[104] The first part of the pacification was the taking of the oath of fealty by a large number of Indian chiefs (fifty-three in all).[105] After this was over the chiefs embraced the Portuguese and Christian Indians with whom they had been at war. Outside the meeting place the Portuguese threw away the balls for their muskets and the Indians broke their bows. Then they retired to the house of the Jesuits, built for them on the island by

---

[103] Leite, *Novas cartas Jesuíticas*, pp. 275 f. Concerning the administration of Pedro de Melo, see "Memoria dos governadores."

[104] Azevedo, *Cartas de Vieira*, I, 549-571.

[105] The oath read: "Eu, . . . Principal de tal nação em meu nome e do todos meus súbditos e descendentes, prometo a Deus e a El Rei de Portugal a fé de Nosso Senhor Jesu Christo; e de ser (como já sou de hoje em diante) vassalo de S.M. e de ter perpetua paz com os Portugueses, sendo amigo de todos seus amigos e inimigo de todos seus inimigos; e me obrigo de assim o guardar e cumprir inteiramente para sempre." *Ibid.*, p. 566.

the Indians, where a legal *termo* was drawn up which all signed. The Jesuits remained at the meeting place for fourteen days, during the day visiting formally with each chief in turn, and at night watching the various dances performed by each tribe. The actual evangelization of all these Indians did not begin until some months later.[106] This was the single greatest achievement of the Jesuits up to that time. It is true that Vieira evidently overreached himself when he estimated the number of those who made peace with the Portuguese as 100,000, but some idea of the size of the celebration can be obtained by considering that fifty-three Indian chiefs and their people took part in it.[107]

In the same letter of February 11, 1660, Vieira spoke also of the last three *entradas* that had been made up the Amazon. All of them, he said, had been successful. The *entrada* up the Rio Negro had netted over 600 slaves, as certified by the Jesuit who accompanied it. On another expedition they waged war against a tribe along the Tocantins, their reason being that tribe's attempt to keep other Indians the year before from coming to live near the Portuguese. They took 240 of them as slaves.[108] The third *entrada* brought back a thousand Indians, free and slave.[109]

The problem of ecclesiastical jurisdiction also provoked Vieira to action. On February 11, 1660, he asked the Jesuit general to petition the Holy See for episcopal powers for the Jesuit superior in Maranhão. Vieira was impelled to do this as a result of the clash between the vicar of the parish church of Belém and the Jesuits. The vicar claimed that the Jesuits who worked in the Indian *aldeias* were subject to his authority in matters concerning the care of souls, and he tried to enforce his claim with excommunications. In order to avoid difficulties of this kind, Vieira felt that the Superior of the Missions should be made, by papal brief, the "ecclesiastical ordinary of all the Indians of our parishes and missions" (*ordinario de todos os Indios das nossas freguesias e doutrinas*). As Vieira pointed out, the Jesuits, in practice, had been exercising this spiritual jurisdiction over the Indians for over

---

[106] *Ibid.*, p. 568. The evangelization began in the spring of 1659.

[107] *Ibid.*, pp. 564-568.

[108] Vieira did not criticize this act of war against the Indians, although earlier (cf. *supra*, p. 91) he inveighed against an almost identical case. The justification of the later war must have been more secure.

[109] *Ibid.*, pp. 549-554.

ten years.   He felt that the Portuguese secular priests were un-
suited for this jurisdiction because they did not know the *língua
geral*, and the Indians did not trust them.[110]
    During these years internal troubles and problems within the
Order also occupied some of Vieira's time, but his real difficulties
lay in another sector.[111]   Early in 1661 the troubles of the Jesuits
with the colonists and government officials reached a critical stage.
Repeated complaints of the people to the Jesuits in Maranhão and
Pará in 1659 and 1660 had had no effect.[112]   On January 12, 1660,
the Town Council of Belém had written to the officials of São Luiz,
suggesting a united front of complaints against the Jesuits' temporal power.   But São Luiz turned down this proposal.[113]   One
last series of appeals was made in 1661 by the Town Council of
Belém to Fr. Vieira.   On January 15, the town council in a long
reclamation, declared the utter helplessness of the colony without
more Indian workers, and said that the law of 1655, which allowed
resgates, should be observed.[114]   Vieira waited a month before
answering, and in his reply he asserted that the people were
wrong in blaming all their troubles on the lack of slaves.   There
were other reasons, as for instance, the type of land in the country,
all crisscrossed with rivers; the growing lack of game and fish in
nearby places; the lack of a market where things could be bought
and sold, which necessitated that each family must be a miniature

---

[110] Leite, *Novas cartas Jesuíticas*, pp. 277-281.

[111] Some of Vieira's more important correspondence, which did not touch directly
on Indian policy, was the following: 1) letter to King Afonso VI, December 4, 1660,
praising Governor Pedro de Melo, and suggesting him as a councillor for the Overseas Council. (Azevedo, *Cartas de Vieira*, I, 571-575); 2) letter of Vieira to the
Jesuit general, March 18, 1661, in answer to the general's request for information
concerning complaints by Fr. Richard Carew (Leite, *Novas Cartas Jesuíticas*, pp.
282-288); 3) letter of same to same, March 21, 1661, on urgent reasons for erecting
a novitiate in São Luiz. He lists as their property a *fazenda* with more than forty
slaves; an *aldeia* of Indians; a large pasture, the best in Maranhão, and a good
quantity of cattle (*ibid.*, pp. 289-297); 4) letter of same to same, March 24, 1661,
in which Vieira defends himself against the accusations of Fr. João Maria Grozoni
(*ibid.*, pp. 298-312); 5) fragment of a letter of Vieira to two Jesuit missionaries in
Ceará, June 11, 1661, telling of the death of four Jesuit fathers during the past
year, and praising the work of the foreign Jesuits helping them (Azevedo, *Cartas
de Vieira*, I, 591 f.).

[112] Berredo, *Annaes históricos*, II, No. 1020-1022.

[113] *Ibid.*, No. 1023.

[114] *Ibid.*, No. 1028.

state in itself; the war at home, which caused prices to rise; the vanity of the people who spent money beyond their means. Vieira concluded that the people should not blame the entire situation on the lack of slaves, but should better these other conditions also. He added that in Brazil there were the same problems, which were never settled until Negro slaves were introduced from Africa. Besides, Vieira contended, the Jesuits had carried out the prescripts of the law of 1655: more than 3,000 free Indians and 1,800 slaves had been brought from the interior. As for the *entrada* petitioned by the *câmara*, Vieira would see to it as soon as possible.[115] The members of the Town Council of Belém were not satisfied with Vieira's answer, and on February 15 wrote another complaint to the Jesuit.[116] They mentioned, for instance, that a goodly number of Indians had been ransomed but that many of them were sold in Maranhão and Caité, so that the local settlers, who had been along on the expedition, did not reap the fruits of it. To make market places and shops, as Vieira suggested, also required the use of slaves for their construction; the remedy proposed by Vieira of another *resgate* expedition to the Tocantins area would be useless, as the last expedition in that direction lost money. They insisted that they wanted to observe the law of 1655, which permitted them to take Indian slaves according to certain rules. Finally, they reminded the Jesuits of their promise not to use the Indians for their own mills or plantations.[117] Vieira's reply to the paper of February 15 was simply that he could say no more than he had said on February 12.[118] The town council then resolved to send a procurator to see the governor in São Luiz to tell him about conditions, and also to send a supplication to the Court. The complaint to the Court was sent off on April 9.[119] So far all the agitation had been in Belém. The scene now shifted to São Luiz, where some private letters of Fr. Vieira to the bishop who had been confessor of the king were made public in early 1661.[120]

---

[115] *Ibid.*, No. 1030.   His reply was written on February 12.
[116] *Ibid.*, No. 1032.   [117] *Ibid.*
[118] *Ibid.*, No. 1033.   [119] *Ibid.*, No. 1035 f.
[120] *Ibid.*, No. 1037.   The letters (not otherwise identified) were sent to Lisbon, and on the way the ship was stopped by French pirates.   The Carmelite provincial on board succeeded in saving the letters, and he kept them until the bishop confessor died in 1659, after which he sent them to his confreres in Maranhão, who published them.   See Leite, *História da Companhia*, IV, 55.

These letters were full of complaints against the lawlessness of the people concerning the protective legislation for the Indians. On May 17 the procurator or commissary sent by the Town Council of Belém left that city on his way to São Luiz. His arrival in São Luiz and the story he told, together with the publication of the recent letters, was enough to cause a riot in São Luiz, which ended in the imprisonment within the college of all the Jesuits.[121] That the revolt succeeded was due in part to the indecisiveness of the governor, Pedro de Melo, when the fatal moment of the revolt arrived. It must be said, however, that his military guards deserted him at the crucial moment. In a letter to Fr. Vieira which the governor sent off ôn May 23, he asked Vieira what he could have done with five or six faithful soldiers against five or six hundred rioters.[122]

Vieira was sailing from Belém in Pará and stopped midway at the captaincy of Cumá, where the letter of the governor reached him.[123] He immediately returned to Belém, where, he trusted, the news had not yet arrived, and where he could possibly still save the situation in the captaincy of Pará. He arrived in Belém on June 21 and immediately addressed himself to the town council, urging them to repudiate the actions of São Luiz.[124] In the course of his argument he cited the actions of the Jesuits in pacifying the Indians of Marajó Island, who had always been so troublesome in the past. He reminded them of the consequences if the Jesuits were removed also from Pará, which had so many more Indians than Maranhão. He suggested that Pará close the borders against Maranhão and have nothing to do with its neighbor.[125] In reply the Town Council of Belém alleged the misery caused by the temporal rule of the Jesuits over the Indians, and mentioned that they had asked the queen for a judge to decide between them and the Jesuits concerning Indian matters, since at the present time there was no appeal against the decisions of the Jesuits. But they did promise to keep the peace in Pará.[126] This was written on June 23, 1661. On July 7 the emissary that had been sent by Belém to the governor some time before returned to Belém and

---

[121] *Ibid.*, IV, 54.
[122] Berredo, *Annaes históricos*, II, No. 1041.
[123] *Ibid.*, No. 1042.   [124] *Ibid.*, No. 1043.
[125] *Ibid.*, No. 1044.   [126] *Ibid.*, No. 1045 f.

made his report.[127]   The governor had granted part of their request: that the Jesuits be removed from their temporal control
over the Indians.   But the *vereadores* were disappointed in that
open *resgates* were still not permitted by the governor, as they had
wished.[128]   When news of the happenings in Maranhão spread
through the city, the excitement grew.   On July 17 a tumult arose
among the people, who demanded the immediate election of a *juiz
do povo* to settle the Indian question.   The *câmara* elected Diogo
Pinto, one of their number, to this position, and the tumult died
down.[129]   The new judge immediately imprisoned Vieira and his
companions and sent them to São Luiz.   From there the fathers
were sent to Lisbon on the first available ship.[130]   By the following
year, 1662, all the fathers, even those in the faraway missions, had
been rounded up and put into custody.   The revolt was complete.[131]

In Lisbon, Vieira immediately set about repairing the situation,
and was having marked success, when, unexpectedly, on June 21,
1662, a palace revolution unseated the queen regent, Luisa.   Her
son, Afonso VI, became king in fact as well as name.[132]   Unfortunately for his cause, Fr. Vieira had backed the losing faction which
had supported Prince Pedro against his brother the king.   Afonso
now turned on Vieira.   The Jesuit was banished from Court and,
in fact, was in the toils of the Inquisition from 1663 to 1667.   He
returned to royal favor in 1668, when Pedro became regent, but
he never regained his former pre-eminence.   In 1669 he went to
Rome, and there he stayed until 1679.   Upon his return from this

---

[127] *Ibid.*, No. 1052.

[128] *Ibid.*

[129] *Ibid.*, No. 1055.

[130] *Ibid.*, No. 1058-1062.

[131] The fullest treatment on this revolt is that of Berredo, *Annaes históricos*, II,
No. 1026-1100, who includes the texts of many pertinent documents.   For other
correspondence and documentation, see Melo Morais, *Corographia*, III, 139 ff., and
Azevedo, *Cartas de Vieira*, I, 579-583.   For the Jesuit side of the story, see Leite,
História da Companhia, IV, 54-61.

[132] The procurator of São Luiz, Jorge de Sampaio e Carvalho, wrote a long
memorial of twenty-five paragraphs, outlining the colonists' viewpoint, and ac-
cusing the Jesuits of various crimes.   See Studart, *Documentos Brasil*, IV, 109-117.
Unfortunately, before Vieira could answer, the palace revolution occurred.   See
Livermore, *History of Portugal*, pp. 309-312.   Vieira's *Resposta aos capitulos*, as it
is called, was not written until September, 1662, when the Jesuit had already been
driven from the Court to Pôrto.   See Melo Morais, *Corographia*, IV, 186-253.

voluntary exile, he regained for a time some of his former influence over the formation of Indian legislation for Maranhão and Pará: he was partly instrumental in framing the law of April 1, 1680. After that he went to Bahia, where he spent his declining years until his death in 1697.[133]

---

[133] For these and other details, see the various biographies of Fr. António Vieira mentioned *supra*, p. 79. For a succinct account of the salient facts of Vieira's life, see Azevedo, *Cartas de Vieira*, vols. I and II, *passim*. The editor, before each section of Vieira's correspondence, gives biographical details. For the Inquisition proceedings, see BNL, Fundo Geral, Códices 557, 589, 673, 681.

CHAPTER V

A PERIOD OF RETROGRESSION, 1663-1680

These seventeen years were years of anarchy in Maranhão and Pará, during which the Indian was shamefully and flagrantly exploited. The period was highlighted by the struggle for power between the governor and the town councils. These latter bodies had tasted power when they forced the expulsion of the Jesuits, and they were determined not to lose it. Their procurators in Lisbon influenced the new governor, Rui Vaz de Sequeira, immediately after his nomination[1] to complain about the lack of Indians in the state, due to the past activities of the missionaries.[2] The town councils in both Belém and Maranhão forced the incoming governor and *capitão-mor* to promise that they would put into effect no law returning the Jesuits to their former pre-eminence.[3] Furthermore, the town councils, through their procurators in Lisbon, succeeded in wresting from the king a new law on Indian policy, favorable to their interests. It was the law of September 12, 1663.[4] By its provisions the Jesuits were allowed to

[1] He was nominated governor on July 29, 1661. See ANTT, Chancelaria de Afonso VI, Liv. 24, fls. 239 f.

[2] His complaint was considered in the council on August 31, 1661. See AHU, Maranhão, Papeis Avulsos, doc. 31 de agosto de 1661. In the same year he requested and received permission to make *resgate* expeditions. *Ibid.*, doc. 1661.

[3] Sequeira took possession of his post on March 26, 1662, and ruled until June 22, 1667. See BA, 51-VI-46, No. 17, "Memoria dos governadores." Francisco de Seixas Pinto, the new *capitão-mor* of Pará, took possession on April 16, 1662, and ruled until June 5, 1665. See Braga, *História do Pará*, p. 141. Concerning their reception at the hands of the town councils, see Azevedo, *Os Jesuítas no Grão Pará*, pp. 124, 126; Berredo, *Annaes históricos*, II, No. 1078-1085.

[4] For the text, see *Livro Grosso*, I, 29-31. Earlier in the year, Feliciano Dourado, one of the councillors of the Overseas Council gave his opinion concerning the Indian problem as follows: The Jesuits should receive back all they had lost, all except Father Vieira; they should have no temporal power over Indians, but they should be the only Order allowed to work among them, since they do the job better than any other Order. The *Juiz Ordinario* should distribute the working Indians among those who need them. The missionaries, having no temporal power, could not transfer any Indians from one village to another. See AHU, Maranhão, Papeis Avulsos, doc. 24 de fevereiro de 1663.

return to their churches and missions, but their monopoly of the missions was broken. An exception was made in the case of Fr. António Vieira; he was specifically prohibited from returning. The law provided that neither the Jesuits nor the other religious orders should have temporal jurisdiction over the Indians. Spiritual jurisdiction over the Indians would henceforth be shared by all religious residing in Maranhão and Pará. The ecclesiastical ordinary, i.e., the vicar general and the prelates of the religious orders, were to assign religious for, and remove them from, parish work and the care of souls in the *aldeias*. No religious orders would thenceforth be permitted to administer their own *aldeias* of Indians. In temporal matters the Indians would be ruled by their own chiefs. Complaints would be judged by the governors and ministers of justice. At the beginning of each year the *câmaras* were to elect a *repartidor*. This official, together with the pastor of each *aldeia*, would be in charge of distributing the Indians of service. The special business of the *repartidor* was to ascertain how many Indians each colonist needed; the pastor's was to inform the Indians who were called to service. The Indians were to be paid in accordance with the *regimento* of 1655, i.e., two varas of cloth or its equivalent per month. *Entradas* were to be made whenever the town councils approved. Each *entrada* was to be provided with a *cabo de escolta*, named by the *câmaras*, and with a religious missionary, from any of the religious orders, also named by the *câmaras*. Such an accompanying religious obliged himself not to have any slaves ransomed for himself or for his Order. Neither he nor his Order could acquire ransomed slaves within one year after the *resgate* expedition. The *cabo de escolta*, governor, *capitão-mor* and other royal officials were prohibited from sending *resgates* for themselves. In all other respects the law of 1655 and the *regimento* of the governors were to continue in force.[5]

On the same day, the king issued a general pardon to all those inhabitants who had taken part in the recent revolt against the Jesuits.[6]

The official copy of the new law concerning the Indians was brought to São Luiz by the procurator, Jorge de Sampaio e Carvalho, in February of 1664, and it pleased nobody. The governor,

---

[5] *Ibid.*

[6] *Ibid.*, pp. 31 f. A MS copy of the pardon is in AHU, Cód. 1275: Ordens regias registadas na camara do Pará, fls. 13 f.

Rui Vaz de Sequeira, was displeased because the *câmaras* had been given powers he had formerly enjoyed, e.g., the appointment of the leaders of the *entradas* and the supervision of them. The Franciscans, Mercedarians and Carmelites were displeased because they had hoped to displace the Jesuits. The *câmara*, or town council, and the settlers were not in favor of having pastors residing in all the Indian *aldeias*, and concerned with the *entradas* and the distribution of the Indians. A junta of all the local dignitaries of São Luiz was thereupon called, and it was decided to postpone the execution of the law until the king had been heard from again. In Belém, on the contrary, the new law was received with applause by the *câmara* and the *capitão-mor*. A special junta confirmed the decision of the town council.[7] The governor, however, considered the action of the Town Council of Belém a personal affront and he left immediately for Belém to subjugate what he looked upon as rebellion! The presence of the governor and his troops cowed Belém into submission, and matters remained in this state until 1667, when the governor allowed the new law to go into effect in Pará, except for the provisions that limited the governor's power.[8]

In Lisbon, meanwhile, the question of the Indian missions continued to be agitated. On September 13, 1663, the Jesuit Procurator General of the Missions, Father Pero Fernandes Monteiro, wrote a defence of the Jesuit missions and missionaries and asked for the return of most of their former extensive powers. The law of 1663, he maintained, by permitting the governor (*sic!*) and the *câmara* to choose the religious for the *resgates* and by giving the ecclesiastical ordinary a part in choosing pastors for the mission churches, could not be obeyed by Jesuits, since it was contrary to the constitutions of the Order. Monteiro was also opposed to the sharing by all the religious orders in the spiritual jurisdiction over the Indians. Since it was clear to him that the Jesuits as missionaries operated "with greater perfection" (*com maior perfeição*) than the other Orders, and held "the first place in this ministry" (*o primeiro lugar para este mynisterio*), he believed that all the mission churches, including those in the hands of other Orders, should be given to the Jesuits. To bolster his own case,

---

[7] Azevedo, *Os Jesuítas no Grão Pará*, pp. 129 f.

[8] *Ibid.*, pp. 130 f.

Monteiro had unkind things to say about the other Orders. The Mercedarians, he said, did not have a religious major superior in Portugal (since they were a Spanish foundation). Their only house in the state was in Belém. They had taken boys from Belém as novices, whose novitiate was passed on the streets of the city. Even though they might have the requisite virtue, they did not have a missionary sense.[9] The Carmelites, Fr. Monteiro said, were good men, but according to the rules of their Institute they were not missionaries. Moreover, there had been some complaints about a few of them, and they were said to have been the cause of the recent revolt. The Franciscans, he wrote, had been missionaries in the early days of the state, but they could not take care of the situation, so the administration of the Indians was taken away from them, and many of them left Maranhão and Pará, so that in 1652 there were only two of them left there. He added that the Franciscans sent from Portugal recently were very young and not very well educated. Few of them learned the *lingua geral*. Monteiro believed, in conclusion, that the Indians should be entrusted to the Jesuits exclusively. They would try to protect the natives, even though the law did not allow temporal control by the missionaries.[10]

João de Moura suggested the importation of Negro slaves as a means of solving the economic problems of Maranhão. He did this because he realized that it was "not the style for the white people of these parts, or of any other of our colonies, to do more than command their slaves to work and tell them what to do." He was in favor of the formation of a monopolistic company to bring in Negro slaves and take out the products of the colony. The slaves would be paid for with the products of the land, not

---

[9] The question of the Mercedarians in Pará was finally settled on September 9, 1665, when the king allowed them to continue their establishment there, but ordered them to accept only Portuguese candidates in the future. See ANTT, Livraria, Livros do Brasil, Cód. 33, p. 6.

[10] AHU, Maranhão, Papeis Avulsos, doc. 13 de setembro de 1663. Another copy of the representation of Fr. Monteiro is found in BA, 50-V-35, fls. 371 f. There are a few slight variations in the text, e.g., "os capuchos forão os primeiros missionarios daquella conquista," instead of "forão missionarios daquella conquista," as it is in the AHU copy. Manoel da Vide Souto Maior, at about the same time as Monteiro wrote, urged the return of the Jesuits to their former privileged position, with the law of 1655 again in force. See BNL, Fundo Geral, Cód. 1570, fls. 308-318, printed in Studart, *Documentos Brasil*, IV, 77-86.

with money.   As for the Indians, they should be given grants of land, as were the other vassals of the king.[11]   Part of Moura's plan was seconded by the Overseas Council in 1665, when they went on record as favoring the request of the people of São Luiz for African slaves from Angola and Guiné.[12]

In the recent revolt of 1661, all the Jesuits had been sent out of the country, but seven of them returned to Pará shortly after sailing, because of a badly leaking boat.   Since by that time the colonists' tempers had cooled, these seven were allowed to remain in the state, and were divided between Pará and Maranhão.[13]   In 1664 or 1665 these Jesuits, soon joined by others, petitioned the Crown for the return of their three *aldeias* of Indians, originally granted for their support in 1653, and for permission to go freely into the interior at royal expense, to get more Indians for their villages.[14]   But this was not granted; the Indian villages were to remain for seventeen years under the administration of Portuguese lay captains, with all the consequent evils of that system.[15]

As mentioned above, this was the era of the struggle for power between the governors and the *câmaras*.   The fight for supremacy continued through the years 1665-1667.   To the end of his administration, Governor Sequeira maintained his position of preeminence over the rights given the town councils in the law of 1663.   The following governor, António de Albuquerque Coelho de Carvalho, who was named on July 27, 1666,[16] and took pos-

[11] BNL, Fundo Geral, Cód. 1570, fls. 319-326, printed in Studart, *Documentos Brasil*, IV, 94-99.   The paper is without date, but is included among the documents of 1658-1663.

[12] AHU, Livros de registo de Consultas Mixtas, Num. 16, pp. 187 f., doc. 19 de dezembro de 1665.

[13] Azevedo, *Os Jesuítas no Grão Pará*, pp. 128 f.

[14] ANTT, Cartório dos Jesuítas, maço 88.   The document is undated, but from the context it can be said with much probability that it was written in 1664 or 1665.

[15] Leite, *História da Companhia*, IV, 102.   An example of the evils inherent in the lay captain system is contained in a request by the Franciscans for reimbursement for the expenses entailed by Fr. Manoel do Espirito Santo, who had to make a long journey to bring back an Aroan tribe who had fled their village near Belém because of bad treatment.   The friars requested that in the future no lay captains be appointed for this tribe, but that their chiefs rule them temporally and the friars have the spiritual jurisdiction.   See AHU, Maranhão, Papeis Avulsos, doc. 15 de fevereiro de 1667.

[16] ANTT, Chancelaria de Afonso VI, Liv. 28, fl. 202.

session on June 22, 1667, was even more intransigent.[17] Sequeira
had controlled the Indians pretty much as he wished. He had
appointed lay captains, and usurped many of the *câmaras'* powers.
The resulting complaints[18] occasioned a new clarification of the
law of 1663, which the new governor brought with him in 1667.
It was now provided that the pastors should have nothing to do
with the distribution of the Indians of the *aldeias*; the *repartidor*
would be the eldest *juiz ordinário*, appointed by the town council.
In transmitting this information to the *câmara*, Coelho de Carvalho, on August 3, 1667, told the members of that body that he
would thenceforth appoint this *repartidor*. The governors-general,
he said in justification of his action, had always had the power of
executing the orders of the king at their discretion. "You gentle-
men," the governor told the *câmara*, "shall comply with my wishes,
because if you do not, great harm will come to all."[19]

Coelho de Carvalho, moreover, placed the *resgates* under his
jurisdiction by the specious expedient of calling them *descimentos*
instead of *entradas* or *resgates*. This, he argued, gave him the
right to carry them out as he wished, since the town councils had
authority only over *resgates*.[20] Thus the *carta regia* of clarification
which he brought with him at the time of his entrance into his
new position meant nothing. But this intransigence and arbi-
trariness of the governors began to be curbed slightly by the
growing practice of taking *residências* of the officials after their
term of office. Thus, the *residência* of Governor Sequeira found
him guilty enough to be remanded to Portugal for final judgment
in 1669.[21]

[17] See "Memoria dos governadores." He ruled until June 9, 1671. *Ibid.*

[18] See, for instance, the *consulta* of January 26, 1667, in AHU, Pará, Papeis
Avulsos.

[19] "ordeno a Vossas Mercês, que assim o cumprão, e guardem; por que do contrario se seguirá grande prejuizo a todos." Berredo, *Annaes históricos*, II, No. 1155.

[20] The text of the new declaration concerning the distribution of the Indians was
contained in a *carta régia* to Governor Carvalho, dated April 19, 1667, urging his
compliance with the law of 1663, except in the following point: "Hei por bem, que
no que se ordenava que interviessem os Parochos, não intervenhão nem se recorra
a elles, mas que o repartidor seja o Juiz ordinario mais velho em cada anno, e com
esta nova declaração fareis que se execute o que tenho mando sem outra replica
e por acabares de por em ordem esta materia, que se disputa ha tantos annos."
ADE, Ordens MSS. annexos do Regimento e leys sobre as missões, p. 134.

[21] AHU, Maranhão, Papeis Avulsos, doc. 18 de setembro de 1669. I was not
able to ascertain the outcome of the final judgment in Portugal. In 1668 there had

Suggestions continued to pour in to the Overseas Council for the betterment of the condition of the Indians. The proposals made by Fr. Manoel do Espirito Santo, the Custos of the Franciscans in the state, were considered by the council on May 30, 1670. What the friar wanted to avoid was the overworking of the Indians, who were thus left no time to attend to their own livelihood. He blamed the situation on the avarice of the governor and other officials. To solve the problem, he proposed that the state should be ruled by the local inhabitants themselves, not by royal appointees from Europe who generally enriched themselves and oppressed the Indians and colonists at the same time. In such a case, money would remain in the colony, and self-interest would better conditions. In no other way, he felt, could the situation be improved, since even good Europeans were perverted in Maranhão. This proposal the Crown did not accept. The Franciscan further proposed that, during the first year, the free Indians (*índios forros*) in the royal and private *aldeias* should work for the settlers no more than four months, and for themselves the rest of the year. There were Indians of service, he claimed, who in five years had not been allowed one week for their own work. In case of extraordinary need, Indians might be assigned for more labor, but only with the approval of all the religious prelates and the town councils. After the first year of the proposed system, the Indians should be obliged to work for the settlers six months out of the year. Fr. Manoel also advocated the sending of an expedition to look for the "Golden Lake" (*Lago Dourado*). He suggested an expedition of twelve to fifteen canoes and about 300 men, whites as well as Indians, an expedition small enough in numbers to preclude the oppression of the Indians and unnecessary wars in the interior. The king approved this part of his suggestions on August 7, 1670. An expedition subsequently set out, with Fr. Manoel as chaplain, to find the mythical lake, but obviously with no success.[22]

---

been a *devassa* proving the guilt of Captain Aguiar da Costa of Gurupá, accused by both the Jesuits and Franciscans of mistreating Indians. The Overseas Council said the *devassa* proved his guilt. He is ordered to Portugal and a *residência* is ordered to judge his term of office. See AHU, Maranhão, Papeis Avulsos, doc. 13 de outubro de 1668.

[22] The governor was to take care of the outfitting and sending of this expedition. If any unjust seizures of Indians were made on this expedition, these would be

Other Franciscans also made themselves heard during these years. In 1669 and 1670 the provincial of the St. Anthony Province in Portugal suggested various means of bettering the lot of his missionaries and their charges. The financial help promised to the Franciscans on April 21, 1669, for their difficult missions among the Aroan Indians on Marajó and Cabo do Norte had not yet, he said, been paid. This failure was holding back the progress of Christianity since the Aroans wanted only Franciscans as missionaries. Moreover, he suggested the early payment of the *ordinária*, or salary, of the Franciscan missionaries, in arrears for many years. He also suggested that the mission areas be permanently divided among the various Orders, obviously to avoid friction and rivalries. Each mission, the provincial thought, should be supported by twenty families of Indians. He knew of no better way to support the missions in such a poor state. He proposed that Indians brought from the interior by the missionaries should not be permitted to serve outside the *aldeia* in which they were gathered for a total of five years. This would make it possible for the missionaries to teach them the Christian religion without interruptions. The Overseas Council was generally favorable to the provincial's proposals, but they were not immediately put into practice. Something more was needed to arouse the Crown to action.[23]

The problem of the missions continued to plague the highest government circles. During the years 1671-1673, determined to reach a satisfactory solution, the Overseas Council went out of its way to collect as much information as it could on this perennial and pressing issue. A questionnaire on the subject was sent to two ex-governors, Rui Vaz de Sequeira and António de Albuquerque Coelho de Carvalho, to Franciscans, Jesuits, Carmelites, Mercedarians, the Solicitor of the Exchequer (Procurador da Fazenda), the people of Maranhão, and the Solicitor of the Crown (Procurador da Côroa).[24] Nothing quite like this had been done before. The council asked for opinions on a number of questions:

considered as major crimes, subject to the gravest penalties. See AHU, Maranhão, Papeis Avulsos, doc. 30 de maio de 1670.

[23] These several documents of 1669 and 1670 are found together under date of November 23, 1669, in AHU, Maranhão, Papeis Avulsos.

[24] All of this correspondence, which will be cited separately, is in AHU, Maranhão, Papeis Avulsos, under doc. 18 de maio de 1672.

1) Would it be more convenient for the conversion of the Indians to assign to each of the religious orders a certain district in which only this Order could preach to the Indians, form *aldeias* and administer to the Indians spiritually?   How could the Indians best be ruled and distributed?

2) Would it be convenient for religion's sake to undertake *resgate* expeditions, or would it be better not to permit *resgates* at all, but to rely exclusively on the preaching of the Gospel?   If the Indians had slaves should they be allowed to bring them to the nearest Portuguese town for the purpose of selling them?   This would free the Portuguese from the carrying out of private *resgates*, which are forbidden to them.

3) What should be done to make certain that the Indians who, of their own free will, come in from the interior at the invitation of the missionaries, work for the colonists for a salary and without vexation?

4) What should be done about the new Indians brought in by the missionaries to live in their *aldeias*?   Should these Indians be allowed to work for the settlers for a just wage?   How could this problem be settled without provoking the religious and injuring the Indians?

5) What should be the policy concerning Indians brought in by the religious and distributed for outside work before being settled definitely in *aldeias* and instructed in the Faith?

6) Should the *aldeias* be ruled by the Indian chiefs, or should they be put in charge of Portuguese laymen?   Should there be a *procurador geral* to protect the Indians from injustice, and to judge their complaints?

7) Should Indians, especially minors, be taught reading and writing, Latin, and mechanical trades?   Would it be wise to found a secondary school (*colegio*) for those among them who could profit from these studies?   Would education help them to become domesticated and lose their barbarity?

The questionnaire was sent out in 1671, and among the first group to answer it were the Franciscans of the Province of St. Anthony.   In their reply of December 11, 1671, they showed themselves emphatically in favor of assigning specific areas for each Order on a fair, just, and above all, permanent basis.   They believed that the *aldeias* should be placed far from the towns of the whites, as had been done with the Jesuit missions in Paraguay and the Franciscan missions on the Río Charcas in Peru. With regard to *entradas* and *resgates*, the Franciscans observed that in the past the Portuguese settlers had been very greedy. They had captured whole villages of Indians without regard for the laws. They had justified their actions on the grounds that they brought the Indians to the Faith, but conversion, declared the Franciscans, did not imply tyrannical servitude. Clearly, lay captains should not be placed in charge of the Indians, for lay captains were notoriously unjust in distributing the captive Indians. It was these lay captains, through their misdeeds, who made the Indians hate the Portuguese. The missionaries in turn should be allowed to redeem Indian slaves in the name of the king, and place them in the royal villages with the other free Indians, where, after a suitable time, they would be ready to serve the colonists as free men, according to the law. The Franciscans further suggested that the Indians be catechized on their home ground. They should not be uprooted and forced to live in a new locality. When some of the Nheengaibas from Marajó Island were brought by Governor Negreiros to Maranhão, almost all of them died within five years. This experience should not be repeated. The Indians prospered, on the other hand, when, as had happened to the Aroan Indians under the Franciscans and the Nheengaiba tribe under the Jesuits, the missionaries went to them. After three years of this type of missionary work, the Indians willing to live near the whites should be allowed to do so. They could then work for the colonists as the other free Indians did. The Franciscans held that the missionaries of the several Orders should not themselves make use of the Indians, except as rowers and for the service of the convents. Moreover, the Indians recently brought in from the interior should be kept separate according to tribes, and their distribution for work should be carried out by the chiefs and not by lay captains. The Franciscans were absolutely opposed to lay captains; it was unjust, they argued, to take away the authority of the chiefs and the missionaries. The system of lay captaincies might possibly work only if the king was able to find men who were truly disinterested, did not favor one Order over another, and did not interfere with the teaching of the Faith. The friars were emphatically in favor of teaching reading, writing and the mechanical skills to the Indians.   This, they believed, could be easily done by the missionaries themselves.[25]

The Mercedarians, on December 13, 1671, advocated the division of the mission field into four sections, one for each of the Orders.   The size of each section should depend on the numbers of religious in each Order in the state.   They believed that some control over *resgates* was necessary, in order to avoid infractions of the law and a repetition of past abuses.   *Resgates*, as well as the distribution of the Indians captured, should be under the control of the town councils.   Indians taken in an unjust war should be known as *escravos de condição*.   A list of such Indians should be made by the Procurator General of the Indians, who should see that these Indians served only for the period of time necessary to pay for the expenses of the expedition in which they were captured.   Ordinarily this would be for five years.   Thereafter the Indians should be permitted to serve whatever master they wished, but under the watchful eye of the procurator, who would see that no violence was done to them.   The Mercedarians thought that a colonist who needed Indian workers should first approach the missionary in charge of an *aldeia*.   No Indian should be permitted to leave unless his wages were paid in advance.   Upon the completion of the stipulated period of labor, the colonist should bring the Indians back to the *aldeia*.   The system advocated by the Mercedarian friars was, they said, already in use.   It could be improved upon if the Procurator of the Indians should have a hand in it.   The procurator might then allot the requested Indians.   After the term of service was over, the colonist should be obliged to get a signed paper from the missionary attesting that the proper salary had been paid, and that the Indian had not been molested during the period of his employment.   Religious had to have enough Indian families for their support.   The other Indians in *aldeias* should work for the settlers for a just salary, according to the directions of the Procurator of the Indians.   Indians who set up new *aldeias* at the request of the missionaries should be free of outside work for a period of three years.   Lay captains were not favored by the Mercedarians, because they felt that the Indians had a right to be ruled by their own leaders.   Yet it was

---

[25] AHU, Maranhão, Papeis Avulsos, doc. 11 de dezembro de 1671, under document dated 18 de maio de 1672.

dangerous to permit a chief who had been over the Indians in the wilderness to continue in the same capacity in the *aldeias*. Such a chief might be tempted to encourage his subjects to abandon their *aldeia*, and indeed, to encourage Indians in other *aldeias* to follow them. There was also the risk that in the process Portuguese might be killed. As to education, the Mercedarians suggested the establishment of a central school where the sons of chiefs might learn to read and write, study Latin and even *casos de consciência*. By this means an elite group could be formed which would have a great civilizing influence among the Indians. The Mercedarians, finally, believed that the important office of Procurator General of the Indians should be exercised by the *câmara* itself (*o mesmo corpo da câmara*). The officials of the town council were the most worthy people of the country, the permanent inhabitants, and they had, as the Mercedarians believed, the utility of the state uppermost in their minds.[26]

The Carmelites did not believe that it would be wise to restrict each Order to a district of its own. Rather, the Orders should take turns in going into the interior to preach to the natives. Whatever Indians they might bring back and domesticate should be under that Order's spiritual control. Temporal matters concerning the Indians should be in the hands of a secular tribunal. Part of its business would be to see that the Indians were paid a wage comparable to that paid to laborers in Portugal.[27] The Carmelite point of view on *entradas* and *resgates* was extremely favorable to the Europeans. They observed that the religious who went on these expeditions were usually protected by soldiers and Christian Indians. If the pagans did not wish to accept the Faith, if they tried to kill those who brought it to them, and if they made war on the Portuguese and the Christian Indians, the Portuguese could justly wage war against them. Any captives taken in such a war would belong to the victors, who would be at liberty to keep them in, or sell them into, perpetual slavery. These legitimately

---

[26] AHU, Maranhão, Papeis Avulsos, doc. 13 de dezembro de 1671, under document dated 18 de maio de 1672.

[27] The Carmelites, in their preface to the answers, made the point that in Brazil Negroes had solved the manpower problem, but in Maranhão and São Paulo the colonists were dependent completely on Indians, and therefore fought vigorously if any attempt was made to take away their slaves. The fathers suggested that the king disregard the past, and legislate only for the future.

enslaved Indians should be distinguished from other Indians by means of an outward sign. Individual Indian converts who had asked to be received into the Faith ought to be permitted to serve whomsoever they pleased, religious as well as laymen. Indians rounded up in a just war and turned over to the religious would remain as much in captivity as if they had been acquired by laymen. Indians who came of their own will to the religious should remain free, under the control of the secular tribunal. Free Indians living in *aldeias* should be administered by the religious and work for a salary. It would be the business of the secular tribunal to see that they were properly paid, and to distribute them among the colonists who needed them. The Indians should not work during Lent, and they should be permitted to go to Mass on Sundays and holydays. The Carmelites were in favor of lay captains (*maiorais seculares*) for the Indian *aldeias*, nominated by the secular tribunal set up in the state. Officials of inferior position might be Indians of the tribe, chosen, if possible, from among the more pious. All the officials should have temporal power only; the Order in charge of the *aldeia* should wield the spiritual power. The Carmelites were not averse to teaching the Indians reading, writing, mechanical skills and even Latin. The pupils should be administered temporally by the lay captain and spiritually by the religious.[28]

Unlike the Franciscans and Mercedarians, the Jesuits were not in favor of limiting each Order to a specific region. One objection was that not all the Indians of a given section spoke the *língua geral*, and hence it would be difficult to mix them together. Another was the mobility of the Indians. For practical purposes, if a missionary Order was already established in a certain section, it would be well, said the Jesuits, for other Orders to stay out. This would avoid confusion. The Society thought that it might be best for the various Orders to go into districts one after the other, so that the Indians might then choose the Order they liked best. *Resgates* should be carried out in accordance with the law of 1655. It would, of course, be better not to have *resgates* at all, since they had generally been only a pretext for unjust captivity. As in Brazil, the missionaries should administer the *aldeias* and distribute

---

[28] AHU, Maranhão, Papeis Avulsos, doc. s.d. [1671], under document dated 18 de maio de 1672. The make-up of the secular tribunal was not mentioned by the Carmelites.

the Indians for salaried work among the colonists. This avoided the inconvenience of having the Indians work before they were catechized, or of their being separated from their wives for long periods of time. Indians of service were absolutely essential for the missions, since the missions had no other means of support. The missionaries should also be provided with Indian rowers. Indians should be allowed sufficient time to settle properly in their villages and be instructed in the Faith and the ways of civilized society before being sent to work for the colonists. The Jesuits were not in favor of lay administrators; they believed that ideally the missionaries should have both spiritual and temporal power. Yet in this matter they preferred to let the king make up his own mind. They did, however, say that the missionaries and the Indians needed a *procurador geral*. They believed, finally, that the Indians should be taught reading, writing and mechanical arts. Latin, on the other hand, was generally beyond them, and it should be taught only to exceptionally gifted Indians.[29]

These replies of the various religious orders were next sent to two ex-governors for their criticism and suggestions. The first of these, Rui Vaz de Sequeira, in his reply dated February 10, 1672, pointed out that Maranhão and Pará consisted of two towns and four captaincies, with 800 Europeans, all of whom were poor and depended absolutely on Indian labor. He suggested following the *Regimento dos Missionarios*[30] to control the captured Indians, and the *Regimento dos Governadores* of 1655 to control the free Indians. The Jesuit mission prelate should be in charge, in his opinion, of the temporal government of the Indians, with the assistance of the other Orders. Well-managed *aldeias*, he said, were the best guarantee against native revolts. Sequeira insisted that all the inhabitants of the state should be free to go to the interior, but that unjust captivity of Indians should not be allowed. The distribution of Indians should be made justly. The four missionary Orders of the state had the right to accompany the troops into the interior. The implementation of this right in practice, however, still remained to be worked out. The Indians should be

---

[29] AHU, Maranhão, Papeis Avulsos, doc. s.d. [1671], under document dated 18 de maio de 1672.

[30] It is uncertain to what *regimento* Sequeira referred. It is possible he meant the "Regulamento das Aldeias" written for use by the Jesuits by Vieira before 1661. See Leite, *História da Companhia*, IV, 105-124.

brought closer to the Portuguese towns than they then were. Indians brought in from the interior by the missionaries should not be used outside the *aldeia* for a period of three years. There should be a lay captain and a chief governing each village of Indians. Pastors could, if they wished, instruct their Indians.[31]

The second ex-governor, António de Albuquerque Coelho de Carvalho, on February 22, 1672, gave as his opinion that the Jesuits should be in charge of all the missions of the state. The Indians, he felt, respected them more than the other religious. *Entradas* and *resgates* should be under the complete control of the governor, and not of the *câmaras*, since the *câmaras* were motivated by selfish interests. Indian slaves were absolutely necessary. Indians should be settled in *aldeias* near the whites. The government should help the Indians when they were in trouble or need. Some of the *aldeias* Indians should be used to support the convents and colleges of the religious; the other Indians should be distributed, but not by the *juiz ordinário*, who was a member of the *câmara*. The Indians should remain unmolested with the missionaries for two years after they were brought from the interior. In the *aldeias* the chiefs and the procurator general should control the Indians temporally. Great care should be exercised in choosing the procurator. Finally, Carvalho thought that the Indians should be taught reading, writing and mechanical skills.[32]

The people of the state had their say through the procurator of the city of São Luiz, who, speaking for these citizens, stressed the paucity of Indians available for service. There were, he said, only eighty in all of Maranhão and these were kept busy continually by the governor. The procurator of São Luiz insisted that *resgate* expeditions should be strictly supervised, to avoid a repetition of the many injustices committed in the past. In the past some friendly Indians had been treated as enemies, and whole villages had been wiped out. Yet *resgates* as such were necessary. He believed each of the four religious orders should have a special district of its own for missionary activity. He did not, however, say who should make the division or how it should be done.[33]

---

[31] AHU, Maranhão, Papeis Avulsos, doc. 10 de fevereiro de 1672, under document dated 18 de maio de 1672.

[32] AHU, Maranhão, Papeis Avulsos, doc. 22 de fevereiro de 1672, under document dated 18 de maio de 1672.

[33] AHU, Maranhão, Papeis Avulsos, doc. s.d. [1672], under document dated 18 de maio de 1672.

During the years 1672 and 1673 these suggested solutions to the problem of the Indians were considered by the home government. It was obviously difficult to reach a sensible decision. One high official, on August 5, 1673, wrote an opinion in which he considered, among other things, the remark by the Franciscans that the institution of lay captaincies could work if men wholly disinterested, without ambition and without affection for a particular religious order, were appointed to the position. He doubted whether such men could be found who would want to go to Maranhão: "Quis est iste et laudabimus eum," he exclaimed.[34]

Finally, on August 17, 1673, the Solicitor of the Crown, Dr. Mateus Mousinho, concluded the entire matter by announcing the best solution, after all, was the law of September 9 [sic], 1655, which, he added, had never been perfectly observed. It would not help, he said, to make new laws when the obviously good laws of the past were dead letters.[35] The solicitor was of course right, and here the matter rested for some years.

The years 1673-1680 continued to be years of uncertainty and chaos in Maranhão and Pará. The scanty documentation that has come down to us from this period bears this out. Rivalries and complaints were the order of the day.

The greatest rivalry continued to be that between the governor and the *câmaras*, especially the *Câmara* of Belém. It will be recalled that the promulgation of the law of 1663, with the powers over the Indians given mainly to the town councils instead of to the governor, had provoked much strife in 1664, and during the following four years.[36] This strife continued from 1673 to 1679. It would not be of service to follow all these changes of opinion, since the account is bewildering in the extreme.[37] Suffice it to say that the end result for the missions and for the Indians was more uncertainty and more oppression. Lack of documentation pre-

---

[34] *Ibid.*, doc. 5 de agosto de 1673.

[35] "Parecer do Procurador da Coroa, Dr. Mateus Mousinho confirmando e explicando melhor sua opinião de 26 de maio de 1672," *Ibid.*, doc. 17 de agosto de 1673.

[36] See above, p. 120.

[37] For a running account of developments, see Berredo, *Annaes históricos*, II, No. 1180-1230, or Azevedo, *Os Jesuítas no Grão Pará*, pp. 133 f. Concerning Governor Menezes, see "Memoria dos governadores." For a letter blaming the *Câmara* of Belém for observing a royal law against the will of the governor, see AHU, Cód. 1275: Ordens regias registadas na camara do Pará, fls. 15-17, doc. 21 de novembro de 1673. It is printed in *Livro Grosso*, I, 33-35.

cludes the real study of the missions during this period. A gauge of the difficult times might be had in the fact that the Jesuits in 1673 were still trying to get back the three private *aldeias* of Indians which had been taken from them in the riots of 1661.[38] But despite the fact that the condition of the missions during these years seems to have depended on the whim or the good will of the officials of the state, missionaries continued to come. In 1674, for example, a royal letter dispatched on March 1 informed Governor Pedro César de Meneses of the coming to Maranhão of additional Franciscan missionaries, whom he was admonished to treat well and pay promptly.[39]

As long, however, as the officials continued their arbitrary action concerning Indians, the missionaries were helpless. Governor Meneses had the audacity, on March 22, 1674, to write to the king to inform him that an *entrada* had been made into the interior to gather Indians, because the settlers in Maranhão needed them badly. In his answer of October 24, the king severely reprimanded him for not having observed the laws concerning the prior sending to the Court of the vote of the junta concerning the legality of the undertaking, and for taking these matters into his own hands.[40] The governor, however, had presented the king with a *fait accompli*, and there was nothing that could now be done.

If the governor in São Luiz was arbitrary, so was the *câmara* in Belém, which continued to keep a tight grasp on Indian matters, much to the chagrin of the *capitão-mor* of Pará, Marçal Nunes da Costa.[41] In the early part of 1675 he complained to the home government that the *câmara* was not giving to him his fair share of the Indians which were distributed among the colonists.[42] On May 10 the Court reminded the town council that Indians should not be distributed without the participation of the *capitão-mor*.[43]

---

[38] AHU, Pará, Papeis Avulsos, doc. 20 de julho de 1673.

[39] AHU, Registo de Cartas Regias . . . para Maranhão e Pará, Num. 268, p. 3v. Also printed in *Livro Grosso*, I, 35, and in the *Annaes da Biblioteca e Archivo Publico do Pará*, I (1902), 62 f. Hereafter cited as *ABAPP*.

[40] AHU, Registo de Cartas Regias . . . para Maranhão e Pará, Num. 268, p. 7v. Also printed in *Livro Grosso*, I, 36.

[41] Costa was nominated *capitão-mor* on September 9, 1669, but actually ruled only from July 30, 1674, to July 25, 1685. See Braga, *História do Pará*, p. 142.

[42] See AHU, Pará, Papeis Avulsos, doc. 2 de maio de 1675. This is the date of the *consulta* of the Overseas Council.

[43] AHU, Registo de Cartas Regias . . . para Maranhão e Pará, Num. 268, p. 10v,

His complaint did not avail much. Four years later, on January 31, 1679, he was forced to complain again concerning the distribution of the Indians. He said that as a result of his other complaint they had given him "one or two Indians," which was obviously not sufficient.[44]

At about the same time the Franciscans complained also concerning the arbitrary actions of the officials of the Town Council of Belém, who were trying to deprive the friars of an *aldeia* which had been granted to them long years before for the upkeep of their missions. The Franciscans pointed out to the king that they had had this *aldeia* for forty years. They used the Indians living in it for hunting, fishing and rowing. Their Indians, they said, were treated like sons; they had never had a single complaint from any of them. Their possession of the village, or rather, its administration, was legal and above dispute. They therefore asked the king to order the governor and the officials of the town council not to interfere in any way with the Indians of this village.[45]

By papal bull of August 30, 1677, the See of São Luiz was erected, the first in the state of Maranhão and Pará. This meant that a large area would no longer be dependent ecclesiastically on Bahia, since the new see embraced the whole Amazon region included within the state of Maranhão and Pará.[46] Before the first bishop, Dom Gregorio dos Anjos, took possession of his see in 1679, a revision of the law of 1663 was made to give him a voice in Indian matters.[47] According to the law of 1663 the *câmaras*

or Cód. 1275: Ordens regias registadas na camara do Pará, fl. 18. Also printed in *Livro Grosso*, I, 36.

[44] AHU, Registo de Cartas Regias . . . para Maranhão e Pará, Num. 268, p. 22v. Printed in *Livro Grosso*, I, 48.

[45] AHU, Pará, Papeis Avulsos, doc. 3 de julho de 1675. In ADE, "Regimento e leys sobre as missões do Maranhão," pp. 40-42, the name of the *aldeia* is given as "Goarabiranga." *Santuario Mariano*, IX, 395-398, calls it "Guarapirangá," and locates it twelve leagues up the Amazon, on the north side of the river.

[46] "Innocentius XI oppidum S. Ludovici de Maragnano á dioecesi Brasiliensi avellit; civitatis jura tribuit ei, in eaque constituit Sedem Episcopalem reservato jure Patronatus Regibus Lusitanis fundationis ac dotationis titulo. Romae, 30 de Augusto, 1677," BA, 46-XI-8, fl. 165. See also Cândido Mendes de Almeida, *Direito civil eclesiastico Brasileiro antigo e moderno em suas relações com o Direito Canonico* (Rio de Janeiro, 1866), p. 588.

[47] AHU, Registo de Cartas Regias . . . para Maranhão e Pará, Num. 268, pp. 20v-21. On Bishop Anjos, see Cézar Augusto Marques, *Diccionario historico-geographico da Provincia do Maranhão* (Maranhão, 1870), pp. 49-51.

had been authorized annually to appoint an official who would take care of distributing the Indians to the settlers for work. On December 4, 1677, this part of the law was changed. It was declared that the bishop and the missionary of the Order whose turn it was to accompany the *resgate* expeditions should propose three names to the governor, from which the leader of the expedition would be chosen by the governor. Formerly the distribution of the Indians for work was taken care of by a *repartidor* elected by the *câmara* annually. Now the bishop, with the pastor of the *aldeia* and the minister of justice, would take care of this distribution, collaborating with the Indian chief and the governor or captain-general. If the bishop was not present, his delegate should take his place. Until the bishop arrived in the state, the two actual prelates of the Jesuit and Franciscan Orders were to have this position. In default of these, or of one of them, the actual prelate of the other Orders should take his place. For the rest, the law of 1663 was ordered to be kept in observance.[48]

The town councils now began to lose their importance in the state. The home government at this time decided that something should be done to control the self-importance of the *câmaras*. On December 4, 1677, the king pointedly told the Town Council of São Luiz to give up the practice of summoning the governor to the council chambers every time it wanted to propose a piece of business. Since the governor represented the king in all state business, it was not fitting that he should be at the beck and call of the *câmara*.[49]

The same *Câmara* of São Luiz began immediately to complain concerning the new method of distribution of the Indians introduced in December of 1677. Already on June 3, 1678, the *câmara* protested to the king against the method in which the religious prelates, Jesuit and Franciscan, had acted in the recent *repartição* of the Indians. They had acted clearly in accordance with the new regulations promulgated the year before, but the *câmara* complained nevertheless. The king answered only on March 16, 1679. He declared that since the new bishop was then on his way to the state the reasons for the complaints would no longer exist. The

---

[48] *Ibid.* The royal letter is also printed, with slight variations, in *Livro Grosso*, I, 44 f. and in *ABAPP*, I, 65 f.

[49] For the text see *Livro Grosso*, I, 43 f.

new regulations, in any event, were to be observed, until such time as the king might decide otherwise.[50]

The new bishop, Dom Gregório dos Anjos, arrived in the latter part of 1679, and immediately made his presence felt throughout the state. His was a strong character that brooked no opposition. He had been given to understand that he would control the Indian situation, but he found that the governor also had something to do with the distribution of the Indians. This interference was apparently justified on the basis of the official copy of the law of December 4, 1677, which the governor followed. In reply, however, to the bishop's complaint, the king, on March 24, 1679, made clear that the governor should have no part in the distribution. His Majesty explained that the section of the law upon which the governor based his authority had been gratuitously inserted by the scribe who had made the copy.[51]

During the course of the year 1679, the king received some good advice concerning the solution of the Indian problem from royal officials cognizant of the situation. One of them, Domingos António Tomás, gave a formal opinion to the king on November 3 of that year. To him there seemed to be two great evils to be corrected in the state of Maranhão-Pará: 1) the short terms of the governors, who therefore felt that they had to enrich themselves as rapidly as possible, and 2) the constant unjust enslavement of of Indians who had done no wrong. Tomás was of the opinion that the best way to take good care of the Indians would be to place them in *aldeias* under control of their Indian chief and missionaries. He preferred the Jesuits for this task, but admitted that any religious order with sufficient members was capable of doing it. The second part of his solution would be to introduce more African slaves into the state, in order thus to spare the Indians.[52] On the same day another official, Simão da Costa e Sousa,

---

[50] For the text, see AHU, Registo de Cartas Regias . . . para Maranhão e Pará, Num. 268, p. 23v. It is also printed in *Livro Grosso*, I, 48 f.

[51] For the text see AHU, Registo de Cartas Regias . . . para Maranhão e Pará, Num. 268, p. 24. Also printed in *Livro Grosso*, I, 49, and *ABAPP*, I, 69. On March 21, 1679, the king commanded that the salary of the coming bishop be paid from the tithes of Maranhão and Pará. If that did not suffice, then the tithes of Bahia were to be used. See *ibid.*, I, 68.

[52] "Parecer que Domingos António Tomás deu a S.A. sobre o Maranhão e Pará. . . ." BA, 50-V-37, fls. 394-397.

gave as his opinion that any new Indian legislation should outlaw Indian slavery altogether; the Indians should work for a salary like any other worker, and the religious should teach them religion and protect them.[53] Still another paper written on the same day by an anonymous author was content merely to petition for an end to Indian slavery in Maranhão and Pará.[54]

Some of the above ideas were to be followed in the next year, 1680, when a new, more comprehensive law was to be passed—the famous law of April 1, 1680. With it began a new era in Portuguese-Indian relations. It was destined to be an important step forward in the direction of a fundamental solution of this vexing problem.

---

[53] "Parecer que Simão da Costa e Sousa deu a S.A. sobre a administração do Maranhão e Pará," *ibid.*, fls. 398-404.

[54] "Petição a S.A. para que se não façam escravos Indios do Maranhão e Pará," *ibid.*, fls. 384-387.

CHAPTER VI

THE FORMATION OF A PERMANENT INDIAN POLICY, 1680-1693

We have discussed thus far the gradual and halting formation of the Indian policy in the Amazon Valley from its inception until 1680. We have seen the various solutions proposed by the interested parties: the missionaries, the royal officials, the colonists acting through their town councils, and finally the home government, all of which alternated between extreme Christian charity and callous indifference regarding the Indian of Maranhão and Pará.[1] The landmarks along the way are the various laws passed concerning the Indians. The law of 1611 allowed enslavement and lay captaincies; the law of 1624 abolished lay captaincies and placed the Indians in charge of the Franciscans. But from the beginning this protective hedge caused complaints and eventual non-observance. The Jesuits attempted in 1637-1643 to take over comprehensive control of the Indians, but all their plans were thwarted by the untimely shipwreck of the missionaries. In 1652 Fr. Vieira succeeded in obtaining protective legislation for the natives, only to see it torn down by the colonist-inspired law of 1653. In 1655 Vieira succeeded in repairing the legal edifice he was building, but the truce was only temporary, and in 1661 the revolt ended his attempt for the time being. There succeeded another period of lay control of the Indians after 1663, which was finally amended in 1677 to give a measure of supervision to the new bishop. In 1680 there occurred another attempt by the Jesuits to take over complete control of the natives of Maranhão and Pará. This attempt, too, was destined to fail within four years, but from the very failure emerged the final permanent solution destined to last for almost seventy years until the secularization of the missions under the rule of the Marquis of Pombal.

In the formation of the new provisions of 1680, Father Vieira played a prominent part. It will be recalled that he was in Rome

---

[1] See Heinrich Handelmann, *Geschichte von Brasilien* (Berlin, 1860), pp. 109 f.

from 1669 to 1679.[2] Upon his return to Portugal in the latter year, he began his last active campaign in favor of the Indians of Maranhão and Grão Pará. It pained him to know that these missions, once so flourishing, were in decay, "given over to secular captains, and almost deserted."[3] It pained him still more to realize that his great pre-eminence of the 1650's was no more.[4] In January, 1680, however, he was able to do something for the Indian missions in Maranhão and Pará at a joint meeting of the councillors of the Council of State and the Overseas Council and other high functionaries, called to propose a plan for the temporal and spiritual administration of the state of Maranhão-Pará.[5] He was called to this junta because he was a recognized specialist in matters concerning the region in question. Opposition to his ideas was not lacking among the participants, but many of his opinions prevailed because of the strong support given him by the president of the meeting, the Duke of Cadaval.[6] Vieira had not changed his ideas very considerably since 1655. He suggested in 1680 that *entradas* into the interior be prohibited; that the government and distribution of the Indians be given to the Jesuits; that the missionaries, that is, the Jesuits, decide the place and time of the *resgate* expeditions; and finally, that Negroes be substituted for the Indian workers as far as possible. After giving his opinion at the junta, he sent a written copy of it to the duke, together with an old plan of his, giving the details of the government of the *aldeias*, and the distribution of the Indian workers.[7] On March 9, 1680, the Overseas Council gave its opinion that the suggestions of Fr. Vieira should be followed in the new legislation. The council added a suggestion of its own, however, at the end. It was in favor of sending more Franciscans to Pará for the missions on the island of Marajó, and the other islands of that district, since the friars were used in the missions of that district and there were no complaints concerning them.[8]

---

[2] See above, p. 116.

[3] Leite, *História da Companhia*, IV, 62.

[4] Azevedo, *História de António Vieira*, II, 210 f.

[5] *Ibid.*, p. 211; Azevedo, *Os Jesuítas no Grão Pará*, p. 136.

[6] Azevedo, *História de António Vieira*, p. 211.

[7] *Ibid.*; The title of Vieira's plan, probably written about 1655, was: "Modo como se há-de governar o gentio que há nas aldeias do Maranhão e Grão Pará." It is found in BA, 49-IV-23, f. 137-141.

[8] AHU, Maranhão, Papeis Avulsos, doc. 9 de março de 1680. The opinion of

Several laws and royal orders were passed on April 1, 1680. The most fundamental of these was entitled "Law concerning the liberty of the Indians of Maranhão." Its principal provisions can be summarized as follows:

1) No Indian would thenceforth be enslaved.

2) Any person of whatever quality or condition guilty of capturing or ordering the capture of Indians, secretly or publicly, under any title or pretext whatsoever, would be subject to arrest by the *ouvidor geral* of the state. Such persons would be sent on the first available ship to Portugal, where they would be punished by the king. Indians thus captured were to be given their freedom by the *ouvidor* and placed at his discretion in any of the *aldeias* of free Catholic Indians.

3) The bishop, governor, religious prelates and pastors of villages were required to inform the king of any infractions of the law, so that the proper measures might be taken.

4) In the event of an offensive or defensive war against the Indians, the Indians taken as prisoners should be treated as were prisoners of war in Europe. The governor alone would have the power to dispose of these captives of war. He should see to it that they were placed in *aldeias* of free Catholic Indians, to promote their conversion, assure their service to the state and preserve their liberty. Under no condition was the maltreatment of the Indians to be permitted. [9]

While the basic "Law concerning the liberty of the Indians of Maranhão" prohibited the further enslavement of the Indians and assigned them to the *aldeias* under the control of the religious missionaries, it made no provision for the repartition of the *aldeia* Indians among the settlers. To provide for this need, a second law, "Provision concerning the distribution of the Indians of Maranhão and the delivery of their conversion into the hands of the

---

the council concerning the Franciscans reads as follows: "Pareçeo tambem que V.A. mandasse escrever ao P. Provincial dos Capuchos de S. Antonio que mande sogeitos capazes para aquelle estado, e maior numero delles para continuarem as missões e se estenderem pela Ilha de Joannes e mais Ilhas circumvecinhas daquelle districto, em que se empregão porque destes religiosos não há queixas e dão bom exemplo." For other royal orders of that time, see *Livro Grosso*, I, 49-59.

[9] *Ibid.*, pp. 57-59. Varnhagen, *História Geral*, III, 339-341, also gives the full text. Leite, *História da Companhia*, IV, 63, gives a part of the text. A MS. copy of the law is found in ADE, Varias Ordens MSS annexos a Regimento e leys sobre as missões do Maranhão, pp. 88-93.

religious of the Society of Jesus,"[10] was promulgated on the same day.

In the introduction, the prince regent admitted how absolutely necessary for the conservation of the state was the constant supply of *gente de serviço*, to be used especially in the cultivation of the soil and the search for drugs. He wished to use all possible means to augment this supply, such as bringing Negroes from Guiné each year, conserving the free Indians at present in the *aldeias*, and bringing in more free Indians for this task. To gain these ends, he ordained that this distribution of Indians take place in the following manner:

1) All free Indians belonging to free villages who have been taken from the villages shall be returned thither at once; for this end he ordered the pastors to give a list of those absent to the governor. The governor, in turn, was commanded to take care of this task immediately, not admitting any contrary request, so that every available Indian would be free for the distribution.

2) After all available Indians had been returned, the number of those capable of working should be ascertained from lists made up by the pastors. These workers should be divided into three parts, the first of which should remain always in the *aldeias*. The second part would be distributed among the inhabitants according to the form prescribed by the king on March 17, 1680 (i.e., the bishop, prelate of St. Anthony and one man elected by the *câmara* have charge of this distribution; these three would also see that the Indian was paid his just wage).[11] The third part would be used by the missionaries for bringing in new Indians from the interior. The king went on to say that since this last third was the most important for the welfare of the state, the missionaries could freely select Indians of more intelligence and prestige to accompany them.

3) Because of moral obligation to use the most efficacious means for the Indians' conversion and the inconveniences which would otherwise follow, the king ordained that the Jesuits, and only they,

---

[10] For convenience, the principal points of this law will be numbered, although the original was not so divided.

[11] The king gave this opinion in a *consulta* of the Overseas Council, dated February 29, 1680. See AHU, Maranhão, Papeis Avulsos, doc. 29 de fevereiro de 1680. The actual law concerning this method of *repartição* was passed on March 30, 1680. See *Livro Grosso*, I, 49 f. for text.

could go into the interior to convert the Indians to the Faith, reduce them and domesticate them. The king declared that he did this because of the great knowledge and practice the Jesuits had in this matter, and because of the confidence the Indians had in them. He felt that it would be only in this way that the Indians could hope for the liberty which the new law secured for them. With the removal of the fear of unjust captivity and the hope of good treatment in the future, the Indians could, through the industry of the Jesuits, be converted to the Faith and be educated for civil society in their villages, always as near as possible to the towns of the Portuguese.

4) The Indians, the king continued, were owners of their property and land, just as they had been in the interior, and their property could not be taken from them. The governor was ordered to assign to them, with the consent of the missionaries, convenient spots of land for their cultivation; these fields could not be taken away from them, nor be changed without their consent, nor would the Indians be obliged to pay any tribute or rent for these lands, even though they had been given in *sesmaria* (as a land grant) to the Portuguese. The reason was that *sesmarias* were always given with a clause in the grant prohibiting prejudice to a third party, which condition was certainly present in this case, since the Indians were the first and natural lords of all these lands.

5) Since the king's principal purpose in this state was the conversion of the natives, and since many of these lived far in the interior and did not care to come near the Portuguese, he recommended highly to the Jesuits that they penetrate as far as possible into the interior, and build there the necessary residences and churches, to bring these faraway Indians to the Faith and conserve them in it. The Jesuits should teach them to live with Christian decency and leave off their barbarous customs; they should exhort the Indians to cultivate the land, and to make use of the drugs and fruits of the soil, so that the Indians could bring them down the rivers and exchange them with the Portuguese. In this way the king hoped to advance the Indians spiritually and temporally, and to make affairs convenient for the settlers also, since with this system the settlers would be spared the expense and trouble of those long trips to seek drugs, and the Indians living closer to the Portuguese could be used exclusively in the fields, without

being consumed, as they have been until now, by long voyages into the interior.

6) The king particularly recommended to the superiors of the Society of Jesus that the first of the missions to be undertaken by the fathers into the interior would be on the other side of the Amazon River in the Cabo do Norte region, so that prudent and industrious men could take care of the conversion of these Indians, and keep them in obedience to the Portuguese.

7) Since for all these expeditions and residences a larger number of Jesuits would be required, and since it was certain that people born in a climate who learn the Indian languages when young could do the work better, the king allowed the Jesuits to have in São Luiz a novitiate with twenty novices, who should eventually be used only in the missions of this state. If they would be sent by their superiors to other countries, other Jesuits would have to be sent to take their places. The king assigned a fit *ordinária* for these novices in a separate royal order.[12]

8) The king further ordered that the missionaries who departed on the expeditions into the interior should not take soldiers with them, in order that the pagan Indians might lose the fear they had of unjust enslavement and harsh treatment. The missionaries should with peaceful and mild means bring the natives to the Catholic Faith and communication with the Portuguese. Only when the missionaries went into some section that was unsafe because of the proximity of barbarous Indians should the governor give them the necessary soldiers and arms for protection; the missionaries should themselves, however, select the soldiers they deemed best for the job.

9) It was thought necessary for the success of the missions into the interior that the Indians who would accompany the Jesuits be from among those whom the Jesuits themselves educated. Therefore the king declared that the third part of the Indians in the *aldeias* held by other religious orders or by secular priests, which normally should have to be given to the Jesuits to accompany them on their missions, would instead be applied to the third part of the Indians given for the service of the colonists, with

---

[12] The royal order was dated April 1, 1680. It provided for 250$000 for the twenty novices each year, from the taxes of Bahia and Rio de Janeiro. *Livro Grosso*, I, 56 f.

the other religious being compensated for this with an equal number of Indians from the Jesuit *aldeias*.

10) The prince regent declared that any *aldeias* in the state which had no pastors should be given over to the care of the Jesuits, since it was his intention eventually to entrust all of them to the Jesuit Order. They must keep also all *aldeias* they ever indoctrinated. To avoid all confusion in the matter, the regent ordered that at the advent of this royal decree the Jesuits must be restored to all the *aldieas* they possessed at the time of the arrival of Governor Ignacio Coelho,[13] since according to the decree of John IV they were the legitimate pastors of all the *aldeias*.

11) It was ordered that the same Jesuit fathers should administer and indoctrinate any Indians they brought from the interior, since it was convenient that only one Order rule *aldeias* in the same province or kingdom, just as was done in India and Brazil. This was so ordered to avoid discord and other great inconveniences. Another reason was that the said Order had, by its very rule of life, a great zeal, application and experience in mission matters, all of which made the Jesuits very agreeable and acceptable to the Indians.

12) Finally, the regent ordained that the bishop, the governor and the prelates of the Orders keep him informed of all that happened in the said missions, using for this purpose the Conselho Ultramarino and the Junta das Missões.[14]

Several other laws were passed at about the same time. By the *alvará* of March 31, 1680, the governor and the bishop were forbidden to engage in business or farming, or to meddle in any way with the taking of Indians from the *aldeias*. They had no right to any Indians of service except those given to them in the official distribution of the Indians.[15] By the law of April 1, 1680, five to six hundred Negro slaves were to be brought each year to

---

[13] I.e., February 17, 1678. Governor Ignacio Coelho da Silva ruled from this date until May 20, 1682. See "Memoria dos governadores."

[14] The complete text is found in *Livro Grosso*, I, 51-56. The local *juntas das missões* were formally set up in São Luiz and Belém on March 7, 1681. See Leite, *História da Companhia*, IV, 63.

[15] ADE, Varias ordens MSS annexos a Regimento e leys sobre as missões, pp. 93 f. An exception was made in the case of the present governor, Inácio da Silva Coelho, who was permitted to continue his growing of cacao as an example to the settlers.

the state to be sold to the settlers for moderate prices.[16] By another law of the same date, the religious orders (other than the Society of Jesus) would be allowed to keep any Indian *aldeias* they administered before the coming of the bishop, that is, before 1679.[17]

This corpus of laws set up, in theory, a formidable missionary empire for the Jesuits. This marked the last of Vieira's triumphs in Indian legislation. He did not, however, have a hand in carrying it out. He left Lisbon for Bahia on January 27, 1681; he would never return to Maranhão and Pará.[18]

The new legislation arrived in Belém, now the seat of government of the state,[19] on May 21, 1680, and it was there promulgated immediately.[20] Meanwhile, the people of São Luiz got wind of the latest legislation, and they were prepared to oppose it even before they received the official text. They held various meetings to discuss what they would do. The bishop was loud in denouncing the laws, even though he had not read them, and he set out for Belém to protest to the governor. He changed his mind after his arrival. He now declared that he would submit to all the provisions of the laws that were not contrary to his episcopal jurisdiction.[21] Actually, Dom Gregório refused to admit that his authority did not extend over the Indian missions and churches. As bishop he claimed the right of visitation, but this the Jesuits opposed. Such a pretended right, they argued, was against the rules of their Institute and the laws of the king. The matter raised by the bishop was never really settled; it continued to plague the

---

[16] Leite, *História da Companhia*, IV, 64. Leite lists (pp. 64-67) twenty *despachos e ordens* given out at this time. Eighteen of them are found in substance in what I have mentioned on pp. 141-146. Of two of them, including the one on Negro slaves, I could not find the original. It is found in substance, however, in the *alvará* setting up the *estanco* or monopoly in 1682. See *infra*, p. 148.

[17] *Ibid.*, p. 65. I could not find the original of this provision. Leite gives no exact source, since he says (p. 67, note): "Tôdas ou a maior parte destas Ordens régias encontram-se na Biblioteca de Évora, Cód. CXV-2-12."

[18] Leite, *História da Companhia*, IV, 67 f.

[19] In 1673 Governor César de Meneses began to maintain two residences, one in São Luiz and the other in Belém, which latter he began to use more frequently, as being more geographically central. See Braga, *História do Pará*, p. 87.

[20] The decrees announcing the new laws and demanding obedience to them can be found in AHU, Cód. 1275: Ordens regias registadas na camara do Pará, fl. 21, and in ANTT, Livraria, Cód. 33: Decretos de 1663-1702, p. 62.

[21] Azevedo, *Os Jesuítas no Grão Pará*, pp. 140 f.

missionaries to the very end of the mission system in 1759.[22] The *câmaras* also were alarmed by the new laws, and became the focal point of resistance to the new provisions, reluctant as they were to give up their partial control of the Indians, the only real source of wealth in the state. They sent two procurators to the Court to plead their case in 1681.[23] In view of all this, the king, on June 6, 1681, sent a special royal order to the *ouvidor* of Maranhão instructing him to carry out the provisions of the new laws even in the face of the opposition of the *Câmara* of São Luiz.[24]

The year 1681 was filled with accusations and complaints growing out of the situation created by the new laws. On October 14 the Overseas Council considered some of them in an effort to work out an amicable solution.[25] The council considered first of all a letter of Governor Inácio Coelho da Silva dated April 10, 1681. In it the governor reported that he had given the Jesuits the administration of all the missions of "Xingú, Capitania do Norte [Cabo do Norte] e Rio das Amazonas." He had also divided the domesticated Indians into three parts, as the law demanded: each third came to about 100. The hundred Indians were divided among the settlers for work. But the bishop and the *Câmara* of Belém kept asking for more and more Indians, so that finally only the Jesuits kept their one-third intact. He also reported that in December, 1680, some of the people had protested the method whereby the bishop was distributing the Indians. Dom Gregório replied that he had been appointed by the Holy Father in Rome to be the overseer of all the Indians. So nothing could be done, concluded the governor. The second complaint was from the *ouvidor geral* of Pará, who stated that the bishop was continually demanding jurisdiction over the Jesuit missionaries, was sending religious (non-Jesuits?) as pastors, and was excommunicating the Jesuits. The third letter is from the *câmara*, dated April 10, 1681. The *vereadores* stated very simply that the law was throttling the state; they asked for an entire change of law as soon as possible.

----

[22] *Ibid.*, p. 140.

[23] Varnhagen, *História geral*, III, 307. The names of the two procurators were Inácio Coelho da Silveira and Francisco da Motta Falcão. Calmon, *História do Brasil*, II, 393.

[24] AHU, Registo de Cartas Regias para Maranhão e Pará, Num. 268, p. 28, printed in *Livro Grosso*, I, 60.

[25] AHU, Maranhão, Papeis Avulsos, doc. 14 de outubro de 1681.

Fourthly, the Jesuits in their letter (undated) asked merely that all the laws be observed and delinquents punished. A letter from the bishop is mentioned in the *consulta*, but the contents are not given. The council gave out the following opinion concerning all these complaints and reports. They suggested that nothing be done concerning the governor's and bishop's reports until a new governor should arrive in the following year. They further suggested that it might be better to have the *câmara* take care of the distribution of the Indians, since the membership in the *câmara* changed yearly, and various men would have an opportunity to perform this difficult job, and all would then be satisfied. Concerning the bishop, the council maintained that he had no right to appoint missionaries as pastors: this had been agreed upon at the junta held in Lisbon in January, 1680. The council finally suggested to the king that he send letters to the various contending parties: to the governor, telling him to await the coming of the new governor in 1682; to the *câmara*, telling it to submit; to the bishop, commanding him to be fair in the distribution of Indians and to cease persecuting the Jesuit missionaries. This was done as suggested on November 17, 1681.[26]

When the procurators sent by the *câmaras* of Maranhão and Pará arrived in Lisbon at the end of 1681 they found, to their dismay, that a still more bitter remedy was being prepared for their state: the establishment of a monopolistic company to assure, among other things, that the promised Negro slaves would be furnished. There can be no doubt, however, that this solution was primarily intended by the Court as a remedy for the chronic economic illness of the state of Maranhão and Pará, and for the unrestricted use of Indians as unwilling workers.

By the *alvará* of February 12, 1682, the *Estanco do Maranhão e Pará* was created, a monopolistic company designed to furnish Negro slaves to the colony in return for the equivalent value in local products. An agreement was made with the rich Portuguese merchants, Pedro Álvares Caldas, Manoel Pinto Valdês, António da Gama de Pádua, António Rodrigues Marques, Luis Corrêa da Paz and Pascual Pereira Jansem, who was placed in charge of the operation in the state. The concession was for a period

---

[26] The letters, all dated November 17, 1681, are found respectively in AHU, Registo de Cartas Regias . . . para Maranhão e Pará. Num. 268, p. 29v.; *ibid.*, pp. 29v-30; and *Livro Grosso*, I, 61.

of twenty years, and it gave the company, during that period, a complete monopoly of trade.[27] More specifically, the charter ordained the following:

1) During the period of its existence, the company was obliged to introduce, at the rate of 500 a year, as many as 10,000 Negroes into the state, if such a number proved to be needed.

2) The company would furnish all the articles of trade required by the inhabitants.

3) Negroes and merchandise would be sold for established prices.[28]

4) The colonists would be given an ample extension of time to pay for the slaves they bought.

5) The company was authorized to send experts to the state of Maranhão and Pará to find and encourage the growing of such products as cacao and vanilla.

6) Only the company, during the period of its concession, would be allowed to trade with the state.

7) The company was required to send at least one ship a year to Pará and one to Maranhão. Foreign ships could also be sent if the captain and most of the crew were Portuguese.

8) Ships sent by the company to Angola or elsewhere in Africa to obtain slaves were to receive every assistance from the Portuguese government officials. Such ships were to be exempt from all taxes except the special taxes levied on those who brought slaves to Maranhão and Pará.

9) The company was free to build factories in the state and could send *entradas* to the interior, without concern for the governor or any other official or person.

10) The company, in each urban center of Maranhão and Pará, could have no more than 100 Indian families, brought from the interior at its own cost, to grow food and other supplies for the sustenance of the Negroes. The company was obliged to pay the Indians the ordinary wage for this work. At the beginning, before obtaining their Indians from the interior, the company was

---

[27] The complete agreement is given in AHU, Cód. 1275: Ordens registadas na camara do Pará, fls. 22-30.

[28] At the end of the document there is appended a list of prices for fifteen items, e.g., "Hum Negro, Pessa da India—sem mil reis; huma libra de cobre—mil reis; hum quintal de ferro—catorze mil reis; huma vara de pano de sentio ordinario—seiscentos reis; pano de linho fino—ao respeito, etc." The rest of the items listed had no determined price ("Os outros ao respeito"). *Ibid.*, pp. 29 f.

to be assigned twenty families of Indians from the *aldeias*, for the immediate needs of the company representatives.   These Indians were to be provided with a priest.

11) The governors and other officials were not to interfere in any way with the affairs of the company but were, on the contrary, to give it every assistance.

12) Any debts owed to the company at the end of the twenty years were to be taken over by the Royal Exchequer.

13) The contract earlier given to José Hordovicos to send 600 Negroes to Maranhão, to be paid for in three years, was to be carried out by means of the ships of the company, which would bring the goods given in payment for the slaves to Portugal where it would dispose of them for the Crown.

14) Civil and criminal suits involving the company were to be heard by a special court in Portugal.

15) Complaints against the company were to be heard by the Overseas Council.[29]

The creation of the company coincided with the arrival of the new governor, Francisco de Sé de Meneses, who took office on May 27, 1682.[30]   His was the double burden of implementing the new Indian legislation and of setting up the new monopoly.   It was not an easy thing to do.   The privileges of the new company respecting *entradas* and Indian workers were particularly galling to the people of the southern captaincy of Maranhão, where Indians were more scarce.   Complaints were numerous, but the people feared to do more than complain, since the governor threatened to send the malcontents to Portugal, where they would have to clear themselves in the royal courts.[31]   Things went from bad to worse in Maranhão.   The promised Negro slaves did not arrive; the goods brought in by the company were of inferior quality and extremely high price, whereas the products of the country received very low prices from the company officials.   If people wanted to order some goods from Lisbon, these were brought in by the company, which charged an exorbitant tax for this service.   The Jesuits were able to secure an exemption from this tax for goods brought in or taken out, if they were for

---

[29] AHU, Cód. 1275: Ordens regias registadas na camara do Pará, fls. 22-30.
[30] See "Memoria dos governadores."
[31] Azevedo, *Os Jesuítas no Grão Pará*, pp. 141 f.

the good of the missions.[32] This naturally caused more resentment among the people. Besides, there were simply not enough Indians in Maranhão to satisfy everybody. Before this time, of the two cities, Belém had been the more boisterous and obstreperous in its complaints and revolts, but this was no longer true. The governor now resided in Belém, supported by his soldiers, and this in itself had a dampening effect on the ardor of the people of Belém. On the other hand, São Luiz was now the capital of the subaltern captaincy, removed from direct control of the governor, and with a weak *capitão-mor*. The bishop was strongly antagonistic to the new order of things, as were the secular priests and the friars of the various Orders. Pamphlets and broadsheets began to appear. Remarks from the pulpits influenced much. As Azevedo says, the "pulpits were the newspapers of the epoch, preparing souls for revolution."[33] When a preacher proclaimed from the pulpit that the solution of all their troubles was in their own hands, and the *capitão-mor* did nothing about the situation, conspirators, led by Manuel Bequimão, or Beckman, a wealthy landowner, met near the Franciscan convent in February, 1684, to plan the revolt.[34] Besides Manoel Beckman,[35] the leaders of

---

[32] The appeal by the Jesuit procurator was considered in the council on March 18, 1682, even before the arrival of the governor in Belém. See AHU, Maranhão, Papeis Avulsos, doc. 18 de março de 1682. The *provisão* granting their request was passed on June 1. See ANTT, Chancelaria de Afonso VI, Liv. 52, fls. 80 f. The Franciscans in 1684 obtained permission to send out tax-free annually 100 arrobas of cacao and cinnamon, the returns of which would be their *ordinária*. See AHU, Maranhão, Papeis Avulsos, doc. 10 de fevereiro de 1684.

[33] Azevedo, *Os Jesuítas no Grão Pará*, p. 143.

[34] *Ibid.*, p. 144. For sympathetic accounts of the revolt, see Varnhagen, *História geral*, III, 306-312, and João Francisco Lisboa, *Jornal de Timon: Aponiamentos, noticias e observações para servirem á historia do Maranhão* (3 vols.; São Luiz, 1865), III, 181-275. This work will hereafter be cited as *Jornal de Timon*. Leite's account in *História da Companhia*, IV, 72-85, is based on a contemporary Jesuit account, written in Vieira's style, entitled: "Informação a Sua Majestade sôbre o sucedido no Maranhão em Fevereiro de 1684." This document shows the part played by the other religious orders in the revolt. There is no Franciscan friar mentioned by name in this connection, but the initial meeting was held "in" (according to Leite's source) or "near" (according to other authors) the Franciscan convent just outside of São Luiz. See Frei Francisco de N.S. dos Prazeres Maranhão, "Poranduba Maranhense, ou Relação histórica da provincia do Maranhão," *RIGHB*, LIV (1891), 85-91. Perhaps the largest group of contemporary letters is in BA, Códices 51-IX-32 and 51-IX-31, which give most of the official correspondence of the period 1684-1685. Another MS account of the uprising is in BNL, Fundo Geral, Cód. 851, fls. 219 ff.

[35] Manoel Beckman had been in trouble for seditious activities earlier. On Jan-

the revolt were the latter's brother, Tomás Beckman, and Jorge de Sampaio e Melo, who had earlier been procurator of Maranhão in Lisbon. The revolt began on February 25, 1684,[36] with the seizure and the imprisonment of the *capitão-mor*, Baltazar Fernandes.[37] The conspirators placed guards around the Jesuit college and abolished the monopoly. A few days later the twenty-seven Jesuit fathers in the college were sent on two ships to Pernambuco. The revolt was formalized by the singing of the *Te Deum* in the principal church of São Luiz. Letters were sent to the *Câmara* of Belém and to Bishop Anjos, who was making an ecclesiastical visitation at the time in Pará.[38] A meeting of the more important men was called, which approved all that had been done. The governor and bishop, however, were not under the control of the revolutionists, and this was fatal to their cause. Mainly because of the suggestion of these two officials the Town Council of Belém refused to co-operate.[39] Manoel Beckman sent his brother Tomás fo Lisbon to explain the happenings, but Tomás arrived too late. Word of the revolt had already been received there, and Tomás was imprisoned until the fleet bearing the new governor, Gomes Freire de Andrade, left for Maranhão early in 1685.[40] Andrade had orders to use a firm hand in putting down the revolt, but this was not necessary. The people of São Luiz received him with respect when he arrived in March, 1685. As a matter of fact, the spirit of revolt was practically dead. The lack of co-operation between the two captaincies and of quick results from the change ot government effected by Beckman had caused spirits to calm long before the arrival of the new governor.

---

uary 24, 1680, a royal letter was sent to Governor Inácio Coelho da Silva in which Beckman was accused of stirring up the people. He was ordered to prison in 1680, but must have been released shortly thereafter. See AHU, Registo de Cartas Regias . . . para Maranhão e Pará, Num. 268, p. 24v.

[36] Textbooks usually give the date as February 24. The contemporary document quoted by Leite, however, states that the revolt began on February 25, the feast of St. Mathias. 1684 was a leap year. See Leite, *História da Companhia*, IV, 73.

[37] See "Memoria dos Governadores."

[38] Leite, *História da Companhia*, IV, 73.

[39] Calmon, *História do Brasil*, II, 394.

[40] Andrade received his commission on January 25, 1685. See ANTT, Chancelaria de Pedro II, Liv. 17, fl. 59.

Gomes Freire de Andrade immediately checked the discipline and reliability of the troops and with great energy restored the deposed authorities and declared the monopoly re-established. Manuel Beckman meanwhile had fled to the interior. One of his followers, Lázaro de Melo, betrayed the hiding place of his friend to Andrade. Beckman and Sampaio were captured, and, after a trial, were hanged on November 2, 1684. Five others received lesser sentences.[41]

The revolt of São Luiz in 1684 had been a protest against the inequities of the monopoly and against the Indian policy adopted in 1680. It is difficult to say which of the two causes had been predominant in the minds of the people. But it is doubtful that the revolt would have taken place without the active support of the rest of the clergy in the captaincy. The reason for this support was the exclusive policy of the Jesuits in regard to the missions. The Jesuits learned from this that the ideas of Vieira concerning monopoly of the missions were simply unworkable. After 1686 the Jesuits as we shall see, abandoned in part their monopolistic ideas. It would be one more step towards a workable mission system.[42]

The Jesuits were formally returned to Maranhão on September 23, 1685, with the same privileges as before, although their power was destined not to endure long before the next revision of the laws in 1686. All the clerical members of the conspiracy were pardoned. But the monopolistic company was abolished in 1685. This was the only victory gained by the revolutionists.[43]

An unforeseen result of the revolt was the cancelling of a new law of September 2, 1684, passed before news of the revolt had reached Lisbon. It was highly favorable to the settlers, since it allowed once more the controversial lay captains for the Indian *aldeias*. The law had been passed in answer to the representations of the procurators sent by the *Câmaras* of São Luiz and Belém, and would have been, if carried into practice, a sad testimony to the fickleness of the home government. The main provisions of the law were as follows. It allowed private administrators of *aldeias* of free Indians. A site near a *fazenda* would be selected for a prospective village. Then the settler, having gained the

<hr/>

[41] Leite, *História da Companhia*, IV, 84; Azevedo, *Os Jesuítas no Grão Pará*, p. 145.
[42] Leite, *História da Companhia*, IV, 87.
[43] *Ibid.*, pp. 84 f.; Azevedo, *Os Jesuítas no Grão Pará*, pp. 145 f.

previous permission of the governor, would approach the prelates of the Jesuits and the Franciscans to obtain a religious capable of influencing pagan Indians to come to live in this village. When the Indians came, they were to be ruled spiritually by the religious who brought them in, and temporally by the governor's representative. Many rules were given to safeguard the free working conditions of the Indians.[44] When news of the revolt reached Lisbon, it was decided to restore things as they had been; the law of September 2, 1684, became a dead letter.[45]

For the time being, then, the same laws for the protection of the Indians were kept in force, but the need for further changes soon became apparent. As early as September 2, 1684, the king had written to the Jesuit provincial concerning the lack of Jesuits in Pará, which had not been touched by the recent revolt. The king made the point that there were not enough Jesuits or Franciscans in Pará, and that the men of these two Orders were the best missionaries in the state. Especially, he continued, was there a lack of Jesuits in Pará, since they had only eight priests and twelve lay brothers there, whereas they should have many more priests and less lay brothers, according to the terms of the income the king had settled upon them recently. The king called the provincial's attention to this obligation and demanded he satisfy it with missionary priests who were Portuguese, and not with foreigners, since these latter were not as convenient as the Portuguese for good political and spiritual government.[46] On the same day, the king forbade the governor to sign the notarized document concerning the *ordinária* of the Jesuits unless they had the required number of priest missionaries in the colony.[47]

Another problem was created by Bishop Dom Gregório in his effort to gain private control over more and more Indians. According to the law of 1680 he had the power to distribute the Indians destined for the service of the settlers, when acting with

[44] For the text, see AHU, Cód. 1275: Ordens regias registadas na camara do Pará, fls. 34-39, or ADE, Ordens MSS annexos a Regimento e leys sobre as missões do Maranhão, pp. 105 ff.
[45] *Jornal de Timon*, II, 308 f.
[46] *Livro Grosso*, I, 64.
[47] ADE, Regimento e leys sobre as missões do Maranhão, pp. 53 f. Printed in *Livro Grosso*, I, 66 f. On the *ordinária* given by the king to the Jesuits, see above, p. 144.

the prelate of St. Anthony and one man elected by the *câmara*. But he preferred to act alone. This led the king to reprimand him on September 9, 1684.[48]

The Jesuits themselves decided that the Indian laws ought to be changed. Leite speaks of the dilemma the Jesuits posed for themselves after the revolt of 1684. Should they forsake the mission of Maranhão and Pará entirely, or should they adapt themselves to the environment, and give up their primitive rigidity concerning the participation of other religious in the work and the strictness of their protection over the Indians? They considered the first course more in accord with the *letter* of the rules of their Institute; the second more in accord with the *spirit* of the Jesuit rules: a spirit of adaptation and charity, even at the cost of their own prestige.[49] They decided to keep on with their endeavors in Maranhão-Pará, but they would no longer try to keep the other Orders from obtaining a share of the official missionary work. They would also be more generous in meeting the demands of the colonists for Indian laborers to be taken from the missions under their control.

The perennial Indian problem now entered another "período de debates, consultas, memoriais e propostas."[50] The people of Maranhão and Pará made themselves heard through their procurators in Lisbon, who became particularly active in 1685 and 1686. Naturally, because of the recent revolt, Maranhão did not press too many complaints at this time; but Pará, feeling itself in a peculiarly advantageous position because it had taken no part in the recent trouble, multiplied complaints and requests. The council considered them on January 17,[51] October 2[52] and November 17, 1685.[53] The burden of the complaints concerned the oppressiveness of the Jesuit control over the Indians. The people of Belém asked that the missionaries have only spiritual control over the Indians. The commendatory letter the king wrote to the *Câmara* of Belém on February 28, 1685,[54] gave the people of Pará even

---

[48] *Livro Grosso*, I, 69 f.   A MS copy of this letter is found in AHU, Registo de Cartas Regias . . . para Maranhão e Pará, Num. 268, p. 39.

[49] Leite, *História da Companhia*, IV, 87.

[50] *Ibid.*, p. 89.

[51] AHU, Pará, Papeis Avulsos, doc. 17 de janeiro de 1685.

[52] *Ibid.*, doc. 2 de outubro de 1685.

[53] *Ibid.*, doc. 17 de novembro de 1685.

[54] AHU, Cód. 1275: Ordens regias registadas na camara do Pará, fl. 40.

greater confidence that their petitions would be heard. The procurators even wrote long treatises on the history of the state, treatises slanted to agree with their views on economic progress. João de Sousa Ferreira wrote his *Noticiario Maranhense* at this time,[55] and Manuel Guedes Aranha, his *Noticias do Maranhão*.[56] Discussions continued in 1686, with the Overseas Council, as usual, endeavoring to hear all sides of the controversy. Some of the more specific complaints were settled immediately. Thus the king, on February 20, 1686, ordered a *devassa* to be taken in the case of the Indians taken by former Governor Francisco de Sá de Meneses from their rightful work.[57] Two letters were sent to Governor Gomes Freire de Andrade on February 25 concerning complaints about the distribution of Indians by the Bishop, the Franciscan prelate and the man elected by the *câmara*. The governor was ordered to see to it that the distribution was done in a just manner.[58]

The more general complaints were referred to a special junta which met in early December of 1686 for the purpose of recommending new Indian legislation on the basis of Governor Andrade's reports. As early as October of 1686, the Overseas Council had laid the groundwork for this junta by inviting a Jesuit to answer the charges made by the *Câmara* of Belém against the Jesuit control of the Indians. His answer consisted of an apology for their work and a plea for more monetary assistance from the king.[59]

---

[55] João de Sousa Ferreira, "Noticiario Maranhense, em que tempo se descubrio o Maranhão; por quem; que governadores o tem governado; como está, como se pode augmentar a sua capacidade," BGUC, Cód. 448, pp. 317-506, published in *RIHGB*, LXXXI (1917), 289-352.

[56] Manuel Guedes Aranha, "Noticias do Maranhão, seu descobrimento, situação e costumes de seus naturais e governadores que nêle havia, enviado pelo Câmara do Estado, por seu Procurador Manuel Guedes Aranha. S. Luiz do Maranhão, 8 de agosto de 1685," BA, 51-VI-46, Num. 5, 54 pages. The identical work, with the title "Papel politico sobre o estado do Maranhão apresentado em nome da Camara ao Sr. Rei D. Pedro II por seu procurador Manuel Guedes Aranha, 1685," is found in BNL, Fundo Geral, Cód. 1570, fls. 221-297. It has been printed with the latter title in *RIHGB*, XLVI (1883), Parte I, 1-60. The last ten pages of this essay are devoted to the recent happenings in Maranhão.

[57] *Livro Grosso*, I, 71.

[58] AHU, Registo de Cartas Regias . . . para Maranhão e Pará, Num. 268, p. 47. On March 2 two letters were sent to the governor, ordering reprisals for Indian attacks on a party seeking drugs in the interior. See *Livro Grosso*, I, 72 f.

[59] AHU, Maranhão, Papeis Avulsos, doc. 13 de outubro de 1686. See also Leite, *História da Companhia*, IV, 89.

On December 2 the special junta of seven men[60] formed to recommend the new law considered the special report sent in by Governor Andrade. The governor's opinion was that *resgates* were absolutely necessary for the welfare of the state of Maranhão and Pará, and that they would not be unjust if carried on in a humane way. Continuing his opinion, he made the surprising statement that, to his way of thinking, Indian slaves were much more important to the colony than Negro slaves. He insisted that one Indian was worth two Negroes!

> Native slaves are much different in worth from those who come from Guiné and Angola, and in this respect a settler esteems more the service of one Indian than that of two Negroes; for the former as *filhos do mato* are conversant with it, and since they have been brought up along the rivers and rapids, they know how to row canoes and make them; they are industrious in hunting and fishing, providing food thereby for themselves and their masters; they have skill and ability to apprehend all the work they have to do for the whites, which one does not find in the Tapanhunos, or black Negroes, because as soon as these leave off being *boçais* [i.e., as soon as they learn Portuguese], they waste much time and they never do anything more but domestic service.[61]

The governor's conclusion was that the enslavement of Indians on the *resgate* expeditions should be permitted, under the watchful eyes of the missionaries. With this the junta agreed.[62]

The recommendations of the junta were incorporated in the *Regimento das Missões do Estado do Maranhão e Grão Pará*, issued

[60] Roque Monteiro Paim, president, Conde de Cadaval, Lopes de Oliveira, Bento Teixeira, Saldanha, João Vasco . . . , Conde de Sampayo. AHU. Maranhão, Papeis Avulsos, doc. 2 de dezembro de 1686.

[61] "Os escravos naturais fazem hua incomparavel differença no prestimo aos que vem de Guiné e Angola, e a esse respeito estima hum morador mais o serviço de hum Indio que o de dous negros; porque estes como filhos do mato são practicos nelle, e como criados nos rios e guarapes se sabem remar as canoas e fazelas, são dustrissimos na cassa e pescaria sustentando-sse della e seus senhores; tem genio e habilidade para aprenderem com presteza tudo o que vem obrar aos brancos, o que senão acha nos Tapanhunos, ou negros tintos, porque primeiramente que deixem de ser buçais gastão largo tempo e nunca os occupão mais que para o serviço domestico." AHU, Maranhão, Papeis Avulsos, doc. 2 de dezembro de 1686.

[62] *Ibid.* The same *consulta*, entitled "Consulta da Junta feita por ordem de S. Majestade relativa aos negócios da Missão dos Padres da Companhia de Jesus, no Estado do Maranhão, e sôbre uma informação de Gomes Freire a tal respeito. Lisboa, 2 de dezembro de 1686," is in BA, 51-VI-25.

on December 21, 1686.   In its preamble the king made clear why
new legislation was necessary.   He and his father, he declared,
had taken all care to give a convenient form to the *redução do
gentio* of the state of Maranhão and Pará into the bosom of the
Church, and to the distribution and service of the Indians after
they were brought to live in villages.   They had tried to satisfy
the good of all concerned.   In 1680, the king continued, he had
promulgated the latest law, aimed at the remedy of all the damages
that had been done.   But experience had shown that this law was
not sufficient to secure this good purpose, because malice had discovered new ways of avoiding its observance.   Not only that,
insisted the king, but the temerity and ambition of the inhabitants
of Maranhão rose to such a degree that they unjustly drove the
fathers of the Society of Jesus from the state; for this they were
punished, and the Jesuit fathers were restored to their former
place.   Now, however, the king had been informed by Governor
Gomes Freire de Andrade concerning all that pertained to the
Indian question, and the king, trusting fully in the zeal and truth-
fulness of Andrade, saw fit to have the information of Andrade
considered by ministers of knowledge and virtue, from which deliberations the new *regimento* proceeded.   The principal provisions
of the *regimento* may be summarized as follows:[63]

1) The fathers of the Society of Jesus were to have the spiritual,
political and temporal jurisdiction of the *aldeias* actually administered by them.   The Franciscan fathers of the Province of St.
Anthony were to enjoy the same authority in their own *aldeias*.[64]
The Indians were to serve those colonists who had a right to their
labor, and were to be ready to defend the state when necessary,
in a just war.

2) There were to be two *procuradores dos índios*, one in São Luiz
and one in Belém.   The former was to be given as many as four
Indians for his own service; the latter, as many as six.   These
Indians were to be assigned to them by the missionaries.   The

---

[63] For the text, see *Collecção chronológica (1683-1700)*, pp. 468 ff.   Leite, *História
da Companhia*, IV, apêndice D, pp. 369-375 also gives the full text.   He took the
text from the printed copy of the "Regimento e leys sobre as missões do Maranhão," issued by Pombal in 1755, and found in the ADE, Cód. CXV-12, 1-15,
impressa.

[64] For the time being, the Carmelites and Mercedarians still remained excluded
from the post of missionary.

original assignment was not to be permanent; the Indians might be changed from time to time at the discretion of the missionaries.

3) The *procuradores* were to be chosen by the governor from among the candidates proposed by the superior of the Jesuit missions. The procurators were to be governed by a *regimento* issued by the Jesuit superior after consultation with the missionaries of the *aldeias*. The *regimento*, together with his opinion of it, would be submitted by the governor to the king for his confirmation. The *regimento*, however, would be observed by the procurators even while they were awaiting the king's pleasure.

4) Besides the missionaries, only the Indians with their families were to reside in the Indian villages. Under no circumstances were whites or half-breeds to be permitted to live there. Lower-class people guilty of transgressing the law in this regard were to be whipped publicly; nobles were to be exiled for five years to Angola. These penalties would not be subject to appeal.

5) Absolutely no person would be allowed to go to the Indian villages to get Indians for his service, or for any other purpose, without the permission of the lawful authorities.[65]

6) No person whatsoever would be permitted to keep Indians beyond their allotted terms of service. First offenders were to be sentenced to two months in jail and a fine of 20$000 for the expenses of the missions. The sentence was to be doubled for second offenders. For a third offence, the guilty were to be exiled to Angola. Again no appeals were to be allowed.

7) Indians from the *aldeias* were not to be encouraged to marry privately owned slaves, and thus increase the slave population. If such a marriage was forced, the party to it that was in slavery would be declared free. In any case, even in voluntary cases, the *aldeia* Indian was not to leave the village.

8) A white settler inducing an Indian woman to divorce her Indian husband, so that he might live in adultery with her, was to be exiled for ten years to Angola. The Indian woman was to be kept in the *aldeias*, and the local *Junta das Missões* would decide what punishment she should be given.

9) The missionaries in charge of the *aldeias* were urged to increase the number of Indians in the *aldeias*, for upon that increase

---

[65] The "lawful authorities" were the governor or *capitão-mor*, with the advice of the Jesuit superior of the missions. See below, p. 161.

depended the security of the state, the defence of the cities, the service of the settlers and the expeditions to the interior.

10) The missionaries were admonished to establish *aldeias* in places convenient for trade and commerce with the inhabitants of the cities and towns of Maranhão and Pará.

11) Since the commerce in the state consisted in the goods and services of the Indians, the prices and wages were to be fixed. The prices of goods sold by or to the Indians were to be determined by the *câmara* with the advice of the governor, the *ouvidor geral* and the *provedor da fazenda*; the wages of the Indians were to be determined by the governor with the advice of the prelates of the Jesuits and the Franciscans, but only after hearing the opinion of the *câmaras*.

12) The wages of the Indian workers were to be paid in two installments, half when they left for service and half at the end of their period of service. The method of payment would be established by the governor, with the counsel and assistance of the missionary prelates, to avoid the possibility of tricking the Indians or of not paying them.

13) In order to avoid the complaints of the white inhabitants concerning the distribution of Indians, and in order that the governors[66] might know the number and quality of the Indians available for service, on occasions when they might be necessary for the welfare of the state, the names of all Indians between the ages of thirteen and fifty were to be entered once every two years in two registers signed and numbered by the governor. One of the registers would be kept by the Jesuit superior of the missions; the other by the clerk of the Royal Exchequer (*escrivão da fazenda*).

14) In order to allow ample time for expeditions into the interior, the term of service for the Indians would thenceforth be six months at a time for Pará and four months for Maranhão. The term as set for Maranhão could be changed by the governor with the advice of the mission superior. The division of the Indian workers should be in two equal parts when the working term was for six months, and in three equal parts when the term was for four months.

15) The Jesuits were not to receive any Indians in the general distribution, but their colleges of São Luiz and Belém would each

---

[66] The text followed by Leite has "os governadores"; the *Collecção chronológica* text has "Os Padres," i.e., the missionaries, an obvious misreading.

be given an *aldeia* of Indians for support. The Indians of these villages were to work exclusively for the Jesuits and their missions.

16) Every Jesuit residence located at a distance of thirty or more leagues from São Luiz or Belém would be assigned twenty-five Indians by the governor for use in mission work. It was realized that without Indian help it would be impossible for the Jesuits to take care of their outlying missions. The Jesuits were to supply Indians for their other residences from the *aldeias* which they had. The only exception was the *aldeia* and district of Mortigura in Pará. Since this district was so large, they were to be given Indians for its work.[67]

17) The distribution of the Indians of service was to be made by the governor, or in his absence, by the *capitão-mor*, together with two men elected by the town council, always with the advice and consent of the Jesuit superior of the missions, and of the pastors of the *aldeias* concerned. But neither the governor, nor the captain, nor the men elected by the *câmara* were to enter any Indian village for this purpose.

18) No layman would be allowed to enter an Indian village without the express permission of the governor or *capitão-mor*, who, however, were not to grant it until they had consulted with the Jesuit superior of the missions. Each certificate of permission was to be signed by the governor or *capitão-mor*, as the case might be, and by the superior, and it had to be presented to the pastor of the *aldeia* before the bearer was allowed to approach the Indians.

19) Since there was a lack of Indians in the *aldeias de repartição*,[68] any settler planning an expedition to the interior was required to find out ahead of time how many Indians were available. Only half of the Indians needed were to be taken from the *aldeias* of service Indians; the rest of the Indians needed were to be taken from the other *aldeias*, for the usual salary. The missionaries

---

[67] The *aldeia* of Mortigura was one of those originally cared for by the very early Franciscan missionaries. It was one of the nine original *aldeias* in the vicinity of Belém. But everything fell to ruin after 1636, and in 1653, when the *aldeia* was given to the Jesuits for their support by *Capitão-mor* Inácio do Rego Barreto, everything had to be rebuilt. See Leite, *História da Companhia*, III, 279; 299 f.

[68] I.e., *aldeias* whose Indians were distributed for work outside, either for the government or for private persons. By far the majority of Indian *aldeias* were of this variety. There were also *aldeias* given to religious orders in lieu of royal grants of money, and *aldeias* deep in the interior, far away from any white settlement. See Leite, *História da Companhia*, IV, 97 f.

were to make sure that the Indians did not excuse themselves from such expeditions, except for valid reasons.

20) No Indian male under thirteen years of age could be assigned to work for the colonists. Indian females were generally to be exempt from labor, except at the time of harvest and as wet nurses. The rectors of colleges and prelates of the missions were to assign the necessary women for these tasks for specified periods of time and for a predetermined salary. These prelates were authorized to grant extensions of time, but only for just cause. They were to avoid placing women in situations which might endanger their virtue.

21) Each Indian village was to have at least 150 inhabitants. Whenever Indians from different tribes were not able to live together amicably, they were to be placed in separate parishes *(freguesias)* within the same district.

22) Indians newly obtained from the interior were not to be assigned for work for at least two years. During this period they were to be taught the Catholic Faith, grow the necessary crops and make their adjustment to the new environment. The agreements made between the missionaries and the Indians prior to their removal from the interior were to be kept inviolably. The governor was to be held accountable in his *residência* for any violation of these agreements. Indians who did not wish to move would not be forced to do so. The missionaries were to be urged to stay with them, to bring about their conversion and to establish villages and parishes in the interior for them. It would not do for the Indians who were willing to become Christians to be removed from their ancestral homes against their will.

23) The governors were to give assistance to the missionaries who made *entradas* into the interior.

This was, in fine, the *regimento* of 1686, and it was to be followed essentially for almost seventy years. It was a carefully thought-out piece of legislation, which endeavored to, but inevitably did not, take care of every eventuality.

One of the earliest clarifications had to do with the meaning of "twenty-five Indians," as mentioned in paragraph 16. The Court was called upon, on March 23, 1688, to declare that "twenty-five Indians" really meant "twenty-five Indian families."[69] A more

---

[69] AHU, Registo de Cartas Regias . . . para Maranhão e Pará, Num. 268, p. 59v. It is printed in *Livro Grosso*, I, 92. See also Leite, *História da Companhia*, IV, 91.

important difficulty that was not solved until 1693, was the province and authority of the Franciscans, and later, of the Carmelites and Mercedarians, in mission work. The law of 1686 gave some rights to the Franciscans, but said nothing about the other two religious orders active in the state.

Despite its deficiencies, the law of 1686 was a masterpiece of legislation, designed to protect the Indian and to place him under the almost complete control of the missionaries, especially of the Jesuits. Most of the weak points of earlier laws had been strengthened. Lay captaincies, the bane of Frei Cristovão and the Franciscans, were effectively abolished. The governor, who formerly interfered in Indian affairs extensively, now had to consult with the mission superiors at every step. *Entradas* and *resgates* of an unofficial private variety were no longer allowed. Safeguards were set up against the exploitation of the Indian workers, including women and children. The Indians were given two special advocates, the two *procuradores dos índios*, whose selection was largely in the hands of the Jesuit mission superior.

Royal laws and provisions on the Indians did not, of course, cease to be promulgated after 1686. Leite mentions a series of legal diplomas sent out by the king during the years 1686 to 1693, which, taken together, formed the essential Indian policy until 1755.[70] The first of the important changes in the basic law was the result of penetration by the French into the northern part of Pará. In early 1687, Governor Artur de Sá e Meneses[71] was erecting a fort in the Cabo do Norte region when he surprised some Frenchmen who had with them ten Indian slaves, captured in Portuguese territory. He took them from the French and distributed them among the Portuguese soldiers. The Overseas Council, on September 15, 1687, commended him for his good work.[72] In the same year, two Jesuit missionaries, Fr. António Pereira and Fr. Bernardo Gomes, were killed by their charges, because, it was said, of the influence of the French interlopers. The council, on February 9, 1688, approved the actions of the

---

[70] *Ibid.*, p. 90.

[71] Governor Meneses was nominated on December 19, 1686. See ANTT, Chancelaria de Pedro II, Liv. 33, fl. 134. He took possession of his post on June 14, 1687 and ruled until May 17, 1690. See "Memoria dos governadores."

[72] AHU, Pará, Papeis Avulsos, doc. 15 de setembro de 1687.

governor, who sent out a punitive expedition to the area.[73]   This success of the French naturally concerned the home government. The king now decided, by an *alvará* of April 28, 1688, to revoke that part of the law of April 1, 1680, which forbade the enslavement of Indians, and to restore some of the provisions of the law of April 9, 1655, which allowed enslavement of Indians in certain well-defined cases.   In the introduction to the new *alvará*, the king, Pedro II, mentioned that the law of 1680, which forbade all manner of enslavement, was defeating its own purpose, since he had heard that in Maranhão and Pará a still greater danger was threatening the Indians' souls than that offered by the *resgates* formerly practiced in the state, for the Indians there wage war among themselves and capture slaves and "bring them to sell in strange lands."[74] To offset this danger, the king set up the following rules concerning *resgates* and *cativeiros* of the Indians:

Concerning *resgates dos índios* the king now ordained that they be officially taken care of by the royal treasury.   Those Indians who were taken captive in wars with other Indians or who were *presos a corda* or who were captives to be sold might be ransomed by the Portuguese when there was danger to the lives of the said Indians.   A self-sustaining method of financing these ransoming expeditions was next set up: The king would at the outset furnish 3,000 *cruzados* which would be used to buy trade goods most useful in ransoming Indians.   2,000 *cruzados* would be used for *resgates* in Pará and 1,000 for Maranhão.   These goods would be transported to the state and deposited in São Luiz and Belém in the hands of bonded agents approved by the Jesuit prelates of the missions.   Some Indians would be given to these agents as payment for their work.   The custodians of the articles were to give them out at the order of the said Jesuit prelates, who should be obliged to make these *resgate* journeys each year, with a military leader and soldiers appointed by the governor.   The Indians ransomed on such expeditions would be distributed by the *câmaras*

---

[73] AHU, Pará, Papeis Avulsos, doc. 9 de fevereiro de 1688.   See also ANTT Cartório dos Jesuítas, maço 88, for the "Treslado do exame que se fes por ordem de justiça na cidade do Grão Pará a hum Indio da nação Maraunú sobre as mortes dos PP. António Pereira e Bernardo Gomes em 1687."   The king pardoned the Maraunú Indians in 1691.   See the decree of February 17, 1691, in AHU, Registo de Cartas Regias . . . para Maranhão e Pará, Num. 268, p. 72.

[74] ". . . os levão a vender a terras estrangeiras. . . ."   For the text of this law, see *Livro Grosso*, I, 97-101.

to those settlers who had the most need of them for the work on their plantations and fields. Those citizens who received the ransomed Indians must deposit with the custodian an amount of trade goods equal to the amount expended for the ransomed Indian or Indians, so that in this way the amount of trade goods would always remain the same. Those who received the Indians would also pay a tax of three milreis a head to the *depositario*, which money would be used for the good of the missions: for *entradas*, and other necessary things. The custodians of this money and these goods were to give a complete account of all these expenditures to the governor, who was commanded to send copies each year to the Overseas Council. The king further commanded that the *ouvidor geral* take great care to see that the governor and the missionaries fulfill their obligations concerning the *resgates*.

The king laid down the following regulations concerning *cativeiros dos índios*. Enslavement could take place on the occasion of wars with the Indians in the following cases: firstly, in a defensive war, which was to be understood as one in which Indians under the leadership of a chief actually invaded the villages and lands of the state and principally when the pagan enemy Indians impeded with armed force the missionaries on *entradas* into the interior, thus stopping the preaching of the Holy Gospel. Secondly, enslavement would be allowed in an offensive war, when there was a certain and infallible fear that the enemies of the Faith were gathering together to attack Portuguese lands, and when it was impossible to impede in any other way this action of the enemy Indians. All other means were to be exhausted first, especially peaceful persuasion. A just war would also be occasioned if the enemy Indians had carried out grave and notorious hostile actions, and had not rendered condign satisfaction for them, but in this latter case, the king allowed imprisonment only during the time the war lasted. In all cases, the governor was commanded to justify the offensive war by juridical documents of the missionaries assisting in the territory invaded; this verification was to be completed before the war began. The king declared further that the first proof of the legality of the operation would be the opinions in writing of the prelates of the Jesuit and Franciscan missionaries of the captaincy in which the war was to be carried on. Without their opinions the war was not to be carried on at all. The governor was ordered to inform the home government each year of all these wars, with all the necessary documents, sending one group of documents to the Overseas Council and the other to the Council of State, so that the king could examine all the circumstances of these wars and determine their justice or injustice. If all this were not done, all the Indians taken would be set free, and the governor and *ouvidor geral* would be considered guilty of a grave misdemeanor, which would be taken up in their respective *residências* at the end of their terms of office. The king put all these rules into effect at once.[75]

Reaction to the new *alvará* was not long in coming. The *alvará* did not entirely please the Jesuits. Father João Betendorff, the outstanding and most influential Jesuit missionary in the state of Maranhão and Pará, who had considerable influence at Court[76] and who was still in Lisbon, was most unhappy over the clause concerning the *resgates* expeditions, with which the Jesuits were now necessarily connected. This was bound to irritate the settlers, and the Jesuits wanted to avoid as much of their ill will as possible. The Jesuits tried to renounce their new responsibility by claiming that the part demanded of them in the *resgates* was against the rules of their Institute.[77] They did not make clear in what way the Jesuit Institute had changed since 1653-1661, when Vieira had advocated the very thing they were now rejecting. The fact remains, however, that most of the Jesuit missionaries refused to accompany *resgate* expeditions during the following years, thereby creating endless trouble in Maranhão and Pará.[78]

It had been the French interloping activity that had occasioned the passing of the law of 1688. This same activity had occasioned other effects even earlier. One of these was the division of the territory of Cabo do Norte between the Jesuits and the Franciscans. On December 21, 1686, the king sent a letter to Governor Gomes Freire de Andrade authorizing him to divide the territory of Cabo do Norte between the Franciscans of St. Anthony and the Jesuits.[79] After telling the governor to build forts and other de-

---

[75] The royal decree promulgating the new regulations was dated April 30, 1688. See ANTT, Livraria, Cód. 33: Decretos de 1663-1702, p. 129.

[76] Leite, *História da Companhia*, IV, 93.

[77] *Ibid.*

[78] *Ibid.*

[79] For the text, see Berredo, *Annaes históricos*, II, No. 1356. The king admitted in this letter that the area was a Franciscan area ("e vos valereis ao mesmo tempo

fences against the encroaching French, the king added that the governor should make use at the same time of the Franciscans of St. Anthony and the Jesuits, to hold the loyalty of the Indians of that region. In order to avoid squabbles over jurisdiction between the rival Orders, the king instructed Governor Andrade to draw a clear line of demarcation between their respective territories.[80] The governor followed the royal order and separated the area of the missions of the Franciscans in Cabo do Norte, which the friars had had for some time, from the area of the proposed missions of the Jesuits. The latter began mission work there only in 1687, with the ill-fated mission of Fathers António Pereira and Bernardo Gomes, who were killed that same year by the Indians.[81] Shortly after the death of their two missionaries, the Jesuits abandoned the area entirely, since, as they told their Father General in Rome, there was no fruit to be expected from these Indians of Cabo do Norte, and the mission was a great detriment to the missionaries. They preferred to occupy themselves in other missions where their work would be more fruitful.[82] They worked in the region less than ten years, seven years of which were occupied with exploration and map making, and two years in mission work.[83] The Franciscans also were under no illusions concerning this mission field. Governor Francisco de Sá de Meneses, after listening to their reports, described Cabo do Norte as an *aspera e perigosa missão*, in 1685. And Father João de Santo Atanásio, a veteran Franciscan missionary of Cabo do Norte, told the king on October

dos Missionarios Capuchos de Santo Antonio que tem as missões do Cabo do Norte . . . e aos Padres da Companhia de Jesus tenho ordenado que fação huma nova Missão para o Cabo do Norte. . . ."

[80] *Ibid.* ". . . e para que huns e outros a fação sem competencias de jurisdicções, procurareis dividir as suas residencias e missões, com a distincção que seja util, para não terem duvida no que pertence a huns e outros. . . ." The exact division line is not known today.

[81] See above, p. 163.

[82] The Jesuits said: ". . . como destes Índios [of Cabo do Norte] se não esperava fruto algum, e ser de grande detrimento aos Missionários, os largou totalmente e se ocupou em outras missões aonde fez maior fruto." "Carta Ânua de 1696," quoted in Leite, *História da Companhia*, III, 265. The Jesuits actually gave up these missions before 1690. See letter of the king to Governor Coelho de Carvalho, dated July 5, 1691, where this is mentioned. *Livro Grosso*, I, 126.

[83] The king had recommended this region to the Jesuit attention in the law of 1680. See above, p. 144. Vieira began the explorations immediately, and these continued until 1687, when mission work began. See Leite, *História da Companhia*, III, 254-260.

12, 1685, how the Indians were being corrupted by gifts from the French traders, and were turning against all the Portuguese, even against the Franciscans. He mentioned that the friars had difficulty in obtaining Indian rowers to take them to Belém, and had to pay four of their Indians in advance for this work, so little did the Indians trust the Portuguese.[84] It was as a result of these intelligences that the king had urged the Jesuits to enter the Cabo do Norte mission field actively in 1686, to help keep the allegiance of the Indians. He felt that the Jesuits "were more suited for this purpose" than the Franciscans.[85] At almost the same time, the king ordered Governor Andrade to seize any Frenchmen found in the region, but not to kill them, since France and Portugal were at peace.[86]

Except for the episode of Cabo do Norte, the Jesuits were highly successful after 1686 in their mission work. An item not to be overlooked in their success was the constant and quick protection they received from the home government, the rapid response they received to any complaints they made. Thus, on March 23, 1688, Governor Artur de Sá e Meneses was rebuked for complaining that the Jesuits had too many free Indians under their control.[87] On the same day the governor was informed that if the twenty-five Indian families promised to each Jesuit house could not be found in the neighborhood, the Jesuits had the right to go to the sertão themselves to gather them.[88] Again, on March 23, after the royal treasurer of the colony had inquired which of the Jesuits was to receive the ordinária and whether students would also receive it, the reply was that all of them were to be paid.[89] On the same day, the governor was told to give every possible assistance to the Jesuits, and to observe the Regimento das Missões and the

---

[84] The governor wrote the letter on January 22, 1685. It was considered in the council on October 12 of the same year. See AHU, Pará, Papeis Avulsos, doc. 22 de janeiro de 1685, and AHU, Maranhão, Papeis Avulsos, doc. 12 de outubro de 1685.

[85] ". . . padres da Companhia de Jesus, que forem mais a proposito a este fim. . . ." Berredo, Annaes historicos, II, No. 1356.

[86] Letter of the king to Governor Andrade, February 20, 1686. Livro Grosso, I, 70 f.

[87] AHU, Registo de Cartas Régias para Maranhão e Pará, Num. 268, p. 58.

[88] Ibid., p. 59v. Also printed in Livro Grosso, I, 92.

[89] AHU, Registo de Cartas Régias para Maranhão e Pará, Num. 268, p. 59.

other Indian laws *ad unguem*.[90] When the Jesuit procurator complained of the lack of shipping space, the king, on March 23, commanded the ship captains on the run from Maranhão or Pará to the Azores or to Portugal to take on board whatever the Jesuits wanted to send, on the grounds that this helped support the churches and residences of the Jesuits and benefited the missions.[91] August 20, 1688, the Crown ordered a citizen of Belém, José de Brito, sent in chains to Portugal for trial for having distributed defamatory broadsides against the Jesuits, in which he had suggested their expulsion.[92] With such protection, the Jesuits were able to extend their missions in every direction except Cabo do Norte. They were well supplied with all the things necessary for the missions as a result of their ample salary. On January 4, 1687, the king had ordained that the Jesuit salary be increased from 350$000 to 700$000, because of the Order's importance to the well-being of the state.[93] Besides the royal salary, they enjoyed the income from their *aldeias* of Indians and from various properties they had inherited from benefactors.[94] The king referred to their improved financial position on March 22, 1688, when he suggested they expand their activities to the Rio Madeira and the Rio Negro, both far in the interior.[95]

Pedro II did not always treat the other religious orders so gently. On March 22, 1688, for example, he upbraided the Franciscans for attempting, after the manner allowed to the Jesuits, to take Indian families from the interior for use in their *aldeias*. The *regimento*, the king pointed out, gave the Franciscans the right only to set up *aldeias* of free Indians, not *aldeias* of Indians for their own service.[96] However just, according to the law, this censure may have been, it was evident that full partnership of the

---

[90] *Ibid.*, p. 59v.

[91] *Livro Grosso*, I, 94.

[92] *Ibid.*, p. 105.

[93] AHU, Registo de Cartas Régias . . . para Maranhão e Pará, Num. 268, pp. 54 f. According to Azevedo, *Os Jesuítas no Grão Pará*, p. 245, their salary was increased to 950$000 in 1692.

[94] See the two packets of documents concerning the inherited properties of the Jesuits of Pará and Maranhão in ANTT, Cartório dos Jesuítas, maço 82.

[95] *Livro Grosso*, I, 84 f.

[96] *Ibid.*, p. 85; or AHU, Registo de Cartas Regias . . . pará Maranhão e Pará, Num. 268, p. 60v.

other religious orders with the Jesuits in the mission field was still to be achieved.

It would, of course, be wrong to say that the Jesuits were never scolded by the king. When the king's instruction of March 23, 1688,[97] ordering the licensing of all boats passing Gurupá either up or down river, to put a stop to the contraband trade, was disregarded by the Jesuits, the king was incensed. On October 17, 1690, he sent sharp letters to the new governor, António de Albuquerque Coelho de Carvalho,[98] and to the captain of the fort at Gurupá, Manoel Guedes Aranha,[99] pointing out to them that the Jesuits had to obey the law like anyone else or face judicial proceedings. The Jesuits were also brought to order concerning the teaching of the língua geral to the Portuguese youth, a thing most important in dealing with the Indians. The Jesuits were given an order to do this on April 20, 1688, but they delayed in carrying it out. On November 30, 1689, the Câmara of Belém complained to the king about their dereliction of duty. The king on February 20, 1690, again ordered the Jesuits to comply with the law.[100] These evidences of royal displeasure were, however, exceptional. Actually, the Jesuits were very much favored by the Crown.

The favoritism shown the Jesuits did not discourage the other religious orders. The Franciscans continued to be active as missionaries, especially in the vicinity of São Luiz and Belém, on Marajó Island, and on the north bank of the Amazon, from Cabo do Norte westward.[101] At about this time (1690), the Carmelites

[97] Livro Grosso, I, 87 f.

[98] Ibid., p. 108. Governor Carvalho was nominated on January 26, 1690. See ANTT, Chancelaria de Pedro II, Liv. 20, fls. 212 f. His rule extended from May (?), 1690, to June 11, 1701. See "Memoria dos governadores."

[99] Livro Grosso, I, 109. Aranha was named to the three year term on March 23, 1688. See ANTT, Chancelaria de Pedro II, Liv. 34, fl. 62.

[100] AHU, Pará, Papeis Avulsos, doc. 30 de novembro de 1689. The importance for plantation owners to know the Indian tongue was evident. Later on, the more prevalent charge against the Jesuits was that of not teaching Portuguese to the Indians. See AHU, Registo de Cartas Regias . . . para Maranhão e Pará, Num. 270, p. 28v, doc. 12 de setembro de 1727.

[101] From various sources we can gather some idea of the missions cared for by the Franciscans at this time. There is, for instance, the letter of King Pedro II to Governor Artur de Sá e Meneses, commanding him to construct a fortress at Torrego, on the north side of the Amazon, and, for pacifying more Indians, to use "os padres de Santo Antonio, que assistem para aquella parte, e que com elles [i.e., these Indians] tem adequerido opinião e respeito." See Livro Grosso, I, 71,

also entered the mission field, beginning their work in the Rio
Negro district. They were preferentially placed in charge of missions in the far west, close to those of the Spanish Jesuits.[102] After
1693 they were to have a substantial number of these missions,
set up as buffers to the advance of Fr. Samuel Fritz and the other
European Jesuits working for the Spanish Crown.[103] The Mercedarians in Pará likewise became active as missionaries in the
Amazon territory during the years 1687-1690, in the Rio Urubú
region, north of the Amazon River.[104]

The local *Juntas das Missões*,[105] in São Luiz and Belém, which
came into being as the result of the law of 1680, were quite active
in carrying out their prescribed work. Their business was to determine the practical adaptation to circumstances of the necessarily
general provisions of the royal laws. In 1687 or 1688, for example,
they determined that the Indians should be paid two varas of cloth

---

letter of February 24, 1686. There is a list of outstanding men of the St. Anthony
Province, including some Pará missionaries of this period, in ANTT, Santo Antonio
dos Capuchos, maço 8. On the Franciscan missions on the island of Marajó, see
above, p. 106. Another Franciscan mission was that of Guarapirangá, twelve
leagues up the Amazon River, also on the north side. See *Santuario Mariano*,
IX, 395-398. There was also that of Orobucára, 100 leagues up the Amazon, on
the north side, which mission, however, was taken over by the Jesuits before 1678.
Ibid., pp. 399 f.

[102] André Prat, *Notas históricas sobre as missões Carmelitas no extremo norte do
Brasil, seculo XVII-XVIII* (Recife, 1941), pp. 36-39.

[103] Among the primary sources for the Carmelite missions of this time is a series
of documents presented to the Conselho Ultramarino by Fr. Victoriano Pimentel,
the Carmelite superior, in 1705, concerning his years of activity in the upper Amazon region, where his particular task was to stop the advance of Fr. Samuel Fritz
and the other Spanish Jesuits. He wrote his *Relação* on September 7, 1705. See
the packet of papers in AHU, Maranhão, Papeis Avulsos, under doc. of November
14, 1706. Concerning the activities of Fr. Samuel Fritz, which do not form an
integral part of my study, see the documents in ADE, Cód. CXV-2-15, No. 10.
For a comprehensive general treatment, see Azevedo, *Os Jesuítas no Grão Pará*,
pp. 263-268.

[104] *Livro Grosso*, I, 106, doc. n.d. Other than this letter, I have found no other
documentation on this subject.

[105] Many of the papers of these years of the local *Juntas das Missões* are not in
the Portuguese archives, because they were never sent from São Luiz and Belém.
There are extant many complaints of the king that the said papers of the junta
had not been sent to him, as ordained by the law of April 28, 1688. See *Livro
Grosso*, I, 110; 112; 114, documents of 1690 and 1691. For a similar complaint of
February 3, 1691, see AHU, Registo de Cartas Regias . . . para Maranhão e Pará
Num. 268, p. 76.

per month, while the Indian women should receive three varas, or, if married, four.[106] Most of their time, however, was devoted to problems concerning the legality of defensive and offensive wars against the Indians. Thus we find the report of the respective junta concerning the justness of Indian wars in 1689-1690,[107] 1691,[108] and 1692.[109]

The new era of mission endeavor was also signaled by the death of Dom Gregório dos Anjos, the Bishop of Maranhão, whose pugnacious activity in Indian affairs we have already considered. Fortunately for the peace of the state, his health began to fail, and after a long illness, he died in 1689.[110] Frei Francisco de Lima, a Carmelite, was appointed to succeed him on October 19, 1691, but he never took possession of his see.[111] The see remained vacant until 1697, when Frei Timóteo do Sacramento arrived as the new bishop.[112]

The recent legislation passed for the protection of the Indians was generally applauded by the missionaries and by others who had the welfare of the Indians at heart, but it continued to be a thorn in the flesh of the colonists who believed only in the unrestricted exploitation of the natives. There were, of course, some loopholes in the law, that made it possible for unscrupulous colonists to profit. Such people were in the habit of assigning to their friends, for a price, the Indians that had originally been assigned

---

[106] ADE, Varias Ordens MSS annexos a Regimento e leys sobre as missões, p. 87. It was also determined that the Procurador dos Indios must be present when the Indians receive their payments.

[107] AHU, Maranhão, Papeis Avulsos, doc. 16 de fevereiro de 1693.

[108] *Ibid.*; and doc. 10 de fevereiro de 1693.

[109] *Ibid.*, under doc. 1690. The largest part of the papers of the local *Junta das Missões* of Belém is still in the *Arquivo Público de Belém do Pará*. They are in a very bad state of preservation. As far as I know, they have never been utilized in any comprehensive way by any historian of the missions, other than by Father Serafim Leite. See *História da Companhia*, III, xix.

[110] Governor Meneses wrote to the king on November 28, telling him of the death of Bishop Anjos. For the letter, see AHU, Pará, Papeis Avulsos, doc. 28 de novembro de 1689.

[111] For the decree of October 19, 1691, nominating him for bishop, see ANTT, Livraria, Cód. 33: Decretos de 1663-1702, p. 148v.

[112] See Miguel de Oliveira, *História eclesiástica de Portugal* (2nd ed.; Lisbon, 1948), p. 453. For the *consulta* of the Overseas Council on the new bishop's request for an *aldeia* of Indians, as his predecessor had had, see AHU, Maranhão, Papeis Avulsos, doc. 16 de março de 1697.

to themselves. The king was alarmed at the practice, and on February 16, 1691, he forbade it except in two cases. The labor of Indians assigned to a colonist could be sold or given as a marriage dowry, and it could be given also as security for the payment of debts.[113] On the following day, the king sent a letter to Governor Coelho de Carvalho, commanding him to observe the *regimento* of 1686 and also the law of 1688 concerning *resgates*. He was forbidden to make any exceptions as he had been doing. He was told to disregard the complaints of the colonists. The king urged him and the other officials to be just in the distribution of the Indians. They were to assign a fair share of the Indians to the *villas* of Maranhão and Pará, and not permit them all to go to Belém and São Luiz.[114] This was another example of the chronic shortage of Indians of service. Actually the problem was never solved to the satisfaction of everybody concerned.

A shortage of another kind came to a head in 1692. This was a shortage of Jesuit missionaries in the field. If we can believe two documents of 1692, there were only eight Jesuit priests active as missionaries in Maranhão and Pará in that year, five of them in Pará and three in Maranhão.[115]

In view of this situation, it was clear that more missionaries were needed, and since the Society of Jesus was unable or unwilling to meet the demands, members of other religious orders would have to be brought in. In 1691 and 1692, negotiations were begun to allow Italian Capuchins to enter the Amazon mission field,[116]

---

[113] *Livro Grosso*, I, 117. A MS copy is in AHU, Registo de Cartas Regias . . . para Maranhão e Pará, Num. 268, p. 79v.

[114] Letter of February 17, 1691 in ADE, Regimento e leys sobre as missões do Maranhão, pp. 54 f. The letter is also published in *ABAPP*, I (1902), 102 f.

[115] 1) AHU, Pará, Papeis Avulsos, doc. 12 de julho de 1692, which is a petition of some settlers in Pará for more missionaries for the Amazon Valley. They mention five Jesuits active in the whole valley. 2) The "Informação do Estado do Maranhão, dada por Miguel da Rosa Pimentel. Lisboa, 4 de setembro de 1692," BA, 50-V-34, fls. 198-205. Pimentel, the former *ouvidor geral* of Maranhão, speaks of eight Jesuits active in the whole state in 1692, which would leave three for Maranhão. Pimentel suggested allowing other religious missionaries to take part in the work of the missions. To me it does not seem possible that the Jesuits had been reduced to so small a number. Perhaps by far the larger number of their men were occupied in their two colleges in the cities, and on their *fazendas* or farms. Besides, this number probably did not include the Jesuit lay brothers.

[116] On February 15, 1691, Fr. Paulo de Varazze, who was procurator in Lisbon of the Italian Capuchin missions in Angola and S. Tomé, wrote to the Congrega-

but the Court finally preferred to send Portuguese Franciscans of the Province of Piedade, popularly known as *Piedosos*.[117] Their coming was due to Captain Manuel Guedes Aranha who wanted missionaries for the territory of Gurupá. Aranha had received permission to gather several villages of Indians near Gurupá and had asked the Jesuits to take charge of them. When they refused, either for lack of men or because they disliked Aranha, the captain complained to the king. The king wrote to Governor Coelho de Carvalho on February 19, 1691, that he was on the point of sending either Carmelites or Franciscans of the Province of Piedade to Gurupá. He was then uncertain which he would send.[118] The governor answered the king's letter on July 4, 1692. He assured His Majesty that either Order would be welcome in Pará and added that the old convent at Gurupá was being rebuilt for occupancy.[119] Pedro II's choice finally fell on the Franciscans of Piedade. Nine

tion of the Propaganda Fide in Rome, saying that the King of Portugal had asked him to arrange the sending of ten Italian Capuchins to Maranhão. See Archivio della Propaganda Fide, Scritture refferite nei Congressi, Congo, Vol. II, fl. 290. On March 12, 1691, the same priest wrote that the Secretary of State had already written to the governor of Maranhão announcing the arrival of the *Capuchinhos*. *Ibid.*, fl. 293. [This was an easy mistake, since both the Franciscans of St. Anthony and of Piedade were known as "Capuchos."] On January 16, 1692, Fr. Varazze complained that the ten had not yet arrived from Italy. *Ibid.*, fl. 335. On December 24, 1692, the Capuchin admitted that negotiations were not progressing well, and he feared that the Court preferred Portuguese Franciscans. *Ibid.*, fl. 398. On February 3, 1693, he declared that it was certain that seven Portuguese Franciscans would go that year to Maranhão. *Ibid.*, III, 6. One of the friends who assisted the Capuchins at Court was Roque Monteiro Paim, who had been a member of the junta called to recommend new legislation in 1686. The Capuchins never succeeded in getting to Maranhão, but in the early eighteenth century they did secure the convents vacated by the French Capuchins in Pernambuco and Bahia.

[117] For an account of the history of this province, see Bartolõmeu Ribeiro, *Guia de Portugal Franciscano, continental e insular. Esquema histórico de 1217 a 1834 e crónica sucinta da Província dos Santos Mártires de Marrocos* (Leixões, 1946), pp. 17-33. See also Manoel de Monforte, *Chronica da Provincia da Piedade primeira capucha de toda a Ordem e regular observancia de nosso serafico Padre S. Francisco* (2nd ed.; Lisboa, 1751). The first edition was printed in 1696.

[118] Letter of the king to Governor Coelho de Carvalho, February 19, 1691, in *Livro Grosso*, I, 122 f. The king stated: "... e esperar com a brevidade que mais fôr possivel vão para esse estado religiosos missionarios da Provincia da Piedade, ou Carmelitas descalços como tenho resoluto. ..."

[119] AHU, Pará, Papeis Avulsos, doc. 4 de julho de 1692.

of their number arrived in Pará in November, 1693, and they proceeded directly to Gurupá, where a house was ready for them.[120] Meanwhile the regulations on *resgates* were clarified. It will be remembered that the Jesuits were never anxious to exercise any sort of control over these expeditions, such as the law of 1688 gave them. In reply to their fresh complaints, the king, on January 22, 1693, told the Jesuit superior of Maranhão that the *resgates* did not have to be made annually, or at certain times of the year, but only when it was convenient to make them, or whenever the good of souls or of the *aldeias* made them necessary.[121] At least from 1694 to 1702 the Jesuits must have decided that they were not needed, since there were no official *resgates* during these years.[122]

In January, 1693, the Overseas Council debated at length the extent of the governor's authority in Indian matters. In practice, the Jesuit missionary superiors of Maranhão and Pará did not allow the governor to have too much authority over the Indians, although the Indians were vassals of the king and were, as such, under the governor's ultimate control. Other royal officials, such as the *ouvidores* and captains, also raised the problem of the extent of their jurisdiction over the Indians.[123] The king decided that the Jesuits had arrogated powers which the law did not permit them to enjoy. In his letter of February 26, 1693, to the Jesuit superior of the missions of Maranhão, the king made clear that the temporal jurisdiction over the Indians which had been given to the missionaries did not exempt the Indians entirely from the jurisdiction of the governors and the ministers of justice. The missionaries were not authorized to disregard the commands of the governors. The mission superiors were free to complain, whenever

---

[120] Berredo, *Annaes históricos*, II, No. 1373; Reis, "Formação espiritual da Amazônia," *Cultura*, I, 101.

[121] ADE, Ordens MSS annexos do Regimento e leys sobre as missões do Maranhão, pp. 95 f.

[122] Included among the papers of a *devassa* taken on May 26, 1723, is an official list of the number of Indians ransomed and distributed from 1691 to 1714. In 1691 there were nineteen, in 1692, eighty-seven, and in 1693, 310. The next entry is that of 1702. See AHU, Maranhão, Papeis Avulsos, doc. 26 de maio de 1723.

[123] The pertinent papers are in AHU, Pará, Papeis Avulsos, under doc. 28 de janeiro de 1693.

necessary, against the actions of the royal officials, but they were not entitled to oppose them on grounds of jurisdiction.[124]

On March 19, 1693, in a letter to Governor António de Albuquerque Coelho de Carvalho, the king divided the vast territory of the captaincy of Pará—Maranhão was not included—into more or less defined districts and assigned a religious order to each.[125] The territory was divided in such a way as to safeguard, in some instances, the prior rights of a given Order, but once a territory was assigned it remained in the exclusive control of the Order which received it. The Jesuits received the lion's share of the territory, and also the best part from the point of view of future expansion.

The king gave as the immediate reason for this division the petition of the Jesuit fathers to be relieved of their missions in the Cabo do Norte area, and their suggestion that these difficult missions be left to the exclusive care of the Franciscans of St. Anthony, because of the friars' long acquaintance and experience with the Indians of that area, and because the said friars have in that region a hospice and several residences. The king had caused all this to be considered in the *Junta das Missões* in Lisbon, in the presence of ex-Governor Gomes Freire de Andrade, and the junta advised setting up separate districts for the Jesuits, the Franciscans of St. Anthony and the Franciscans of Piedade. This the king was now of a mind to ordain, and he did so in the following way. To the fathers of the Society of Jesus he apportioned all the district south of the Amazon River, from the mouth to the westward, without limitation towards the interior. This section, in the king's mind, was the principal part and the most important part of the state, and he gave it to the care of the Jesuits because they were the first (*mais antigos!*) missionaries in the state, and because of their many virtues.

To the fathers of St. Anthony the king assigned all that lay north of the Amazon River, including the *sertão* of Cabo do Norte, and as far westward as the *aldeia* of Urubucuará, then a Jesuit *aldeia*. The district comprised the Jary and Parú Rivers, and was also without limit towards the interior north of the Amazon.[126]

---

[124] ADE, Ordens MSS annexos do Regimento e leys sobre as missões do Maranhão, p. 109, printed in *Livro Grosso*, I, 139.

[125] *Ibid.*, I, 142-144.

[126] In modern terminology, the territory of the Franciscans of St. Anthony included the island of Marajó, the territory of Amapá (Cabo do Norte), and west-

To the fathers of Piedade the king assigned the district round about the island of Gurupá, and the territory north of the Amazon River, from the *aldeia* of Urubucuará westward, including the Xingú,[127] Trombetas and Gueribí Rivers.[128]

From the Rio Gueribí westward along the shore of the Amazon River the king delineated another district which comprehended the Urubú and Negro Rivers and all the other rivers to the limit of his dominions. This also would be given over to the care of the Jesuits, since they wished this district and had the competent missionaries for the task. But the king ordered that the Mercedarians be allowed to keep the mission they had in this area, since they were laboring there to the king's entire satisfaction, according to information given by the governor. Pedro II further ordered that if at any time the Jesuits did not care to keep this district, or did not send there the necessary fathers, the Mercedarians would be allowed not only to keep the mission they had but to found new missions in that district. If, however, these conditions did not obtain, it would be better if the Mercedarians would not found new missions there, except the one they already had.[129]

The king concluded his letter with several observations of interest. Firstly, he mentioned that it would be very useful for the Jesuits to use foreign Jesuits in their vast territory, because of the great spirit of fervor of the foreign Jesuits. Secondly, he allowed the Franciscans of St. Anthony, and, by extension, the other Orders, to continue to assist in *aldeias* of Indians brought from the respective territory of the Order, even though the new *aldeias* were in the district of another Order. This would be done at least

---

ward along the northern side of the Amazon as far as the neighborhood of the modern town of Prainha.

[127] Inclusion of the Xingú River in the territory of the fathers of Piedade was an evident geographical error, since the Xingú lies south of the Amazon. It was corrected in November, 1694, when it was explained that Manoel Guedes Aranha would bring Indians down the Rio Xingú to a spot near Gurupá. See *carta régia* of November 29, 1694, to the governor in ADE, Regimento e leys sobre as missões do Estado do Maranhão e Pará, p. 80.

[128] In modern terminology, the territory of the Franciscans of Piedade extended from Prainha to Faro, and included also the island of Gurupá.

[129] The man most responsible for the Mercedarians' success was Fr. Teodósio da Veiga, who began his mission in this district after the Maranhão revolt. See above, p. 171, and Leite, *História da Companhia*, III, 383. The Jesuits actually allowed this section to remain in Mercedarian hands. Their district extended from the Rio Jamundá and Faro to the region of Manaos, in present-day Amazônia.

until these Indians could, with certainty, receive the missionaries of Orders other than the one that originally evangelized their group.[130] Thirdly, the king concluded by commanding the governor to promulgate this new ruling through the local *Junta das Missões*. He was given the faculty of changing or altering anything in the ruling which he saw to be impractical, or which would lead to inconveniences. In any case, he was commanded to inform the king of whatever he might do concerning the division of territory.

In the original division of the mission districts of the Amazon, the Carmelites were not included. In 1695 they acquired the mission territory of the Rio Negro and Rio Solimões region, but only because the Jesuits asked the king to be relieved of it in consequence of a lack of priests caused by sicknesses their missionaries had acquired in the Cabo do Norte region.[131] The request of the Society of Jesus to abandon this vast area was acted upon favorably, if unwillingly, by the king who, on November 26, 1694, authorized Governor Coelho de Carvalho to call in the Carmelites.[132] The new missionaries began their work in the Rio Negro-Rio Solimões district in 1695, and they continued it with marked success in the eighteenth century.

The stage was now set for the Golden Period of the Portuguese missions in the Amazon Valley. The several religious orders could at length co-operate towards the same end; the days of constant bickering among themselves were for the most part over. It is true that the Jesuits and the Franciscans complained of the division, the former because they lost so many of the *aldeias* and churches they had built,[133] and the latter because they were al-

---

[130] The occasion for this ruling was the custom of the friars to bring Cabo do Norte Indians to villages near Belém, which would normally now be Jesuit territory.

[131] Leite, *História da Companhia*, III, 376. Leite mentions that the local Jesuits could never have obtained this permission from their father general, so they turned instead to the king.

[132] *Carta régia* of November 26, 1694, to the governor, in ADE, Regimento e leys sobre as missões do Maranhão, pp. 79-83. The governor was to clearly separate the district of the Mercedarians [which the Jesuits also refused] from that of the Carmelites. *Ibid.*

[133] Fr. José Caeiro, the Jesuit, complains in his "Apologia da Companhia de Portugal": ". . . chegaram [os Jesuítas] a fundar 55 aldeias . . . . Esta República fundaram e estabeleceram os Jesuítas, sós, e sem ajuda alguma ou favor dos outros,

most wholly confined to the Cabo do Norte area, which was a most undesirable part, as the Jesuits proved by abandoning it so soon.[134] But the division endured until the secularization of the missions in 1755.

Besides breaking the Jesuit monopoly by the division of mission territory, the Crown also diminished considerably the powers of the Jesuit superior of the missions in the state. Many of the powers granted him in 1680, 1686 and 1688, were now given to the local *Junta das Missões*, made up of the prelates of all the religious orders laboring in the Amazon. For instance, on March 15, 1696, a royal letter stated that the *depositario* with the 3,000 *cruzados* for the *resgate* was to be approved by and report to the junta, and not to the Jesuit superior. Other religious besides the Jesuits were to be in charge of the *resgate* expeditions, each in their turn.[135]

The mission system reached its full flowering at the turn of the eighteenth century. Both Pedro II, who ruled until 1706, and João V, who ruled from 1706 to 1750, were generally favorable to the cause of the missionaries, and believed that the missions were the best means of protecting the Indians from unjust exploitation. The opposition of the people, which arose especially after 1722, was confined to verbal expression and defamatory broadsides. The missions prospered. Exact statistics for all the missions are not available. We do know that in 1696 the number of Christianized Indians in the Jesuit missions alone was about 11,000. In 1730

---

antes com gravissimas oposições e contradições contínuas . . . . Em 1693 se dividiram as 55 aldeias, fundadas e povoadas pelos Jesuítas, entrando ao governo e administração de grande parte delas os religiosos Carmelitas, os Mercenários, e os Capuchinhos [*sic*!] de Santo António, obedecendo os Jesuítas prontamente ao decreto real que assim o ordenava e cedendo, sem dificuldade algumas 27 povoações, que com tantos trabalhos tinham feito e as igrejas que à sua custa tinham edificado. Depois da divisão administraram os Jesuítas 28 aldeias até o ano de 1755. . . ." Quoted from Leite, *Luiz Figueira*, p. 34.

[134] The Franciscans' complaint was embodied in a treatise written by Fr. Luis de Annunciação in 1772, who complained that the Jesuits drove the friars from their best missions in 1655, kept a monopoly on the missions from 1655 to 1691 (?), and in that year maneuvered a division of the missions which left the Franciscans of St. Anthony with Cabo do Norte, a most undesirable part, abandoned by the Jesuits after one short attempt. See ANTT, St. António dos Capuchos, maçó 6. The friars renamed the district "Cabo do Morte." See *ibid*.

[135] The letter is in ADE, Regimento e leys sobre as missões do Maranhão e Pará, pp. 50-52.

the number was 21,031.[136] These Indians were divided among some twenty-eight *aldeias* belonging to the Jesuits.[137] We also know that the Franciscans had twenty-six mission *aldeias* under their charge in 1739.[138] In 1750 Governor Francisco Xavier de Mendonça Furtado reported that there were sixty-three Indian *aldeias* in Maranhão and Pará. Of these, nineteen were administered by Jesuits, fifteen by Carmelites, twenty-six by Franciscans[139] and three by Mercedarians.[140] Azevedo estimates that before the terrible smallpox epidemic which raged in Maranhão and Pará from 1743 to 1750, there were some 60,000 Indians domesticated in the various *aldeias* of the state.[141]

To the middle of the eighteenth century, all these missionaries worked incessantly, converting many thousands of natives, erecting chapels and churches, founding *aldeias*, changing pagan customs, urging the Indians to develop the spirit of industry, teaching them mechanical skills, studying the land and the human beings of the land. It was through the missionaries that the frontiers of Portugal in the Amazon area were spread to the headwaters of the Madeira, the Rio Negro and the upper Amazon.[142] To a foreign observer in 1743, La Condamine, the missions presented a startling picture of prosperity and contentment.[143] Certainly we must say that the mission system offered the Indians the best available protection they could ever obtain against the encroachments of the stronger race into the Amazon region.

---

[136] Leite, *História da Companhia*, IV, 138.

[137] See above, p. 178 n.: "depois da divisão administraram os Jesuítas 28 aldeias até o ano de 1755."

[138] Basílio Roewer, *A ordem franciscana no Brasil* (Petrópolis, 1942), p. 73.

[139] The twenty-six Franciscan missions were divided between friars of three distinct provinces, as follows: nine to the Province of St. Anthony, seven to the Province of the Immaculate Conception (which had entered the mission field in 1706), and ten to the Province of Piedade.

[140] For the text of this "Informação do governador Francisco Xavier de Mendonça Furtado à Mesa da Consciencia," see Azevedo, *Os Jesuítas no Grão Pará*, pp. 228 f.

[141] *Ibid.*, p. 228.

[142] Reis, "Formação espiritual da Amazônia," *Cultura*, I, 102.

[143] Charles-Marie de La Condamine, *Relation abrégée d'un voyage fait dans l'interieur de l'Amerique meridionale, depuis la côte de la mer du sud, jusqu'aux côtes du Brésil et de la Guyane en descendant la rivière des Amazones* (Maestricht, 1778), pp. 87 f.

SUMMARY AND CONCLUSION

The Amazon region is still one of the largest undeveloped areas in the world. A combination of climate, disease and lack of transportation has retarded its development. If this is true today, it was doubly true in the seventeenth century. Today medicine has made vast strides in ridding this area of disease, and modern transportation, especially the airplane, has opened the Amazon Valley to travel. Nothing, however, has been or can be done about the climate and dense vegetation. At the beginning of the seventeenth century all three of these problems—climate, disease and lack of transportation—remained to be solved. When the Portuguese arrived in this part of the world in 1614 determined to settle the country at all costs, they were immediately brought face to face with the economic realities of their situation. They were few in number, in unfamiliar jungle surroundings, dependent on river travel almost exclusively. They knew little of the indigenous plants or agricultural methods. The climate sapped their vitality. Diseases, especially fevers, plagued them. Naturally enough they turned to the natives for help. In fact, the use of Indians became essential to the well-being and economic security, if not the very existence, of the state.

Feeling their cultural superiority over the naked savage, while they were forced to depend on his knowledge for some of their material necessities, the Europeans strove to bring as many Indians as possible under subjection to themselves, to use them to best advantage. Not having sufficient numbers for large-scale expansion into the interior, the Portuguese hit upon the expedient of sending armed expeditions into the backlands to entice or force Indians to move to the coastal areas near the white settlements, where the Indians would be of service to them in those unfamiliar surroundings. Once brought nearer the white settlements, the natives were encouraged or forced to live in *aldeias*, or villages, located conveniently near the plantations and warehouses and mills built by the Europeans. The Indians could then be utilized in rowing, fishing, hunting and manual labor. Such was the origin of the *entradas* and the *aldeias*.

181

From the very beginning of colonization, missionaries were active in Maranhão and Pará. They accompanied the earliest expeditions or came soon afterwards. They soon realized that the success of their work with the pagan Indians would depend largely on the correct regulation of *entradas* and *aldeias*. But they were not able to achieve both goals immediately. It would take time to work out a system that was feasible. The earliest missionaries in Pará, the Franciscans of St. Anthony Province, were at first able merely to accompany the *entrada* expeditions as chaplains, and to exert a moral influence on the Portuguese soldiers to avoid unnecessary cruelties. Meanwhile they endeavored to convert the Indians under great handicaps. Upon returning from these expeditions, the friars were forced to watch helplessly the exploitation of the natives in the *aldeias* by the lay captains placed in charge of them. Here in the administration of the *aldeias*, the first Franciscans argued, was the place to begin their protective tutelage, if they hoped to influence and convert the pagan Indians. These new villages of Indians became the focal point of much of the early strife over the protection of the Indian. Who would control the *aldeias*? This was to be a decisive question throughout the seventeenth century. The Franciscans were of the opinion that lay control of the *aldeias* produced generally dubious results. The friars became convinced during the years 1617-1623 that only through missionary control of the *aldeias* could the Indians be adequately protected. Accordingly, when Frei Cristóvão de Lisboa entered the state in 1624 with supreme ecclesiastical powers, he brought with him a royal order prohibiting lay captaincies, annuling those already granted, and turning over the government of the Indian *aldeias* to ecclesiastics. With the passing of this law, missionaries of Maranhão and Pará could, for the first time, attempt to intervene decisively in Indian affairs. According to this new system, for we can now speak of a rudimentary system, the missionary, living with or visiting frequently his Indians in their villages, was able to aid materially in the Europeanization and Christianization of his pagan charges. Supervision and tutelage it was, without a doubt, from the beginning. There was no thought of leaving the Indian to his own devices. The Indian, in the missionaries' minds, had to be Christianized, and for that he had to become more cultured in the European sense. Since he would not do this successfully if left to himself, he had to be made in some way to do so. The process of cultural and religious change was to be forcibly accelerated. It is beside the point to argue the validity of this viewpoint. It was common doctrine at the time among all colonizing nations.

The Franciscan attempt at control, however, encountered trouble from the beginning. The people of Maranhão and Pará did not appreciate this attempt of the friars to control the most valuable commodity of the colony, even if it was ultimately for purposes of conversion to the Catholic Faith, which they all professed. In Maranhão the law was grudgingly observed, but it was never fully observed in Pará, where there were so many more Indians to exploit. The opposition was strong and tenacious, and the friars, without financial resources of their own, and without strong enough influence at Court, were forced to give way in the years after 1630. Back into power came the system of lay captaincies, not to be effectively dislodged again until 1652. Can it be said, however, in all fairness, that the system of lay captaincies was completely evil? By no means, otherwise how can it be explained that the Indians in Maranhão rendered valiant aid to the Portuguese after the Dutch overran Maranhão in 1641? Can it be argued that the Indians of those years were merely rebelling against harsh treatment by the Dutch? Or was there a spark of love and understanding in the Indians' hearts which influenced them to cast their lot in 1643 and 1644 with the weaker Portuguese forces? We know that without the Indians' aid, Maranhão would not have been regained from the Dutch so quickly. Their aid was admittedly decisive.

In 1652 the mission system of Maranhão saw the entrance of a new force, the Jesuit Order, under the leadership of Fr. António Vieira. Ever since 1638, after the Franciscans had conceded defeat, the Jesuits had attempted to take over as official protectors of the Indians of Maranhão and Pará. Only the shipwreck of Jesuit missionaries in 1643 prevented the implementation of their first attempt. In 1652 the stage was set for another phase of mission and Indian policy development. The Jesuits, more aggressive than the Franciscans, were determined to set up a more workable system in every detail. Prestige at Court was assured through Fr. Vieira's preponderant influence over the king. Financial arrangements were adequately obtained. As for the protective system for the Indians, Vieira put his faith in Jesuit supervision of the two most important economic functions of the colony: control of the placing and governing of the mission *aldeias*, and control of the *entradas* that furnished a continual supply of the necessary Indian laborers from the interior. With these two powers, together with the ample royal salary and continued influence at Court, Vieira felt that much could be accomplished towards protecting and Christianizing the Indians. Vieira, however, had not gauged correctly the temper of the colonists, who saw the Jesuit empire grow with a feeling akin to terror. Something had to be done, they felt. In 1661 something was done. The revolt and expulsion of the Jesuits from both Maranhão and Pará, although speedily suppressed and nullified, was sufficient to influence the Court, to reintroduce, through the law of 1663, the old system of lay control and exploitation. The remaining missionaries of other Orders were not permitted to step into the breach; they and the Jesuits who returned to the state in 1663 had to be content for some seventeen years to be merely spiritual pastors of an oppressed people, with no temporal power to speak of. But economic conditions did not improve for the colonists even with lay exploitation of the luckless native. The Indians deserted their *aldeias* in large numbers, and it became increasingly difficult to replenish the supply. In this situation, Vieira, now an old man, but unbent by his years of persecution by the Inquisition, saw his chance to re-establish the Jesuit dominion in the state. In 1680 a new set of laws gave predominant power once more to the Jesuits, who once again set up the mission system as in 1655. As earlier, the aim was to control the Indian *aldeias* and the *entradas* as completely as possible. But Vieira now went several steps further: he obtained control also of the *distribution* of the Indian workers to the colonists, and he secured permission to form missions in the interior, where there would be no danger of cruelties from white masters, since no white settlements were nearby. Again circumstances militated against complete success. The revolt of 1684 in Maranhão, caused partly by the inequities of the monopolistic commercial company set up in 1682 and partly by the settlers' reaction to the new Indian law of 1680, was a definite setback, even though the revolt did not affect Pará directly. The revolt, however, turned out to be a blessing in disguise to those interested in protecting the Indians, since it defeated the promulgation of a colonist-inspired law of 1684 secured without the consent of Vieira that would have again shorn the missionaries of temporal power and put control of the Indians into the hands of the colonists. As a result of the revolt, the attitude of the home government stiffened against the colonists' demands and the king resolved to keep the missionaries in complete control of the Indians; the *regimento* of 1686 was the result.

In this *regimento* the government policy of giving all control over the Indians to one religious order, as was done in 1624, 1638, 1652 and 1680, was changed. Both the Jesuits and the Franciscans of St. Anthony were now declared official Indian missionaries. The hold of the missionaries over the Indians was strengthened, and at the same time the colonists' most pressing needs for manual laborers were taken care of in the *regimento* by strictly supervised *entradas* and ransoming expeditions (*resgates*). The all-important *entradas* and *resgates* and the distribution of the Indians were to be strictly supervised by the religious. The government of the *aldeias* was placed securely in the hands of the Jesuits and Franciscans, each in their respective missions. Two procurators, or advocates of the Indians, one in each captaincy, were to protect the welfare of the Indians, especially when they worked for the settlers. Prices of goods sold by or to an Indian were fixed to prevent cheating. The paying of the wages of the Indian workers—those between thirteen and fifty years old—was strictly regulated. No Indian could be forced to work for the settlers more than six months of the year, nor could he be allowed to work outside the *aldeia* until two years after his arrival from the interior, to allow time for his adequate instruction in the Faith. Besides this, an attempt was made, through the legal provisions of the *regimento*, to cut off all unnecessary contact of the village Indian with the whites by allowing no one but the missionary to reside in the *aldeias* with the Indians. Specific and heavy penalties were laid down for every unlawful act against the Indians. An attempt, in short, was made to close every foreseeable loophole.

The *regimento* of 1686 was a realistic law: it recognized and endeavored to provide for the colonists' legitimate need of Indian laborers, while at the same time it tried to afford the Indian maximum protection against cruel exploitation by placing him under the vigilant care of the missionaries. Under the circumstances, it was the greatest protection that could have been provided in Maranhão and Pará, if the state was to continue to exist. In

1693, with the inclusion of the other religious orders in the missionary work on an equal plane with the Jesuits, and with the division, in the same year, of the missionary territory between the various Orders, the Portuguese protective system was completed.

The missions prospered in the eighteenth century, and so did the Indians.   If the state as a whole had progressed equally well, perhaps the secularization of the missions in 1755, the expulsion of the Jesuits in 1759, and the replacing of the Indians under lay, and finally, in the nineteenth century, under military control, would never have happened.   The mission system, paternalistic as it was, was not a perfect system for the aborigines, especially in the Amazon region.   But nothing better or as good was invented after the secularization of the missions in 1759.   It is significant, I believe, that in the twentieth century Brazil is again relying upon the missionary very extensively in the Amazon Valley, to civilize and Christianize the unassimilated Indians.

GLOSSARY

Adjunto—adjutant, assistant.

Ajuda de custo—a royal pecuniary grant to help defray traveling expenses.

Aldeia—a village, especially a village for Indians.

Aldeia de repartição—an Indian village whose adult inhabitants were used as workers for the benefit of white settlers.

Alvará—a royal decree beginning "Eu, el rei" and ending with the signature "Rei." The effect of an *alvará* did not continue more than one year, unless, as was usually the case, a clause to the contrary was inserted.

Autos—affidavits gathered before and during the course of a trial or lawsuit.

Cabo da escolta—the military leader of an armed escort which accompanied an expedition into the interior.

Câmara—town council or city council, with many judicial and administrative rights, exercised within its jurisdiction under the authority of the governor or captain of the province.

Capitão-mor—a royal appointee who was the subordinate governor of a captaincy within a state, and was answerable only to the governor-general of the state and to the king.

Capitania—1) the territory ruled by a *capitão-mor*; or 2) when used in connection with Indians, the right of administration of Indian villages.

Cargo dos índios—official care of the Indians, given to a religious order or a lay person.

Carta régia—a royal provision, of its nature permanent, which began with the name of the person or authority to whom it was addressed, after which it continued, "Eu el Rei vos envio muito saudar." It was signed "Rei."

Casus conscientiae—Case of conscience. It is a Latin term used in ecclesiastical circles to define a disputation in moral theology or church law in which moral questions are proposed and answered.

Cativeiro dos índios—the act of capturing Indians and keeping them in slavery for long periods.

Clérigo—literally, a cleric. In seventeenth-century documents, however, it is used synonymously with "secular priest."

Consulta—an ordinance or decree of a council; a conclusion reached after deliberations in council.

Custos, Custódio—a term used in the Franciscan Order to designate the religious superior of a group of missionaries of the same Order. He has powers equivalent, but subordinate to, the provincial superior of the home province.

Degredados—those exiled or expatriated in punishment for petty crimes. Synonymous with "desterrados."

Depositário—an official with whom money or goods are deposited for safekeeping.

Descimento—an expedition composed of soldiers and missionaries, or of missionaries only, used to bring Indians, by force or persuasion, from their homeland to localities near white settlement.

Devassa—a judicial investigation.

Entrada—An expedition similar to a *descimento*, but in which soldiers and force were more often employed.

Escravos de condição—Indian slaves taken in an unjust war against the natives, whose status as slaves was uncertain.

Fazenda—1) plantation; 2) property of any kind.

Freguesia—a parish and the compass of land belonging to it, or under the jurisdiction of the respective pastor.

Gente de serviço—Indians used for the service of white settlers, lay or ecclesiastic.

Governador geral—an official appointed by the king who was supreme in civil and military administration within the state, and was considered the king's representative in all political matters.

Igreja matriz—the mother church, which usually became the cathedral church upon the advent of a bishop.

Índios de corda—Indians captured by other Indians in war and kept as privileged slaves until they finally became victims of ceremonial cannibalism at the hands of their captors.

Índios de serviço—See "Gente de serviço."

Índios encomendados—Indians granted in the Spanish style to individual settlers for a set period of time, during which they must serve the settler and his heirs.

Índios presos à corda—See "Índios de corda."

Juiz ordinário—The eldest member of the town council, who was granted judicial powers over less important cases.

Junta—meeting, assembly.

Língua geral—The Tupí Indian language, used by most of the Indians in the Amazon region.

Memorial—a treatise containing an exposition of facts and circumstances, and soliciting attention to them.

Mercê—a gift, reward, granted by the Crown for meritorious service.

Lei—a royal provision by its very nature permanent. It began with the name of the king and his various titles, and ended with "Rei."

Ordinária—annual salary paid by the king to missionaries.

Ouvidor—literally, a "listener." The highest judge in a *comarca*, or district.

Parecer—opinion.

Procurador da Fazenda—Procurator, or Solicitor, of the Exchequer, or Treasury.

Procurador da Coroa—Procurator, or Solicitor, of the Crown.

Procurador dos índios—an official appointed to look after the interests of the Indians.

Provedor da Fazenda—superintendent of the treasury.

Provisão—a general term used for a royal decree, letter, or *alvará*.

Redução do gentio—the subjection of the Indians to Portuguese rule.

Regimento—charter, or set of instructions to govern the actions of an official in the carrying out of his functions of office.

Relação—a written account or treatise.

Repartição dos índios—the distribution of Indian workers among the settlers.

Repartidor dos índios—the official in charge of the distribution of Indian workers.

Resgate—1) an expedition sent to ransom Indians who are slaves of other Indians, especially as "Indians of the cord"; or 2) trade goods used for the purpose of ransoming.

Residência—official examination into the administration of an official, after his term was completed.

Requerimento—request, or petition.

Requerimento em contrário—a petition against a prevailing practice.

Sargento-mor—literally "sergeant-major." A military officer in charge of the military defence of the state, under the authority of the captain or governor.

Sertão—the interior, backland, wilderness.

Sesmaria—allotments of land granted to colonists by the king or the governor.

Subsídio de mantimentos—money granted by the king to be used for provisioning for a voyage.

Termo—an official written declaration taken during or at the conclusion of a judicial process.

Vereador da câmara—an alderman or councilman of the town council.

Viático—money furnished by the king for traveling expenses.

Vila—a town duly recognized as such by law.

EQUIVALENTS OF MONEY, WEIGHTS, AND MEASURES[1]

Arroba—a dry weight equal to approximately 32 lbs.

Cruzado—a coin equal in value to 400 *réis*. The value of a *cruzado* in dollars has been estimated as follows: from 1580 to 1640, the *cruzado* was worth about $7.00; in 1646, $3.00; in 1662, $1.60; in 1668, $1.35; in 1688, $1.00.

Légua—a league, a measure of distance of approximately 4.10 miles.

Milreis—1000 *réis*. Milreis, like *cruzados*, varied in modern value as follows: from 1580-1640, they had the approximate buying value of $17.50; in 1646, $7.50; in 1662, $4.00; in 1668, $3.35; in 1688, $2.50.

Pipa—a liquid measure equal to about 126.6 gallons.

Pataca—a coin of Portuguese India equal in value to 300 *réis*.

Real (pl. *réis*)—The real was the unit of Portuguese currency. The value of the real fluctuated as follows: 1580-1640, $.0175; in 1646, $.0075; in 1662, $.004; in 1668, $.0033; in 1688, $.0025.

Vara—a unit of measurement equal to approximately 43 inches.

---

[1] The money equivalents were computed from data given by Lucio d'Azevedo, *Épocas de Portugal económico*, p. 488 f. The dollar equivalents are as of 1928. Hence the numbers given should be roughly doubled to conform to the present value of the dollar. The weights and measures equivalents were taken from J. Villasana Haggard, *Handbook for translators of Spanish historical documents* (Austin, 1941), *passim*.

SELECTED BIBLIOGRAPHY

I. Bibliographical Guides

Almeida, Eduardo de Castro e. *Inventario dos documentos relativos ao Brasil existentes no archivo de marinha e ultramar, organisado por Eduardo de Castro e Almeida.* 6 vols. Rio de Janeiro, 1913-1921.

Anselmo, António. *Bibliografia das bibliografias portuguesas.* Lisboa, 1923.

Azevedo, Pedro A. de, and António Baião. *O arquivo da Torre do Tombo. Sua historia, corpos que o compoem e organização.* Lisboa, 1905.

Basto, Arthur de Magalhães. *Catálogo dos manuscriptos ultramarinos da biblioteca municipal do Pôrto.* Lisboa, 1938.

Cardozo, Manoel S. "A guide to the manuscripts in the Lima Library, the Catholic University of America, Washington, D. C.," reprinted from *Handbook of Latin American Studies, 1940.*

Castañeda, Carlos Eduardo & Jack Autrey Dabbs (eds.). *Calendar of the Manuel E. Gondra Manuscript collection. The University of Texas Library.* Mexico, D. F., 1952.

Catalogo da exposição de historia do Brasil realizada pela Biblioteca Nacional do Rio de Janeiro. 2 vols. Rio de Janeiro, 1881.

Collecção Pombalina. Biblioteca Nacional de Lisboa. Inventario. Secção XIII-Manuscriptos. Lisboa, 1889.

Dias, A. Gonçalves. "Exames nos archivos dos mosteiros e das repartições publicas para collecção de documentos historicos relativos ao Maranhão," *Revista do Instituto Geográfico e Histórico Brasileiro,* XVI (1853), 370-384.

Ferrão, António. *Os arquivos e as bibliotecas em Portugal.* Coimbra, 1920.

Ferreira, Carlos Alberto. *Inventário dos manuscritos da Biblioteca da Ajuda referentes à America do Sul.* Coimbra, 1946.

Figanière, Frederico Francisco Stuart de. *Catalogo dos manuscriptos portuguezes existentes no Museu Britannico.* Lisboa, 1853.

Figueiredo, A. Mesquita de. *Arquivo Nacional da Torre do Tombo. Roteiro practico. Notas colligidas por A. Mesquita de Figueiredo.* Lisboa, 1922.

Fitzler, M. A. Hedwig & Ernesto Ennes (eds.). *A secção ultramarina da Biblioteca Nacional. Inventários. I. Códices do extincto Conselho Ultramarino. Estudo e notas por M. A. Hedwig Fitzler. II. Códices vindos de Moçambique por iniciativa de António Ennes. III. Códices do Arquivo da Marinha. Publicados, anotados e prefaciados por Ernesto Ennes.* Lisboa, 1928.

Fonseca, Luisa Lima da (ed.). "O Maranhão. Roteiro dos papeis avulsos do século XVII do Arquivo Histórico Colonial," *Congreso do Mundo Português,* XI (1942), 197-218.

Garraux, Anatole Louis. *Bibliographie brésilienne: catalogue des ouvrages français & latins relatifs au Brésil, 1500-1898.* Paris, 1898.

Guia das bibliotecas Brasileiras. Rio de Janeiro, 1941.

Hill, Roscoe R. (ed.). *The national archives of Latin America.* Cambridge, Mass., 1945.

Jones, C. K. *A bibliography of Latin American bibliographies.* Second ed., rev. and enlarged by the author with the assistance of James A. Granier. Washington, 1942.

Lima, Oliveira (ed.). *Relação dos manuscriptos portuguezes e estrangeiros de interesse para o Brasil existentes no Museu Britannico de Londres, coordenada por Oliveira Lima.* Rio de Janeiro, 1903.

Marques, João Martins da Silva (ed.). *Arquivo Nacional da Torre do Tombo. Ensaio de um manual de heuristica e arquivologia. Vol. I: Index Indicum.* Lisboa, 1935.

Moraes, Rubens Borba de, and William Berrien (eds.). *Manual bibliográfico de Estudos Brasileiros.* Rio de Janeiro, 1949.

[Palha, Fernando.] *Catalogue de la bibliothèque de M. Fernando Palha.* 2 vols. Lisbonne, 1896.

Reis, António Simões dos. *Bibliografia das bibliografias brasileiras.* Rio de Janeiro, 1942.

Rivara, Joaquim Heliodoro. *Catalogo dos manuscriptos da Biblioteca publica Eborense. Tomo I, que comprehende a noticia dos codices e papeis relativos ás cousas da America, Africa é Asia.* Lisboa, 1850.

Sodré, Nelson Werneck. *O que se deve ler para conhecer o Brasil.* Rio de Janeiro, 1945.

II. PRIMARY SOURCES

A. UNPRINTED[1]

1. *Arquivo Histórico Ultramarino, Lisbon*

Papeis Avulsos (Miscellaneous Papers): on Pará (1616-1778) - 38 *caixas*, or boxes; on Maranhão (1610-1777) - 5 caixas; 31 *maços*, or bundles.

Códices (Codices).
Livros de registo de decretos relativos ao Brasil e outras possessões, 1702-1737. 3 vols.
Livros de registo de Consultas de Partes, 1617-1656. 39 vols.
Livros de registo de Consultas Mixtas de todas as capitanias, 1643-1704. 7 vols.
Registo de Cartas Régias, Avisos e Offícios para Maranhão e Pará, 1673-1796. 5 vols.
Registo de Consultas do Maranhão, 1673-1732. 1 vol.
Registo de Ordens Régias, Offícios e mais papeis relativos ao Pará, 1717-1796. 2 vols.
Catálogo do resumo das Ordens Régias aos governadores e capitães gerais do Pará, 1708-1755. 1 vol.
Collecção das representações, propostas e providencias sobre as ruinas que aos povos do Estado do Gram Pará e Maranhão fizerão os denominados Jesuitas, até o fim do reinado do Senhor Rey Dom Joam Quinto. 1 vol.
Consultas da Mesa da Consciência e Ordens, 1755-1799. 2 vols.
Catalogo das cartas que contem este 2º. livro dos papeis que as instruem, escritas

---

[1] Listed in this bibliography are only the larger collections of documents the author consulted in the various archives. Single documents used from sections not listed here are identified fully in the footnotes.

deste reino para as capitanias do Grão Pará e Maranhão e das mesmas capitanias para ele, sobre as demarcações e tratado dos limites, e sobre o estabelecimento do estado politico, civil e militar das mesmas capitanias, a que se dé principio no anno de 1752. Cód. 1213 (1724-1752); Cód. 1214 (1752-1755).

Collecção de cartas e Ordens Régias dirigidas ao senado da Camara e mais authoridades do governo do Pará, ao quais se encontrárão trasladadas em dois livros existentes no archivo do mesmo senado. Copia feita em 1797. Cód. 1275.

Consultas do serviço de partes de todas as conquistas, 1643-1652. Cód. 278.

Consultas do Conselho Ultramarino. Cód. 917 (1749-1750); Cód. 918 (1751-1755).

Registo de cartas oficiais para todas as conquistas e mandadas do Ultramar, 1644-1806. Códs. 275, 277.

2. *Arquivo Nacional da Torre do Tombo, Lisbon*

Livros da Chancelaria
Filipe II: Livro 1.
Filipe III: Livros 1, 11, 18, 27, 28, 31, 34, 35, 36, 39, 40.
João IV: Livros 1, 2, 11, 13, 14, 15, 17, 19, 21, 22, 23, 24, 25, 26, 27.
Affonso VI: Livros 2, 24, 26, 28, 29, 30, 38, 40, 41, 46, 52, 54.
Pedro II: Livros 7, 17, 20, 24, 26, 27, 30, 33, 34, 40, 53, 54, 56, 59, 62.
João V: Livros 49, 69, 79, 93, 115, 129.

MSS. da Livraria
Manuscritos relativos ao Brasil. 50 vols.

MSS. Miscelaneos. 6 vols.

Leis e regimentos, 1506-1800. 5 *maços.*

Códs. 962, 968, 1114, 1116, 1148.

Cartório dos Jesuitas. 120 *maços.*

Armário Jesuítico. 1 cod. 1 *caixa.*

Santo António dos Capuchos. 12 cods. 25 *maços* (no. 18 missing).

Ministerio do Reino
Consultas do Conselho Ultramarino, 1730-1825. 13 *maços.*

Consultas de Mesa da Consciência e Ordens, 1731-1833. 13 *maços.*

Registo de consultas da Mesa da Consciencia e Ordens, 1755-1832. 11 vols.

Papeis Diversos, Ultramar. 10 *maços.*

Circulares, 1654-1803. 2 vols.

Leis dos portos do Brazil. Registo, 1605-1761. 1 vol.

Decretamentos, 1688-1754. 1 *maço.*

Ultramar e Ilhas. Correspondencia, representações e outros papois diversos. 4 *maços.*

Ordem de Cristo. 3 *maços.*

Colecção Especial
Documentos do século XVII. 1 *maço.*

MSS. Communs. Cód. 2066.

3. *Biblioteca Nacional, Lisbon*

Colecção Pombalina, made up of 758 codices:
Códices 159, 160, 161, 162, 163, 249, 453, 459, 471, 475, 478, 482, 620, 621, 622, 623, 624, 625, 626, 627, 628, 629, 630, 631, 632, 641, 642, 643, 645, 647, 653, 686.

Fundo Geral, consisting of 9000 codices and 100 *caixas*:
Códices 172, 175, 176, 251, 302, 467, 568, 589, 665, 681, 682, 1460, 1527, 1570, 1680, 4516, 4529, 7627, 8396.
Caixas 10, 11, 16, 29, 71, 72, 217.

4. Arquivo Distrital de Évora

Regimento e leys sobre as missões do Maranhão e Pará, Cód. CXV-2-12.
Ordens MSS. annexos a Regimento e leys sobre as missões do Maranhão e Pará.

5. Other Archives in Portugal

Biblioteca da Ajuda: This library contains many documents, although it is famous chiefly for its printed books. Neither the books nor the documents are indexed or catalogued. The author used Ferreira, *Inventario dos manuscritos da Biblioteca da Ajuda referentes à America do Sul*, copying all documentation on Maranhão and Pará.

Biblioteca Pública do Porto: Concerning Maranhão and Pará, this library is important chiefly for travel books of the eighteenth century and maps of the same period. The author here used Basto, *Catálogo dos manuscriptos ultramarinos da biblioteca municipal do Pôrto*.

Biblioteca Geral da Universidade de Coimbra: This library and archive has, with few exceptions, nothing concerning my subject other than eighteenth and nineteenth century copies of earlier documents. There is a partial index and catalogue available at the library.

Arquivo do Ministerio das Finanças: Concerning Maranhão and Pará, there is nothing in this archive anterior to the Companhia Geral of 1755. There is a partial MS. index and catalogue available at the archive.

6. Archivo Nacional de Simancas, Spain.

Colección de Estado: *legajos* 2615, 2616, 2622, 2623, 2629.
Colección de Secretarías Provinciales: *legajos* 2690, 2691, 2737, 2766.
Colección de Patronato Real: *legajos* 7374 through 7434.

7. Archivo General de las Indias, Seville, Spain.

Patronato Real, *legajo* 272.

8. Archivio Segreto Vaticano, Vatican City.

Nunziature di Portogallo
Letters of the Secretariat of State to the Papal Nuncio in Lisbon. Letters of the Papal Nuncio in Lisbon to the Secretariat of State, 18th century.
Lettere di Vescovi e Prelati. Vols. 1, 106.
Processus Consistorialis, Vols. 105, 124.

9. New York Public Library.

Collecção authentica de todas as leys, regimentos, alvaras, e mais ordens que se expediram para o Brasil desde o estabelecimento destas conquistas. Ordenada por Provisam de 28 de Março de 1754. This collection is incomplete, lacking, of the 39 volumes, volumes 2, 3, 18, 20, 22, 25, 29, 31, 32, 33, 37, 38.

B. Printed

Abbeville, Claude de. *L'arrivée des peres capucins en l'isle de Maragnon et la conversion des sauvages à nostre saincte foy*. Paris, 1623.

SELECTED BIBLIOGRAPHY   195

Abranches, Joaquim dos Santos. *Fontes do direito eclesiastico Portugues*. Vol. I:
Summa do Bullario Portugues. Coimbra, 1895.
Almeida, Cândido Mendes de. *Código filipino; ou ordenações e leis do reino de
Portugal*. 2 vols. Rio de Janeiro, 1869-1870.
————. *Memorias para a história do extincto estado do Maranhão, cujo territorio
comprehende hoje as provincias do Maranhão, Piauhy, Grão Pará e Amazonas*.
2 vols. Rio de Janeiro, 1860-1874.
Almeida, M. Lopes de (ed.). *Collecção dos crimes, e decretos pelos quaes vinte e
hum Jesuitas forão mandados sahir do estado do Gram Pará, e Maranhão antes
do exterminio geral de toda a companhia de Jesus daquele estado*. Coimbra, 1947.
Alonso, B. Sánchez. *Fuentes de la historia española e hispanoamericana. Ensayo
de bibliografía sistemática de impresos y manuscritos que ilustran la historia política
de España e sus antiguas provincias de ultramar*. 2 vols. Madrid, 1927-1940.
Aranha, Manoel Guedes. "Papel politico sobre o estado do Maranhão aprezentado
em nome da camara ao Senhor Rei Dom Pedro Segundo por seu procurador
Manoel Guedes Aranha, anno de 1665 [1685]," *Revista do Instituto Histórico e
Geográfico Brasileiro*, XLVI, I. Pte., 1-61.
Azevedo, João Lúcio de. *Cartas do Padre António Vieira coordenadas e anotadas*.
3 vols. Coimbra, 1925-1928.
Berredo, Bernardo Pereira de. *Annaes históricos do estado do Maranhão*. 3rd. ed.
Florença, 1905.
Betendorf, João Felippe. "Chronica da missão dos padres da Companhia de Jesus
no estado do Maranhão," *Revista do Instituto Histórico e Geográfico Brasileiro*,
LXXII, Pte. I (1909).
Biblioteca Amazonas. Obras publicadas bajo la direccion del D. Raul Reyes y
Reyes, Presidente del Instituto Ecuatoriano de Estudios del Amazonas. Vols.
I-VII. Quito, 1924.
Biblioteca Nacional do Rio de Janeiro. *Documentos Históricos*. 1928-. 90 vols.
to 1951.
Boletim do Conselho Ultramarino. Legislação antiga. Vol. I: 1446-1754. Lisboa,
1867.
*Collecção dos Breves pontificios e leys regias que forão expedidos, e publicadas desde o
anno de 1741 sobre a liberdade das pessoas, bens e commercio dos Indios do Brasil*.
Lisboa, 1759.
Conceição, Apolinario de. *Primazia serafica na regiam de America, novo descobri-
mento de santos, e veneraveis religiosos da ordem serafica, que ennobrecem o Novo
Mundo com suas virtudes e accoens*. Lisboa, 1733.
————. *Claustro franciscano erecto no dominio da coroa portuguesa, e estabelecido
sobre dezaseis venerabilissimas columnas. Expoem-se sua origem e estado presente.
A de seus conventos e mosteiros, annos de suas fundações, numero de hospicios,
prefecturas, recolhimentos, parroquias e missoens, dos quaes se dà individual noticia
e do numero de seus religiosos, religiosas, terceiros e terceiras, que vivem collegiada-
mente tanto em Portugal, como em suas conquistas. Dedicado a sacra, real, augusta
magestade del Rey D. João V, nostro Senhor, por Fr. Apolinario da Conceição,
religioso leigo capucho da Provincia da Conceição em o estado do Brasil*. Lisboa,
1740.
————. *Pequenos na terra, grandes no ceo. Memorias historicas dos religiosos*

da ordem serafica, que do humilde estado de leigos subirão ao mais alto grão de perfeição. Escritas por Fr. Apolinario da Conceição de Nossa Senhora do Rio de Janeiro, do instituto Capucho, e natural da cidade de Lisboa. 5 vols. 1723-1754.

Condamine, Charles-Marie de la. Relation abrégée d'un voyage fait dans l'interieur de l'Amerique, meridionale, depuis la côte de la mer du sud, jusqu'aux côtes du Brésil et de la Guyane en descendant la rivière des Amazones. Maestricht, 1778.

Corrêa, Francisco (ed.). Leys e provisões que el rey dom Sebastião nosso senhor fez depois que começou à governar. Lisboa, 1570.

Cruz, Laureano de la. Nuevo descubrimiento del Río de Marañón llamado de las Amazonas por Fr. Laureano de la Cruz, 1651. New edition. Madrid, 1900.

————. "Nuevo descubrimiento del Río de Marañón llamado de las Amazonas hecho por la religión de San Francisco, año de 1651, siendo misionero el Padre Fr. Laureano de la Cruz e el Padre Fr. Juan de Quincoces, escrito por la obediencia de los superiores en Madrid año de 1653, por Fr. Laureano de la Cruz, hijo de la provincia de Quito, de la orden de San Francisco," in Marcellino da Civezza, Saggio di Bibliografia geografica storica etnografica sanfrancescana, pp. 269-300.

Documentos Historicos. See Biblioteca Nacional do Rio de Janeiro.

"Documentos para a história da conquista e colonização da costa de Leste-Oeste do Brasil," Anais da Biblioteca Nacional, XXVI (1904), 150-526.

Edmundson, George. Journal of the travels and labours of Father Samuel Fritz in the River of the Amazons. London, 1922.

Espada, Marcos Jiménez de la. Viaje del Capitán Pedro Teixeira aguas arriba del río de las Amazonas, 1638-1639. Madrid, 1889.

Evreux, Yves de. Suite de l'histoire des choses plus memorables advenues en Maragnan, en annees 1613 et 1614. Paris, 1615.

Faria, Manoel Severim de. Historia portugueza e de outras provincias do Occidente desde o anno de 1610 até o de 1640, publicada e anotada pelo Barão de Studart. Fortaleza, 1903.

Ferreira, João de Souza. "America abreviada. Suas noticias e de seus naturaes, e em particular do Maranhão, titulos, contendas e instrucções a sua conservação e augmento mui uteis," Revista do Instituto Histórico e Geográfico Brasileiro, LVII (1894), I. Pte., 5-153.

————. "Noticiario Maranhense. Descripção do estado do Maranhão em que tempo se descobriu o estado, por quem, que governadores o têm governado, como está, suas riquezas, e noticias que de presente temos sem muitas mais que não se conhecem, e como se pode augmentar, e sua capacidade, donde vieram os moradores Indios deste Estado, e outras peregrinas circumstancias," Revista do Instituto Histórico e Geográfico Brasileiro, LXXXI (1917), 289-352.

Fonseca, Luiza da (ed.). "Relação de Frei Cristóvão de Lisboa ao Conselho Ultramarino, 29 de outubro de 1647," The Americas, VII (1950), 215-220.

————. "Two petitions of Frei Cristóvão de Lisboa, O.F.M., Custos of Maranhão, to the King, 1623," The Americas, VIII (1952), 357-359.

Fritz, Samuel. See Edmundson, George.

Greenlee, William Brooks (trans. & ed.). *The voyage of Pedro Álvares Cabral to Brazil and India from contemporary documents and narratives.* London, 1938.

Heriarte, Mauricio de. *Descripção do estado do Maranhão, Pará e Rio das Amazonas feita por Mauricio de Heriarte, ouvidor-geral, provedor-mor e auditor, que foi, pelo governador D. Pedro de Mello, no anno de 1662. Por mandado do governador-geral Diogo Vaz de Sequeira. Dada á luz por primeira vez.* Edited by Francisco Adolpho de Varnhagen. Vienna, 1874.

Jaboatão, António de Santa Maria. *Novo orbe serafico brasilico, ou Chronica dos Frades Menores da provincia do Brasil.* 2 vols. 2nd. ed. Rio de Janeiro, 1858-1861.

Jiménez de la Espada, Marcos.
See Espada, Marcos Jiménez de la.

La Condamine, Charles Marie de.
See Condamine, Charles-Marie de la.

Leite, Serafim. *Novas cartas jesuíticas de Nóbrega a Vieira.* São Paulo, 1940.

"Livro Grosso do Maranhão," *Anais da Biblioteca Nacional do Rio de Janeiro,* Vols. LXVI & LXVII (1948). Edited by Arthur Cezar Ferreira Reis.

Maria, Agostinho de Santa. *Santuario Mariano, e historia das imagës milagrosas de nossa Senhora, e das milagrosamente apparecidas, em graça dos pregadores e dos devotos da mesma Senhora.* 10 vols. Lisboa, 1707-1723.

Martins, F. A. Oliveira. *Um heroi esquecido: João da Maia da Gama.* 2 vols. Lisboa, 1944.

Monforte, Manoel de. *Chronica da Provincia da Piedade, primeira capucha de toda a ordem e regular observancia de nosso seráfico Padre S. Francisco.* 2nd. ed. Lisboa, 1751.

Morais, Alexandre José Melo. *Corographia historica, chronographica, genealogica, nobiliaria e politica do Imperio do Brasil.* 5 vols. in 4. Rio de Janeiro, 1858-1863.

Regimento e leys sobre as missoens do estado do Maranhão e Pará e sobre a liberdade dos Índios. Lisboa, 1724.

Reyes y Reyes, Raúl. See *Biblioteca Amazonas.*

Ribeiro, José Anastásio de Figueiredo. *Synopsis chronologica de subsidios, ainda os mais raros para a história e estudo critico da legislação portuguesa mandada publicar pela Academia Real das Sciencias.* 2 vols. Lisboa, 1790.

Ribeiro, João Pedro. *Indice chronologico remissivo da legislação portuguesa posterior a publicação do Codigo Filippino cum hum appendice.* 4 vols. Lisboa, 1805-1807.

Salvador, Vicente do. *História do Brasil, 1500-1627.* Revista por Capistrano de Abreu & Rodolfo García. 3rd. ed. São Paulo, 1931.

Santa Maria, Agostinho de.
See Maria, Agostinho de Santa.

Santuario Mariano.
See Maria, Agostinho de Santa.

Silva, José Justino de Andrade e. *Collecção chronológica da legislação portuguesa compilada e annotada.* 10 vols. Lisboa, 1854-1859.

Silveira, Simão Estácio da. *Relação sumaria das coisas do Maranhão, escrita pelo Capitão Simão Estácio da Silveira.* First edition: Lisbon, 1624. Second edition: Lisbon, 1911.

Sluiter, Engel (ed.). "Document: Report on the State of Brazil, 1612 (Rezão do estado do Brasil)."*Hispanic American Historical Review*, XXIX (1949), 518-562.

Studart, Guilherme (Barão de). *Documentos para a história do Brasil e especialmente a do Ceará.* 4 vols. Fortaleza, 1904-1921.

——— *Documentos para a história de Martim Soares Moreno, colligidos e publicados pelo Barão de Studart.* Fortaleza, 1905.

Wadding, Luca *et al. Annales Minorum seu trium ordinum a S. Francisco institutorum.* I-. Quaracchi, 1931-. 29 volumes published to date.

III. SECONDARY SOURCES

Abreu, João Capistrano de. *Capitulos de história colonial, 1500-1800.* 3rd. ed. Rio de Janeiro, 1934.

Agia, Miguel. *Servidumbres personales de Indios.* Edición y estudio preliminar de F. Javier de Ayala. Sevilla, 1946.

Almeida, A. Duarte de. *História do Brasil. Documentário-histórico-geográfico. Descoberta. Colonização e independência do Brasil. Regimen republicano. 1500-1936.* Lisboa, 1936.

Almeida, Cândido Mendes de. *Direito civil eclesiastico brasileiro antigo e moderno em suas relações com o direito canónico.* Rio de Janeiro, 1866.

Almeida, Fortunato de. *História da igreja em Portugal.* 4 vols. Coimbra, 1910-1921.

Almeida, Rubem. "A contribuição dos Antoninos para a historia do Maranhão," *Revista de Geografia e história do Maranhão,* II (1947), 113-123.

Amaral, Lia Arez Ferreira do. "Ravardière no Maranhão," *Congreso do Mundo Portugues,* IX, 239-250.

Amazonas, Lourenço da Silva Araújo e. *Diccionario topographico, historico, descriptivo do comarca do Alto-Amazonas.* Recife, 1852.

Anais da Biblioteca Nacional do Rio de Janeiro. 1876-.

Annaes da Biblioteca e Archivo Publico do Pará. 10 volumes. 1902-1926.

Azevedo, Fernando de. *A cultura brasileira. Introdução ao estudo da cultura no Brasil.* Rio de Janeiro, 1943.

Azevedo, J. Lúcio de. *História dos christãos-novos portugueses.* Lisboa, 1922.

———. *Estudos de história Paraense.* Pará, 1893.

———. *Épocas de Portugal Economico.* Lisbon, 1929.

———. *História de António Vieira.* 2nd ed. 2 vols. Lisboa, 1931.

———. *Os Jesuítas no Grão Pará, suas missões e a colonização.* 2nd ed. revised. Coimbra, 1930.

Baena, António Ladislau Monteiro. *Compendio das eras da provincia do Pará.* Pará, 1838.

———. *Ensaio corográfico sobre a provincia do Pará.* Pará, 1839.

Baena, António Nicolau Monteiro. *Bosquejo chronológico de veneravel ordem terceira de São Francisco da penitencia do Gram-Pará.* Pará, 1878.

Baião, Antonio, Hernani Cidade & Manuel Múrias. *História da expansão portuguesa no mundo.* 3 vols. Lisboa, 1937-1940.

Barata, Manuel de Mello Cardoso. "Apontamentos para as ephemérides Paraenses," *Revista do Instituto Histórico e Geográfico Brasileiro,* CXLIV (1925), 9-235.

————. *A jornada de Francisco Caldeira de Castello Branco. Fundação da cidade de Belém.* Belém, 1916.

Barros, André. *Vida do apostolico padre António Vieira da Companhia de Jesus chamado por antonomasia o grande.* Lisboa, 1746.

Bayle, Constantino. *El protector de Indios.* Sevilla, 1945.

Braga, Teodoro. *História do Pará. Resumo didactico.* São Paulo, n.d.

————. *Apostillas de história do Pará.* Belém, 1915.

————. *Noções de chorographia do estado do Pará.* Belém, 1919.

Caeiro, José. *Os Jesuítas do Brasil e da Índia na perseguição do Marquez de Pombal.* Bahia, 1936.

Caetano, Marcelo. *Do Conselho Ultramarino ao Conselho do Imperio.* Lisboa, 1943.

Calmon, Pedro. *História da civilização brasileira.* 4th ed. revised. São Paulo, 1940.

————. *História social do Brasil.* Vol. *I: Espirito da sociedade colonial.* 3rd. ed. revised. São Paulo, 1941.

————. *História do Brasil.* 2 vols. São Paulo, 1939-1941.

Castro, Augusto Olympio Viveiros de. "Os Franciscanos no Maranhão," *Revista do Instituto Histórico e Geográfico Brasileiro,* XCVI (1924), 255-285.

Cidade, Hernani. *Padre António Vieira.* 4 vols. Lisboa, 1940.

Civezza, Marcellino da. *Saggio di bibliografia geografica storica etnografica sanfrancescana.* Prata, 1879.

Coleccion de libros que tratan de America, raros e curiosos. Madrid, 1891-. 21 volumes to date.

Congreso do Mundo Portugues. Publicações, memorias e comunicações apresentadas aos congressos da Pre- e Proto-história de Portugal, de história medieval, de história dos descobrimentos e colonização, da monarquia dualista e restauração, de história moderna e contemporânea de Portugal, ao congreso Luso-Brasileiro de historia, da história da actividade cientifica Portuguesa, colonial, nacional, de ciências da população, programas, discursos e mensagens. Comissão executiva dos centenários. Sessão de Congressos. 19 vols. Lisboa, 1940.

Cooper, John M. "Areal and temporal aspects of aboriginal South American culture," *Primitive Man,* XV (1942), 1-38.

Costa, Francisco Augusto Pereira da. *Anais pernambucanos 1591-1634.* Recife, 1952.

Cunha, Amadeu. *Sertões e fronteiras do Brasil. Noticia da época colonial por Amadeu Cunha.* Lisboa, 1945.

Dias, Carlos Malheiro (ed.). *História da colonização portuguesa do Brasil: edição monumental comemorativa do primeiro centenário da independência do Brasil.* 3 vols. Pôrto, 1924-1926.

Diffie, Bailey W. *Latin American civilization, colonial period.* Harrisburg, 1945.

Edmundson, George. "The Dutch on the Amazon and Negro in the seventeenth century. Part I: Dutch trade on the Amazon," *English Historical Review,* XVIII (1903), 642-663.

Ferreira, Alexandre Rodrigues. "Propriedade e posse das terras do Cabo do Norte pela corôa de Portugal. Deduzida dos Annaes Historicos do estado do Maranhão, e de algumas memorias e documentos por onde se acham dispersas as suas

200 THE INDIAN POLICY OF PORTUGAL IN THE AMAZON REGION

provas. Por Alexandre Rodrigues Ferreira. Pará, em 24 de abril de 1792," *Revista do Instituto Histórico e Geográfico Brasileiro*, III (1841), 389-421.

Filho, Cruz. *História do Ceará. Resumo didactico.* São Paulo, 1931.

Fleiuss, Max. *História administrativa do Brasil.* Rio de Janeiro, 1923.

Fonseca, Luiza da. "Frei Cristóvão de Lisboa, O.F.M., missionary and natural historian of Brazil," *The Americas*, VIII (1952), 289-303.

Freyre, Gilberto. *Casa grande e senzala.* 6th ed. enlarged. 2 vols. Rio de Janeiro, 1950.

Ganzert, Frederic William. "The boundary controversy in the Upper Amazon between Brazil, Bolivia and Peru, 1903-1909," *Hispanic American Historical Review*, XIV (1934), 427-449.

Grande Enciclopedia Portuguesa e Brasileira. Lisbon & Rio de Janeiro. Vol. I-.

Guajará, Barão de.
See Raiol, Domingos António.

Handelmann, Heinrich. *Geschichte von Brasilien.* Berlin, 1860.

Herrera, José Chantre y. *Historia de las misiones de la Compañia de Jesús en el Marañón español.* Madrid, 1901.

Julien, Charles André. *Voyages de découverte et les premiers établissements, XVe-XVIe siècles.* Paris, 1948.

Kroeber, A. L. *Cultural and natural areas of native North America.* Berkeley, 1939.

Leite, Serafim. *História da Companhia de Jesus no Brasil.* 10 vols. Lisbon & Rio de Janeiro, 1938-1950.

————. *Luiz Figueira. A sua vida heróica e a sua obra literária.* Lisboa, 1940.

Lima-Barbosa, Mario de. *Les Francais dans l'histoire du Brésil. Traduction et adaptation de l'original Brésilien par Clément Gazet.* Paris, 1923.

Lisboa, Cristóvão de. *Santoral de vários sermões de santos; oferecido a Manoel de Faria Severim, Chantre da Santa Sé de Évora.* Lisboa, 1638.

Lisboa, João Francisco. *Jornal de Timon: apontamentos noticias e observaçoes para servirem á história do Maranhão.* 3 vols. São Luiz, 1865.

Livermore, H. V. *A history of Portugal.* Cambridge, 1947.

Maranhão, Francisco de Nossa Senhora dos Prazeres. "Poranduba Maranhense ou Relação histórica da provincia do Maranhão," *Revista do Instituto Histórico e Geográfico Brasileiro*, LIV (1891), 4-188.

Marques, Cezar Augusto. *Diccionario historico-geographico da provincia do Maranhão.* Maranhão, 1870.

Métraux, Alfred. *La civilisation matérielle des tribus Tupí-Guaraní.* Paris, 1928.

Morais, José de.
See Pinto, José de Morais da Fonseca.

Norton, Luiz. "A colonização portuguesa do Brasil, 1500-1550," *Revista de Historia de América*, XI (1941), 5-46.

Oliveira, Miguel de. *História eclesiástica de Portugal.* 2nd ed. Lisboa, 1948.

Oliveira, Oscar de. *Os dízimos eclesiásticos do Brasil nos períodos da colônia e do Imperio.* Juiz da Fora, 1940.

Palazzolo, Jacinto de. "Primeiros Capuchinhos no Maranhão," *Vozes de Petrópolis*, III (1945), 501-506.

Peres, Damião & Eleutério Cerdeira (eds.). *História de Portugal. Edição monu-

mental comemorativa do 8. centenário da fundação da nacionalidade, profusamente ilustrada e colaborada pelos mais eminentes historiadores e artistas Portugueses. 4 vols. in 2. Barcelos, 1928-1931.

Pinto, José de Morais da Fonseca. "Historia da Companhia de Jesus na extincta provincia do Maranhão e Pará," Cândido Mendes de Almeida, *Memorias para a historia do extincto estado do Maranhão*, Vol. I.

Pombo, José Francisco da Rocha. *História do Brazil*. 10 vols. Rio de Janeiro, n.d.

Porto Seguro, Visconde de.
See Varnhagen, Francisco Adolfo de.

Prado, João Fernando de Almeida. *Pernambuco e as capitanias do norte do Brasil, 1530-1630*. 3 vols. São Paulo, 1939-1941.

Prat, André. *Notas históricas sobre as missões Carmelitas no extremo norte do Brasil, século XVII-XVIII*. Recife, 1941.

Primério, Fidelis M. de. *Capuchinhos em terras de Santa Cruz nos séculos XVII, XVIII e XIX. Apontamentos históricos*. São Paulo, 1942.

Raiol, Domingos António [Barão de Guajará]. "Catechese de Índios no Pará," *Annaes da Biblioteca e Archivo Publico do Pará*, II (1903), 117-183.

Reis, Arthur Cézar Ferreira. "A formação espiritual da Amazônia," *Cultura*, I (1948), 97-118.

——. "A economia do vale do Amazônas no periodo colonial," *Boletim Geográfico*, Rio de Janeiro, V (1947), 50-53.

——. *Sintese da história do Pará*. Belém, 1942.

——. *História do Amazonas*. Manaos, 1931.

——. *Limites e demarcações na Amazônia Brasileira*. Tomo I: *A fronteira colonial com a Guiana Francesa*. Tomo II: *A fronteira com as colonias espanholas*. Rio de Janeiro, 1947-1948.

——. *A política de Portugal no vale Amazônico*. Belém, 1940.

——. "Aspectos econômicos da dominação lusitana na Amazônia," *Boletim Geográfico*, V (1947), 262-274.

——. *Estadistas portugueses na Amazônia*. Rio de Janeiro, 1948.

Restauração e o imperio colonial portugues, A. Lisboa, 1940.

Ribeiro, Bartolomeu. *Guia de Portugal franciscano, continental e insular. Esquema histórico de 1217 a 1834, e crónica sucinta da provincia dos santos martires de Marrocos*. Leixões, 1945.

Rocha, Ricardo da. "Ordens religiosas que contribuiram para a conquista e colonização do Grão Pará," *Revista do Instituto Histórico e Geográfico do Pará*, II (1918), 149-156.

Roewer, Basílio. *A ordem franciscana no Brasil*. Petrópolis, 1941.

——. *Páginas de história franciscana no Brasil*. Petrópolis, 1941.

Sá, Manoel de. *Memorias históricas dos illustrissimos arcebispos, bispos, e escritores portuguezes da ordem de Nossa Senhora do Carmo, reduzidas a catalogo alfabetico que entregou na Academia Real da Historia Portugueza e a seu protector augustissimo el rey D. João V nosso Senhor offerece e dedica o Academico Supranumerario Fr. Manoel de Sá, religioso da mesma Ordem da provincia de Portugal*. Lisboa. 1724.

Saraiva, José Mendes da Cunha. *A fortaleza de Bissau e a Companhia do Grão Pará e Maranhão.* Lisboa, 1947.

Simonsen, Roberto C. *História económica do Brasil, 1500-1820.* 2 vols. São Paulo, 1938.

Sombra, S. *História monetária do Brasil colonial. Repertorio cronológico com introdução, notas e carta monetária.* Revised and enlarged edition. Rio de Janeiro, 1938.

Sousa, António Caetano de. *História genealógica da casa real portugueza, desde a sua origem até o presente, com as familias illustres, que procedem dos reys, e dos serenissimos Duques de Bragança, justificada com instrumentos, e escritores de inviolavel fé e offerecida a el rey D. João V, nosso Senhor por D. António Caetano de Sousa, clerigo regular, e academico do numero da Academia Real.* 20 vols. Lisboa, 1737-1748.

Southey, Robert. *History of Brazil.* 3 vols. London, 1810-1819.

Steward, Julian H. (ed.). *Handbook of South American Indians.* Smithsonian Institution. Bureau of American Ethnology, Bulletin 143. 6 vols. Washington, 1946-1950.

Varnhagen, Francisco Adolfo de (Visconde de Porto Seguro). *História geral do Brasil.* 3rd. ed. 5 vols. Rio de Janeiro, 1926-1936.

————. *História das lutas com os Hollandezes no Brasil desde 1624 a 1654.* Lisboa, 1872.

Vasques, Fernando. *Conquista e colonização do Pará.* Lisboa, 1941.

Vianna, Arthur. "Monographias Paraenses. Os exploradores da Amazonia," *Revista do Instituto Histórico, Geográfico e Ethnográfico do Pará,* I (1900), 282-306.

Vianna, Helio. *Estudos de história colonial.* São Paulo, 1948.

Waetjen, Hermann. *Das hollaendische Kolonialreich in Brasilien. Ein Kapitel aus der Kolonialgeschichte des 17. Jahrhunderts. Mit einer Karte.* Haag. 1921.

INDEX

203

204 INDEX

Aroan Indians, 68, 125, 127
Avelar, S.J., João de, 50
Avelar, Paulo Soares de: requests money for widows of Indians, 57
Azevedo, Lúcio de: quoted, 104 f.
Azevedo, Sebastião de Lucena de: dismissed and exiled, 68; report on *aldeias*, 67 f.
Azorean settlers in Maranhão, 24 f.

Bahia, 25; ecclesiastical division of, 135
Barreiros, António Moniz: bequest to Jesuits, 72; *capitão-mor*, 32; deeds property to Jesuits, 82; forbids Cristóvão de Lisboa's trip to Ceará, 34; gives convent to Jesuits, 49; warfare against Dutch, 56
Barreto, Inácio do Rego: accused, 74; *capitão-mor* of Pará, 75, 83; prepares for *resgate*, 89; *regimento* of, 86; sends money to Portugal, 92
Barros, João de, 8
Barros, Manoel Gomeiro de: holds *devassa*, 75
Beckman, Manoel: hanged, 153; leads revolt, 151 f.
Beckman, Tomás, 151 f.
Belém, Nossa Senhora de: founded, 17 f.
Belém: Carvalho in, 67; complaints against Jesuits in, 155; Cristóvão de Lisboa, O.F.M., visits, 33; Luiz Figueira, S.J., stays in, 50; first ecclesiastical organization, 18; Franciscans in, 170; Franciscans work near, 20; Jesuits in, 105; law of 1680 promulgated, 146; number of citizens in, 1637, 51; number of priests in, 1637, 51; obeys law of 1655, 105; procurators of, active at court, 95; procurators of, and junta on slavery laws, 96; trial of Indian captives at, 102
—Town Council of: accuses governor, 75; against Jesuits' return, 118; asks return of Franciscans, 71; com-

plains about Jesuits, 107, 113; conflicts with governor, 133; does not co-operate with revolt, 152; and law of 1663, 120; organizes *resgate*, 43; receives royal letter, 81; requests *resgates*, 62; Vieira addresses, 115
Berredo, Bernardo Pereira de: quoted, 33 f.
Betancor, Jorge de Lemos de, 24
Betendorff, S.J., João, 166
Botelho, Diogo, Governor: frees Indians, 9
Branco, Francisco Caldeira de Castelo: first *capitão-mor* of Pará, 21; founds Belém, 1616, 17 f.; letter to king, 1616, 23
Brazil: discovery of, 8; early exploitation, 8; role of missions in, 186; and slavery, 84
Brazilwood, 3
Brieva, O.F.M., Domingo: exploration of Amazon, 54
Brito, José de, 169

Cabo do Norte: controlled by Jesuits, 147; granted to Parente, 44; Jesuits abandon, 176; missions divided, 166 f.; missions encouraged, 144; missions definitively confided to Franciscans, 176
Cabo do Norte Indians, 57, 125
Cadaval, Duke of, 140
Caité: Álvaro de Sousa donatary of, 61; Indians sold in, 114; Jesuits in, 105; two Jesuits in, 103; without priest, 1637, 51
Caldas, Pedro Álvares, 148
Caminha, Pero Vaz de: quoted, 1
Camucim, 106; settlement of, 12
Camutá: Figueira visits, 50; given to Feliciano Carvalho, 50; has no priest, 51
Cannibalism: part of Indians' ritualistic feasts, 2
Capuchins, 173
Carcamo, Diogo de: named governor-

of *aldeias* after 1630, 39; excluded from missions, 101; extent of work in 1627, 36; first missionaries in Pará, 18; given charge of Indians, 1618, 20; given office of *pai dos cristãos*, 1652, 76; given two *aldeias*, 67; invited to resume Indian administration, 1647, 60; at junta on slavery laws, 96; later activity of, 170; and law of 1663, 120; and law of 1677, 136; and law of 1686, 163; leave Portugal for Maranhão, 1652, 60; in Maranhão in 1652, 78; more sought for Pará, 154; number of missions, 180; one killed by mob, 42; one shot to death, 1637, 44; opinion of Pero Fernandes Monteiro, S.J., concerning, 121; opinion of Jácome Raimundo de Noronha concerning, 44 ff.; permitted to work in Maranhão, 1652-1653, 95; rebuked by king on March 22, 1688, 169; receive mission questionnaire, 125; receive several missions from Jesuits, 176; release *aldeias* unwillingly, 106n.; request funds, 29; request of Sousa d'Eça for more, 28; return of advised, 69; return to Pará sought, 71; sail from Lisbon, 1624, 32; seek salary increase, 1652, 78; take missions in Pará, 20; to accompany *resgates*, 43; vow of poverty hinders work, 38; work evaluated, 47; work for Indians, 1617-1636, 19 ff.; work near Belém, 20; work summarized, 182 f.

Franciscans of the Province of Piedade: arrive in Pará, 1693, 175; assigned to Gurupá, 174 f.; mission district described, 177

Francisco de Alcântara, O.F.M.: named custos, 1652, 77: prepares for departure to Maranhão, 77

Francisco de Presepio, O.F.M., 74

French: corrupt Indians, 168; dealings with Indians, 63; details of expedition of 1612, 13; early activities in

Amazon, 10; found São Luiz, 13; and Indians of Cabo do Norte, 68; interloping activities, 163; occasion law of 1688, 166; resist Portuguese expedition, 14

Fritz, S.J., Samuel: opens Spanish missions, 171; opposed by Portuguese Carmelite missionaries, 171

Furtado, Diogo de Mendonça, Governor of Brazil: friend of Jesuits, 48

Furtado, Francisco Xavier de Mendonça: Governor of Pará, 180

Gomes, S.J., Bernardo: killed by Indians, 1687, 163, 167

Golden Lake: search for, 124

Guaxenduba: battle of, 14

Gueribí River, 177

Guiné, 122, 142, 157

Gurupá, 24, 89, 170, 174, 177; Azevedo exiled to, 68; Figueira visits, 50; Jesuits given *aldeia* in, 80; revolt in, 105; Jesuits in, 103, 105; Piedade Franciscans given territory of, 174, 177

Hordovicos, José, 150

Igreja Matriz, Belém: law of 1624 read in, 34

India, 59, 104

Indian captives: trial of, at Belém, 1655, 102

Indian chiefs: decorated by king, 57

Indian legislation: against forced labor, 1609, 5; law of 1611, 6; law of 1624, 33 f.; *alvará* of 1638, 52; *alvará* of 1647, 65 f.; law of 1648, 70; *provisão* of 1649, 71; *provisão* of 1652, 81; law of 1653, 86; law of 1655, 96 ff.; royal letter of 1658, 109; law of 1663, 118; law of 1677, 136; *alvará* of March 31, 1680, 145; law of April 1, 1680, 138 ff.; *provisão* of April 1, 1680, 141; law of 1684, 153; junta of 1686, 156; *Regimento das Missões*, 157 ff.;